GROWING THE TARACO PENINSULA

Growing the Taraco Peninsula

Indigenous Agricultural Landscapes

MARIA C. BRUNO

UNIVERSITY PRESS OF COLORADO
Denver

© 2024 by University Press of Colorado

Published by University Press of Colorado
1580 North Logan Street, Suite 660
PMB 39883
Denver, Colorado 80203-1942

All rights reserved
Printed in the United States of America

 The University Press of Colorado is a proud member of the Association of University Presses.

The University Press of Colorado is a cooperative publishing enterprise supported, in part, by Adams State University, Colorado State University, Fort Lewis College, Metropolitan State University of Denver, University of Alaska Fairbanks, University of Colorado, University of Denver, University of Northern Colorado, University of Wyoming, Utah State University, and Western Colorado University.

∞ This paper meets the requirements of the ANSI/NISO Z39.48-1992 (Permanence of Paper).

ISBN: 978-1-64642-612-6 (hardcover)
ISBN: 978-1-64642-613-3 (ebook)
https://doi.org/10.5876/9781646426133

Library of Congress Cataloging-in-Publication Data

Names: Bruno, Maria C. (Maria Christina), 1976– author.
Title: Growing the Taraco Peninsula : indigenous agricultural landscapes / Maria C. Bruno.
Description: Denver : University Press of Colorado, [2024] | Includes bibliographical references and index.
Identifiers: LCCN 2024002493 (print) | LCCN 2024002494 (ebook) | ISBN 9781646426126 (hardcover) | ISBN 9781646426133 (ebook)
Subjects: LCSH: Agriculture—Bolivia—Taraco (Municipio)—History. | Indians of South America—Agriculture—Bolivia—Taraco (Municipio)—History. | Traditional farming—Bolivia—Taraco (Municipio)—History. | Plant remains (Archaeology)—Bolivia—Taraco (Municipio) | Environmental archaeology—Bolivia—Taraco (Municipio) | Botany—Research—Bolivia—Taraco (Municipio) | Sustainable agriculture—Bolivia—Taraco (Municipio) | Taraco (La Paz, Bolivia : Municipio)—Antiquities.
Classification: LCC F3320.1.A47 B78 2024 (print) | LCC F3320.1.A47 (ebook) | DDC 630.984/12—dc23/eng/20240229
LC record available at https://lccn.loc.gov/2024002493
LC ebook record available at https://lccn.loc.gov/2024002494

This book will be made open access within three years of publication thanks to Path to Open, a program developed to bring about equitable access and impact for the entire scholarly community, including authors, researchers, libraries, and university presses around the world. Learn more at https://about.jstor.org/path-to-open/.

Cover photograph by Maria C. Bruno

To my parents, Frank Bruno and Carol DeLaMare Bruno, who raised me with an open heart and mind to explore the world beyond our beautiful Lake Tahoe landscapes and to value the livelihoods of others.

Contents

List of Figures	ix
List of Tables	xiii
Acknowledgments	xv

1. Indigenous Agriculture and Resurgent Communities: Defining Taraco Peninsula Landscapes   3

2. Taraco Peninsula Communities: Space, Place, and Time   24

3. Field Preparation: Earth, Water, and Variability   54

4. Planting: Growing Domesticated Plants   72

5. Tending: Wild Plants and Domesticated Animals   89

6. Harvesting and Processing: Transforming Plants into Food (Part 1)   108

7. Eating: Transforming Plants into Food (Part 2)   126

8. Agricultural Taskscapes: Resurgent Communities of the Taraco Peninsula   164

Notes	183
References	187
Index	225

Figures

1.1. Location of Lake Titicaca in the Andean *altiplano*. 4
2.1. Map of the Taraco Peninsula indicating the location of modern-day communities along the main road. Chiripa, Santa Rosa, San José, and Coa Collu participated in the ethnobotanical study. The four archaeological sites studied by TAP are also indicated. 25
2.2. The community center of Chiripa as photographed in 2017. 26
2.3. Lake Titicaca basin and archaeological sites mentioned in text. 29
2.4. Decorated ceramics from the Taraco Peninsula: (a) Middle Formative period, large cream-on-red bowl from Chiripa; (b) Late Formative period, red-rimmed/Kalasasaya bowls from Kala Uyuni. 34
2.5. Stone monolith placed in the center of the Upper Court at KUAC and the "Lightning Stone" placed at the base of the monolith. 35
3.1. Planting a field with a *yunta* in San José, Bolivia. 55
3.2. Planting a field with a *chaquitaclla* depicted by Guaman Poma de Ayala (1615). 56
3.3. Distribution of planting zones on the Taraco Peninsula. 57

3.4.	Aerial image of Chiripa indicating mapped canals diverting water from springs to fields.	68
4.1.	The *altiplano* maize variety.	86
4.2.	Ubiquity of crop plants through time.	88
5.1.	*Th'aruña*. Using a *chuntilla* to remove a weed from a growing fava bean field.	90
5.2.	Ubiquity of common wild taxa in order of discussion.	99
6.1.	Processing potatoes.	111
6.2.	Processing crops with seeds.	113
6.3.	Site of Kala Uyuni and the four excavation areas: Ayrampu Qontu (KUAQ), Achachi Coa Collu (KUAC), Kala Uyuni (KUKU), and Siwinka Qontu (SQ).	115
6.4.	Western profile of KUAQ excavations.	116
6.5.	Excavation units at KUAC.	117
6.6.	Plan view of excavations at KUKU indicating the architectural subdivisions (ASD) encountered.	119
6.7.	Number of wild taxa present across each type of context at KUKU.	124
7.1.	An outdoor kitchen with clay oven and clay and metal pots. A drying stack of quinoa awaits processing in the background.	128
7.2.	Bowls of *wallaque* waiting to be eaten.	129
7.3.	Local authorities in the community of Coa Collu lay out boiled potatoes, *oca*, and *chuño* on textiles with bowls of *llawja* as a relish.	132
7.4.	Ubiquity of animal food sources through time at all Taraco sites.	135
7.5.	A small *w'atia* to roast potatoes prepared in a harvested field.	141
7.6.	Comparison of crop foods and cacti at KUAC and KUAQ based on average density of plant remains per liter of soil.	147

7.7. KUAC Lower Court (KU-ASD1) indicating the location of the "fish pits" and burial under floor. 150
7.8. Density of carbonized plant materials and contexts across the site of KUKU. 153
7.9. Comparison of crop plants and cacti across the Initial, Expansion, and Terminal occupations of KUKU based on average density of plant remains per liter of soil. 154
7.10. Proto-*keru* and Tiwanaku *keru* from Kala Uyuni. 159
7.11. Comparison of food taxa across different Tiwanaku period contexts at KUKU based on average density of plant remains per liter of soil. 161

Tables

2.1.	Archaeological chronology of the southern Lake Titicaca basin and Taraco Peninsula	30
4.1.	Crop species grown on the Taraco Peninsula	73
4.2.	Ubiquity of *Chenopodium* types through time	82
4.3.	Ubiquity of tuber remains and maize through time	83
5.1.	Ubiquity of woody plant species through time	97
5.2.	Ubiquity of common herbaceous wild taxa in order of discussion	98
5.3.	Ubiquity of cacti and aquatic plants through time	103
5.4.	Diversity indices through time	105
6.1.	Description of context categories in alphabetical order and number of samples of each type	123
6.2.	Patterns in density and richness of carbonized plant remains in different types of contexts at Kala Uyuni	123
7.1.	Ingredients of past Taraco meals and their potential categories of use	139

Acknowledgments

The present work stemmed from my dissertation research in the early 2000s at Washington University in St. Louis. This book's research was generously supported by initial grants from the university's International Studies program and the Department of Anthropology and larger grants from IIE Fulbright, the National Science Foundation, and the Wenner Gren Foundation. I conducted ethnographic and botanical research on the Taraco Peninsula between October 2003 and 2004. Permissions were sought and obtained from all of the participating communities: Chiripa, Coa Collu, Santa Rosa, and San José, as well as the Herbario Nacional de Bolivia (LPB) and the Dirección General de Biodiversidad (DGB). Dr. Juan de Dios Yapita of the Instituto de Lengua y Cultura Aymara (ILCA) translated all of the Aymara interviews into Spanish. The archaeological elements were gathered as a member of the Taraco Archaeological Project (TAP). Between 2003 and 2009, under the co-directorship of Drs. Christine Hastorf and Matthew Bandy, I participated in the excavations at the sites Kala Uyuni, Sonaji, and Kumi Kipa and then analyzed the archaeobotanical samples between Washington University in St. Louis and University of California, Berkeley. I also draw upon TAP excavations and archaeobotanical analyses conducted by William Whitehead and BrieAnna Langlie at the site of Chiripa. As co-directors of TAP, between 2011 and 2019 Dr. Hastorf and I conducted additional fieldwork mapping of Chiripa and Kala

Uyuni, and I continued archaeobotanical analysis at Dickinson College. This research was supported by Dickinson College's Research and Development Committee and Center for Sustainability Education as well as grants from the National Geographic Society and the American Philosophical Society. These nearly annual return trips to the peninsula allowed me to update some of the observations about farming and food that I first collected 20 years ago.

This project was shaped by a graduate program at Washington University in St. Louis that was supportive, innovative, and obsessed with the history of agriculture and pastoralism. The support and expertise from the faculty, particularly David Browman, Gayle Fritz, Fiona Marshall, Patty Jo Watson, T. J. Kidder, and Glenn Stone, allowed me to dream up and get funding for a project that combined both ethnographic and archaeobotanical research. My fellow graduate students nourished me with wonderful food, trips to markets, careful editing, and their own incredible projects that helped to elevate my own. Many thanks to Sarah Walshaw, Elisabeth Hildebrand, Ben Carter, Kevin Hanselka, Karla Hansen, Monte Abbott, Angela Gordon Glore, Michael Glore, Elizabeth Monroe, Kristi Arntzen, Vanessa Hildebrand, Erin Stiles, Liz Horton, and Kate Grillo.

The transformation of my dissertation ideas into this book about sustainability was fundamentally aided by my tenure at Dickinson College. My colleagues in the Anthropology and Archaeology Department, particularly Karen Weinstein, Jim Ellison, and Ann Hill, not only supported my professional trajectory but infused and inspired my research through their own work on food and sustainability in Carlisle, Tanzania, and China. I also found myself surrounded by colleagues in different disciplines engaged in questions about agriculture, food, Latin America, and Indigenous studies that stimulated this work. Many thanks to Siobhan Phillips, Emily Pawley, Heather Bedi, Maggie Douglas, Kristin Strock, Amy Farrell, Susan Rose, Nikki Dragone, Luca Trazzi, Mariana Past, Marcelo Borges, Santiago Anria, Margaret Frolich, Elise Bartosik-Velez, and Carolina Castellanos. I am especially grateful to Jen Halpin and Matt Steinman, of the Dickinson College Farm, who taught me so much about farming and agrobiodiversity in central Pennsylvania that shed new light on my understanding of Taraco agriculture. I am grateful to Jim Ciarrocca for his technical support with ArcGIS, his wisdom in creating permanent datums, and guidance on the detailed mapping of Chiripa and Kala Uyuni. The Center for Sustainability Education, headed by Neil Leary and Lindsay Lyons, provided not only generous support for this project and student participation but also the transformational speakers, discussion groups, and field-learning experiences in Carlisle and Yunnan, China. Finally, thanks to my wonderful network of friends who provided moral support and many delicious meals: Linda Brindeau, Crystal Moten, Toby Reiner, Meg Winchester, Anna Kozlawska, Vincent Stephens, and Diana Dragani.

I'm especially grateful to the students who worked and volunteered as my research assistants in the Dickinson Environmental Archaeology Lab sorting through Tiwanaku samples and updating the database: Chloé Miller, Solai Sanchez, Marc Primelo, Rachel Provazza, Julia McMahon, Nicholas Beard, Michael Sinclair, and Erin Summers. Special thanks to Benjamin West, who focused his analysis on samples from Sonaji and synthesized the data for his senior thesis. Chloé Miller and Will Kochtitzky helped map and collect plants as well as re-excavate raised fields in Chiripa. Amanda Santilli helped to map Chiripa and Coa Collu and created one of the geodatabases used here. Justin Burkett created the GIS database from which several of the figures were created. Finally, *thank you* to *all* of the Dickinson students who took my classes, invited me into discussions, and engaged with these various ideas. You challenged me to think and teach about them in new ways that infiltrated many elements of this work. Your passion for the health of our planet and the well-being of others has been inspiring and gave me the confidence that the message of this book has an audience who will do something with it.

The Taraco Archaeological Project not only provided the material means for this study but a dynamic intellectual home for its elaboration. I'm so grateful for the long field seasons, emails, meetings, and meals in which we exchanged ideas about ancient life on the peninsula with Matthew Bandy, Andrew Roddick, Kate Moore, José Capriles, William Whitehead, Lee Steadman, Kirk Fry, Di Hu, Amanda Logan, Katy Killackey, José Luis Paz, Ruth Fontenla, Jewell Soriano, Alejandra Domic, and Eduardo Machicado. I'm especially grateful for Eduardo's help with many mapping elements of this study. Christine Hastorf's influence can hardly be summarized here, but her support of me, starting as a student from another institution to now co-directors and friends, has been unwavering and continuous. The imprint of her ideas and collaboration is found throughout this book. I'm particularly grateful for her encouragement to not give up on this book. She supported me as an Archaeological Research Facility Visiting Scholar in 2015–2016, and I'm especially thankful to her Archaeobotany dinner group, which provided much needed feedback as I experimented with the structure of the book.

I feel incredibly lucky to be a Lake Titicaca Basin anthropologist/archaeologist; the support and friendships I have gained from this welcoming group of scholars has been invaluable at every stage of this project. Special thanks to Clare Sammells, Alison Kohn, Kate McGurn Centellas,

Nicole Couture, Deborah Blom, John Janusek, Claudine Valleieres, Elizabeth Klarich, Elizabeth Arkush, Chip Stanish, Steve Kosiba, Maribel Perez, Scott Smith, Erik Marsh, Sonia Alconini, Claudia Rivera, and Mabel Ramos. Scott Smith provided especially important feedback during the review process of the manuscript.

I am very grateful to the University Press of Colorado, Darrin Pratt, Allegra Martschenko, and Jessica d'Arbonne for their incredible patience as I developed this project over many years. I am so thankful that the press believed this book was worth waiting for. Reviewers of the proposal and the final manuscript provided critical feedback, and Alison Tartt provided careful copyediting, and Dan Pratt for shepherding the manuscript to its final publication.

Most importantly, I thank the Taraco and Tiwanaku families that hosted me, fed me, and patiently taught me about farming and life in the Titicaca Basin: Facundo Llusco and Lucia Catari, Victor Aruquipa and Petrona Mamani and their children, and Anaclo and Paulina Patty and their children.

Finally, many thanks to my own family, the Brunos and DeLaMares, for their unwavering support of my work even though it took me many miles away from the Lake Tahoe, Bay Area, and Great Basin landscapes that I am so fortunate to call home. This book is dedicated especially to my mother and father, Carol and Frank.

GROWING THE TARACO PENINSULA

1

Indigenous Agriculture and Resurgent Communities

Defining Taraco Peninsula Landscapes

Just before sunrise, I woke to the rustle of the Quispe[1] family getting out of their beds of heavy blankets, handwoven by an elderly neighbor from sheep's wool dyed bright, synthetic yellows, reds, blues, and purples. My adobe wall room was adjacent to the family room, and so while we had our private spaces, the sounds of morning activity were my daily wake-up call. The men slipped on warm pants and the women a colorful wool skirt called a *pollera*. They all donned sweaters, and the kids added a coat. Although it was summer on the Taraco Peninsula, the temperature outside in the morning was a bit chilly, around 10°C (50°F). It was February, and several nightly rains this week had created a damp coolness outdoors.

The Taraco Peninsula is located in modern-day Bolivia and juts into the smaller, southern basin of Lake Titicaca, known locally as Lago Wiñaymarka. Lake Titicaca is the world's highest navigable lake at approximately 3,660 m a.s.l. (figure 1.1). It is situated in what is known as the *altiplano*, or high plain, which extends between latitudes 15° S and 22° S where the Andes split into two ranges (Allmendinger et al. 1997; Clapperton 1993). Taraco families living on the northern side of the peninsula, as we were here, have a view of the snowy eastern Andean range.

The father and son, Julio and Nicolas, headed down to Lake Titicaca to recover the morning's fish catch. Their house, built of a combination of locally made adobes and factory-made bricks with a calamine roof, sits

https://doi.org/10.5876/9781646426133.c001

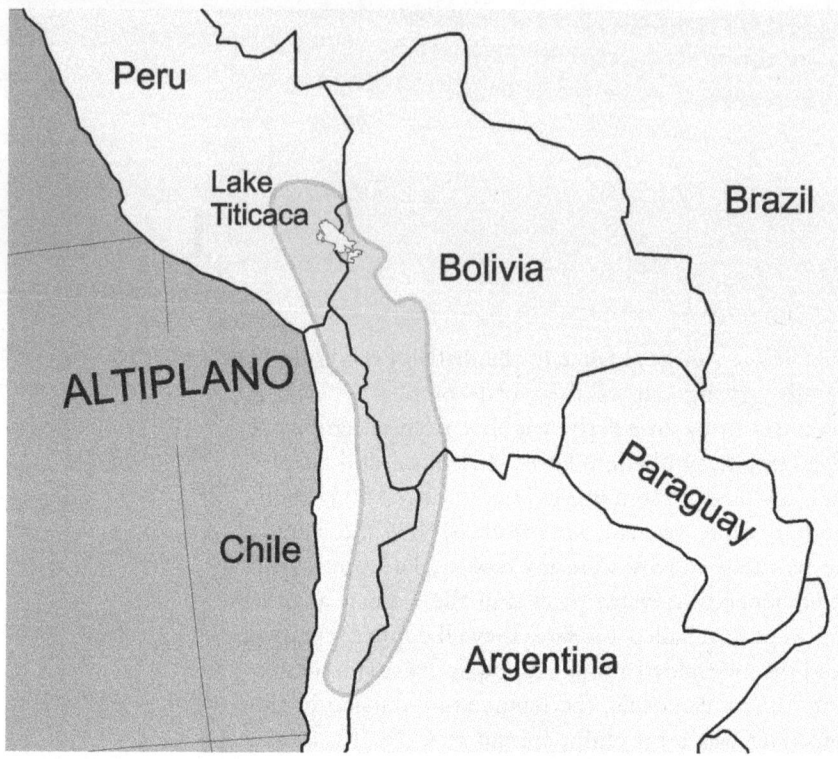

FIGURE 1.1. *Location of Lake Titicaca in the Andean* altiplano

at the top of a ravine, or *quebrada*, cut out by a small stream. They walk down a slightly rocky but gentle slope toward the *Eucalyptus*-lined dirt road, which extends around the perimeter of the peninsula. Past the road the land flattens out where silty brown and black soils are covered in dense green grasses. This flat plain or *pampa* terminates in the shimmering, crystal-blue lake with towering snowcapped mountain peaks in the distance. I can't speak for Julio and Nicolas, but I lose my breath every time I glance upon this striking vista.

They arrived at the lake where their blue and red wooden boat was anchored in an area where they had cleared the thick growth of tall *totora* reeds. They didn't have to walk out quite as far as they do in the winter months because the rains have brought the lake higher up the plain. They then rowed out a few meters to find the floating pieces of Styrofoam that mark where their plastic nets have snagged a variety of native and introduced fish below the cold blue waters.

All along their journey, from hilltop to lakeshore, they passed a landscape filled with fields. In most of the fields that day, potatoes were blooming with purple and white flowers and bright yellow anthers. Some fields had a plant with triangular green leaves, a yellow flower, and a yellowish, red tuber growing underground, known as *oca*. Several fields had alternating rows of maize and fava beans, both tall and green. There were even a few rows of quinoa with bright red stalks and brilliant pink, red, and yellow panicles filled with thousands of tiny white, yellow, and red seeds. Thriving alongside the crops that families in the village had carefully planted in rows between September and December were a variety of wild plant species. One resembles quinoa but is shorter and has dark purple flowers and seeds. Another one, a wild mustard or *ñustasa* (*Brassica rapa* L.), has broad green leaves and bright yellow flowers. Later in the day, the mother, Alejandra, will head out to the fields with a pick to yank out these unwanted species and repair the mounds of earth and furrows around the crops, a task called *th'aruña*. Before this task, however, I helped her put the animals out to graze.

First, we grabbed a bucket filled with the scraps of yesterday's meals and walked a short distance down the hill to the animal pens. The scraps were served to a mama pig and her four little piglets in their small pen. They squealed in delight. We then walked to the nearby sheep pen, opened the small gate, and ushered them to one of the fields uphill from the house that was not in production this year. Here the same wild plants that will later be removed from the potato field were free to grow and thrive, providing food for the sheep. Finally, we moved their cow, tied near the house, down the hill to a grassy patch near the stream. The animals will be moved throughout the day to new pasture areas, most of which are "resting" fields. The teenaged daughter, Valentina, will also go out into the lake in the afternoon to cut down some of the *totora* reeds and pull up a plant growing under the water, called *lima*, to supplement the animals' mostly terrestrial diet. Alejandra will also collect the weedy plants she pulled out of the fields into her light, brightly colored textile called an *aguayo*, strap it on her back, and feed them to the animals.

On the Taraco Peninsula and throughout the Lake Titicaca Basin tasks involving the collection of resources from the lake and tending to domesticated animals and plants occur every day of the year, varying based on the season. I begin with this description of a typical day on the peninsula because it introduces the human and nonhuman actors from which this story of agricultural landscape creation and sustainability unfolds. The patterns of humans, land, water, plants, and animals that I describe here are as I experienced them on the peninsula in 2003 and 2004, when I lived there for 12 months to study agricultural practices for my dissertation research.[2] I have returned on nearly a yearly basis over the past 20 years, and with a few exceptions, these practices have remained largely the same. If we were to zoom back 100, 1,000, or 2,000 years, some of these descriptions would be similar: the general topography and types of soils, the mountains in the distance, some of the animals (fish like *mauri*), plants like quinoa, and activities like weeding. Many aspects would also be very different, depending on the year, the lake would be much lower and more distant, the distribution of soils would be higher up or lower down, instead of sheep there would be llamas, instead of fava beans there would be more quinoa, and perhaps less weeding might have been needed. Additionally, and not inconsequentially, the social and political milieu in which these daily activities took place would be very distinct. The imprint of 500 years of colonization by Europeans and the subsequent struggles of Indigenous communities to regain ownership over the land itself has played an enormous role in what we experience today.

In this book, I trace the long-term history of Indigenous agriculture on the Taraco Peninsula through the interactions of inorganic, organic, and human elements of this landscape across the earliest periods of settled, farming life approximately 1500 BCE to 1100 CE. This, in turn, provides a model of sustainability through flexible yet persistent interactions of humans and their environment. I argue that Indigenous Taraco communities are examples of what Anna Tsing refers to as "resurgent communities" as they have confronted profound environmental and sociopolitical changes and have employed generational knowledge of water, soils, animals, and especially plants to sustain their families and continue to thrive into the present day.

I study the elements of Taraco's past agricultural landscapes through an examination of archaeological evidence preserved within and beneath the modern-day fields and pastures. In 1992, Christine Hastorf began the Taraco Archaeological Project (TAP), which has included the excavation of several Formative (1500 BCE–500 CE) and Tiwanaku (500–1100 CE) period sites on the peninsula as well as a full inventory of all archaeological sites visible on the surface, carried out by Matthew Bandy. From this long-term project a wealth of information about the past lives of the Taraco inhabitants has been recovered and studied. I have been a member of TAP since 2000. While I draw upon the full range of archaeological data related to ancient agriculture in the region, I focus specifically on ancient plant remains as they provide crucial insight into not only the crops people raised and consumed but the impact that a range of agro-pastoral activities had on the ecology of the peninsula. In doing so, I track the development of farming on the Taraco Peninsula and the roles it played as its earliest human communities grew and changed. Elevating the histories of human-plant interactions and agriculture, in turn, disrupts some long-held beliefs about past social and political trajectories in the Lake Titicaca Basin, pushing us to rethink traditional social evolutionary ideas about how these societies changed.

Such a project would not have been possible without the current Indigenous inhabitants of the peninsula. They have not only granted permission to archaeologists to dig up ancient remains in their fields but also have done much of the digging alongside us. Most importantly, however, has been their generosity in teaching us about what it means to live on the peninsula, to see, interact with, and learn from its nonhuman elements. My understanding of how to interpret the archaeological evidence is based on the education they provided me about land, water, plants, and agriculture as they experience it today.

AYMARA FARMERS OF THE TARACO PENINSULA, BOLIVIA

Bolivia is unique in that nearly half of its population belongs to one of 36 Indigenous ethnic groups (INE 2012). Today's residents of the Taraco Peninsula self-identify as Aymara. As with any identity, what constitutes Aymara is complex and fluid. On the peninsula as well as other places in Bolivia, this affiliation is expressed and recognized through shared yet dynamic language, dress, beliefs, and practices. According to the 2012 Bolivian census, approximately 55 percent of the rural population in the Department of La Paz learned Aymara as their first language (INE 2012). Most Taraco inhabitants speak the Aymara language. Although many are bilingual in Spanish, older members of the communities speak only Aymara, and there are some younger residents who speak only Spanish. Linguistic and genetic studies suggest that the wide adoption of Aymara as a common language in the Bolivian highlands was relatively recent. At least two other language groups, Uru and Pukina, also existed in the lake region when Europeans arrived in the fifteenth century (Bouysse-Cassagne 1992). While Uru is still spoken in small pockets of communities in Bolivia and Peru, the Pukina language is now extinct (Adelaar 2004). The Spanish lumped speakers of these three languages together as a single category of "Aymara" for taxation purposes, and this eventually became the unifying term and language for the populations around the lake and much of the *altiplano* (Bouysse-Cassagne 1992). It is unknown what language was spoken by the residents of the Taraco Peninsula when the Spanish arrived. Based on continuities in material culture, many archaeologists argue for Aymara being a long-lived language in the region, starting at least with the Tiwanaku state (Browman 1994; Stanish 2003). Linguistic evidence, however, suggests that Pukina may have been the primary language of the Tiwanaku state, while Uru appears to be the language long associated with lakeshore dwellers (Adelaar 2004; Torero 1987). Genetic studies suggest a long history of population expansion and admixture across the central Andes by both Aymara and Quechua groups, possibly beginning with the spread of agriculture in the Formative period (Barbieri et al. 2011; Batai and Williams 2014). Yet examination of genetic relationships with contemporary Uru and Aymara groups indicates some diversity within these populations, supporting the hypothesis that Uru and possibly Pukina speakers adopted Aymara due to pressures from Spanish control (Barbieri et al. 2011; Bouysse-Cassagne 1992).

Apart from language, there are a variety of cultural practices, including clothing, foodways, rituals, and belief systems, that contribute to one's identification as Aymara in Bolivia today, including the Taraco Peninsula (Albó 1979, 2000; D. Arnold, Aruquipa, and de Yapita 1992; Buechler and Buechler 1971; Canessa 2012). For example, most adult Aymara women wear distinctive clothing. This usually includes a full, brightly colored *pollera*, a sweater, and a shawl draped over the shoulders and pinned at the front (*llecla*). While other styles of brimmed hats are becoming popular, women most commonly don a bowler hat, which became popular in the early twentieth century. As this typical fashion illustrates, contemporary Aymara practices are mixtures of pre-Hispanic Andean, European, and modern influences that reflect the dynamic ways in which Indigenous populations adapted to and also resisted colonial pressures (MUSEF Editores 2019). Likewise, you will meet many women who speak fluent Aymara and prepare typical dishes, yet do not wear a *pollera* and still consider themselves Indigenous. As several scholars of contemporary Indigenous groups point out, it is futile to try and tease out which things are "Indigenous" and which things are "European" because that is not how people understand their practices or what gives them meaning (Abercrombie as cited in Canessa 2012). As Andrew Canessa (2012, 65) states, "Indigenous authenticity is not to be found in 'proving' historical continuities." Rather, we can examine the various elements of what constitutes the daily livelihoods of people who self-identify as Aymara and trace out the dynamic histories of practices as they emerged and shifted.

Although many Aymara now live in the cities of La Paz and El Alto, making a living from a variety of modern economic pursuits, construction workers, clothing manufacturers, transport workers, vendors of all variety of goods, and politicians, they come from a long tradition of farmers, pastoralists, and fisherfolk and continue to have ties to their rural communities. Today, in places like the Taraco Peninsula, many Aymara families continue these practices, producing food for their own households, for extended family in the city, and, in the case of surplus, for sale in local and city markets. Thus, the farming, herding, and fishing practices still carried out each day on the peninsula are particular to this region and contribute to their identities as Indigenous and Aymara. As will be discussed, many of these practices have origins deep in the past; others are more recent.

One aim of this book is to contribute to the literature of contemporary Indigenous livelihoods in the Lake Titicaca Basin and bring to a broader audience the vistas, stories, and histories of the remarkable place and communities of people on the Taraco Peninsula. As Keith Basso (1996) encouraged anthropologists to do in his book on Apache landscapes, *Wisdom Sits in Places*, I aim to evoke a sense of being on the Taraco Peninsula "by presenting a host of local details and taking note of their own and others' reactions to them." I do so with the recognition of my own positionality as a white, non-Indigenous woman from the United States who has had the immense *privilege* to have the opportunity and permission to live and learn from these generous communities and individuals. This has allowed me to study and bring to bear the experience and deep knowledge of the current Taraco residents to my investigations into the past lives of people on the Taraco Peninsula, particularly with regard to farming.

The Indigenous farming systems of the Andes are widely recognized as repositories of traditional ecological knowledge (Altieri 2004; Altieri and Koohafkan 2004) and have been identified by the Food and Agriculture Organization of the United Nations as a "Globally Important Agricultural Heritage System (GIAHS)" (FAO 2011). As I will argue further below, studying and documenting these current systems is of value in and of itself, but this knowledge can also help us better understand the past (P. Anderson 1999; Baleé 1994; Denevan 2001; Ford 1994). I am not assuming or suggesting that the modern Taraco inhabitants are frozen in time and present perfect analogies for the interpretation of past agricultural practices. Rather, my goal is to observe and record the material manifestations of farming, particularly in plant remains, by Indigenous experts on the Taraco Peninsula. I can then compare material patterns from the present and past to identify potential similarities, possible continuities, as well as differences and divergences (Hildebrand 2003; Stahl 1993; Wylie 2002). Together, the ethnographic and archaeological information can be used to provide a deeper and richer long-term history of agricultural landscapes on the Taraco Peninsula.

Finally, I hope that the details presented here of Indigenous agriculture on the Taraco Peninsula across multiple generations can serve as a model for the future. Many aspects of this subsistence farming lifestyle are transforming and will continue to do so. Opportunities for Indigenous people in Bolivia changed significantly in the early 2000s when Evo Morales, an Aymara man who came from a rural village like those I describe here, became Bolivia's first Indigenous president. This opened new opportunities in government, business, and other sectors that were difficult to access previously. Staying "out on the farm" appears to be less desirable by the younger generations, who have a new range of opportunities in urban settings across South America. Of the two Taraco families I lived and spent most time with, *none* of their children have taken up adult residence on the peninsula. Most live in El Alto working various jobs such as police officers, vendors, seamstresses, and minibus drivers, and several of the other children have migrated to Peru, Argentina, and Brazil to work. The adult children return to their family homes to help their aging parents with a variety of tasks, especially agricultural work. This transition away from farming and into more industrial and technologically "developed" economies not only presents challenges for the continuation of unique and important Taraco lifeways but also has global implications in terms of food production, greenhouse gas emissions, and other issues related to the current state of Earth's changing climate. It is not my intention here to suggest that my host sisters and brothers, and their children, live as their parents and grandparents did. Instead, I ask, what if we *all* placed greater value on those lifeways, learned from them, and worked toward maintaining the beneficial aspects of them? What might those of us living in urban, nonproducer, non-Indigenous contexts learn from this example of what Anna Tsing (2017) would describe as "resurgent" communities who have developed viable ways of living through interactions with many nonhuman actors in their surroundings?

While this book highlights how various aspects of Taraco livelihoods have changed dramatically since people began living here permanently about 3,000 years ago, it also illuminates what has persisted. Despite many profound shifts in climate, economy, society, and politics, this examination of Taraco livelihoods reveals some practices, particularly engagements with plants, that have endured over very long periods of time. A large part of what has made these communities successful for millennia has been their ability to adapt, resist, and rebound by building relationships and generational knowledge of this place through agriculture. I argue that the long-term history of Indigenous landscape creation through farming on the Taraco Peninsula is an important example of sustainability.

DEFINING SUSTAINABILITY

Sustainability is something of a "buzzword" that, in the twenty-first century, signals human efforts (or at least the appearance of efforts) to behave, develop, produce, and grow economies in a way that minimizes harm to other entities on Earth and that enables future generations to persist and thrive. This concept emerged out of the late twentieth-century environmental movement as concerns grew over land degradation, air and water pollution, accelerated species extinctions, and human-induced global warming associated with industrialization, modernization, and neoliberal economies spreading across the globe. In 1987 the United Nation's World Commission on Environment and Development codified the term in relation to economic development in the Bruntland report, *Our Common Future*, stating: "Humanity has the ability to make development sustainable to ensure that it meets the needs of the present without compromising the ability of future generations to meet their own needs" (UN Secretary-General and WCED 1987, 16). The term has now been used in a wide variety of contexts, in and outside of development, and is not without criticism (Brightman and Lewis 2017; Murphy and McDonagh 2016).

Here I employ the concept of "sustainability" on two levels. First, in a broad sense, which has been expanded upon by anthropologists and other social scientists, to represent "the connective tissue between ideas of responsibility, rationality, value, and ethics, all embedded in the broader concerns for the future of the world in which we live" (Murphy and McDonagh 2016, xvii). An anthropological approach to sustainability aims to highlight lifeways that provide potential solutions to our current crises of resource depletion and global warming (Brightman and Lewis 2017; H. L. Moore 2017; Pikirayi 2019). It works toward futures that value and support multiple ways of living in the world: "Sustainability . . . might be best understood as the process of facilitating conditions for change by building and supporting diversity—ontological, biological, economic and political diversity" (Brightman and Lewis 2017, 2). A broader (and more ambitious) goal of this book is to elevate the lifeways of Indigenous Taraco residents as an example of how people outside of this specific region might find greater balance and productivity within their places (Altaweel 2008; Denevan 1995; Fisher 2020; Guttman-Bond 2010; Turner et al. 2020). The ways in which they do this are fundamentally connected to their knowledge of and relationships with the nonhuman entities that they share the world with, particularly through their daily activities of farming, herding, and fishing. Anthropologist Anna Tsing (2017, 51) argues that "meaningful sustainability requires multispecies resurgence, that is, the remaking of livable landscapes through the actions of many organisms." As this book will highlight, Taraco farmers are a model for such actions.

Second, in a narrower sense, I examine the idea of "sustainable agriculture." Definitions of sustainable agriculture are often contrasted to modern, industrialized food systems that emphasize high inputs, technology, and monocultures that are rooted in the Green Revolution (Altieri 2004; Gold 2007; Netting 1993). Although these systems have been able to increase overall food production, they have had detrimental consequences to the environment as well as human communities. Definitions of sustainable agriculture from the agronomic and development sectors mimic those of the Bruntland Commission that aim to "balance economic profitability, social equity, and environmental health" (Hand 2016, 10); this could include restoring soils and watersheds, producing in a way that maintains profitability, and better supporting a community (Mason 2003). Fisher (2020, 396), who examines how archaeology can contribute to sustainable agriculture, employs the definition from the Food and Agricultural Organization of the United Nations: "the production of food and other agricultural products, like fiber and fuel, in ways that ensure that future generations will be able to continue to do so and, simultaneously, conserve and, ideally, enhance the environment." Through the course of this book, I detail the elements that created and continue to contribute to the productive, flexible, and enduring food production system on the Taraco Peninsula.

At the heart of understanding sustainability and what it looks like is an inquiry into how humans live in the world and their relationships with their environs and other nonhuman inhabitants and entities. The study of human-environmental interactions is in many ways a peculiar one to Western thinking and science, viewing ourselves (humans) as something distinctive from everything else on earth (environment) (Bateson 1972; Descola 1994). As a result, Western scholars have come up with a variety of ways to think about and understand these relationships, today and in the past (including the concept of "sustainability" itself). To move away from that dichotomy, I take a landscape approach to these human-environmental interactions, for I believe it can help us define and understand sustainability in its multiple dimensions.

DEFINING LANDSCAPES

Much like sustainability, landscape is a useful, although at times, unwieldy concept (Tilley 1994, 37). The term *landscape* has developed and been employed by several disciplines, including art, but particularly geography and anthropology (Jackson 1984). Although the landscape concept itself has shifted "to and fro along a natural-cultural continuum" (Knapp and Ashmore 1999, 6), the most fruitful and useful conceptualizations of it have served to collapse the nature-culture dichotomy to better understand humans as part of environments in both evolutionary and historical senses. It is not my aim here to review all of the definitions of landscape (see Anshuetz, Wilshusen, and Scheick 2001; Balée 1998; Falconer and Redman 2009; Gosden and Head 1994; Hirsch 1995; Knapp and Ashmore 1999); rather, I consider five aspects of the landscape concept that make it useful for an archaeologist interested in studying past agricultural systems. Landscapes are material, historical, lived and grown, social and political, and meaningful. These elements of agricultural landscapes, in particular, not only facilitate investigation into the dynamics of present and past farming systems but also provide important insights into the daily lives of the people, places, and entities that bring them to life.

Material

The first essential element of landscapes is that they are material: they are tangible, physical entities that can be observed at a variety of scales and times (Sauer 1925). One of the most cited definitions of landscape by the archaeologist and historical ecologist Carole Crumley (1994, 6) is "the material manifestation of the relation between humans and the environment." Landscapes are composed of almost an infinite number of physical elements that a researcher could examine, each of which tells a story about a particular moment in place and time. For this reason, scholars have often characterized landscapes as texts, things that can be read and interpreted (Bellentani 2016). The description at the start of this chapter was my depiction of a Taraco landscape at a particular moment in space and time. It highlighted many elements that can be experienced in the Taraco landscape, including the topography, soils, water, plants, animals, humans, as well as built features and activities taking place in this area.

Archaeologists have long looked for patterns in the landscape to "reconstruct" or access subsistence practices (Denevan 2001; Erickson 2006; Knapp and Ashmore 1999). In this study, I focus on several material aspects of landscape as they relate to agriculture. I consider nonorganic elements of the Earth, such as topography, soils, and water. I do this primarily through the study of soil types, lake levels, and settlement patterns as well as remnants of ancient field systems. I examine in even greater detail nonhuman organic elements, including animals but particularly plants. Zooarchaeological studies provide insights into the role of animals, especially domesticated camelids. My own research is archaeobotanical and focuses on patterns in plant remains, such as wood, tuber remains, and seeds. I also consider features and artifacts such as agricultural fields, tools, and vessels. Taken together, this assemblage of material remains provides surprising insights into many aspects of past agricultural landscapes. Of course, each element interacts with the others, and it can be difficult to separate them at times, but I attempt to "zoom in" on certain elements to understand their specific roles in the whole landscape.

The materials that constitute landscapes can be viewed from many scales. If we examine the peninsula from a satellite in space through Google Earth, we might note the patterns of fields across the peninsula, the location of houses, and the height of the lake. If we zoomed in to a particular plot of land and took a soil sample, we could observe the size of the particles that make up the soil and test its attributes, such as levels of pH and organic matter. In the field we could examine actions of organisms like plants and insects that, at once, can threaten or support a growing potato. The materials of landscapes vary depending on not only *where* you observe them but also *when*. The description at the start of the chapter takes place during the rainy season when plentiful moisture makes the peninsula green and bloom with colorful flowers. Just a few months later, the rains disappear and are replaced with clear skies and colder temperatures. The crops are all harvested, and the remaining vegetation on the peninsula becomes a yellowish brown. Across the chapters, I take care to note the different spatial and temporal scales that create Taraco agricultural landscapes. Time is particularly relevant and is the focus of the next aspect of landscape to consider.

Historical

Landscapes are historical. As Tim Ingold (2011, 189) has stated, "Landscape is constituted as an enduring record of . . . the lives and works of past generations who have dwelt within it, and in so doing, have left there something of themselves." Although some features of a landscape are products of the current moment—for example, the weeds growing in Alejandra's field that need to be removed for her crop to grow—aspects of them are the result of past activities. The weeds were growing in the potato field because generations of farmers have been tilling this land, making it hospitable to species that thrive in disturbed soils. Furthermore, the now ubiquitous, yellow-flowered plant *ñustasa*[3] arrived in the region when Spanish colonists brought over their crops and animals. While an examination of landscape can reveal elements that endure or persist, most elements undergo change through time. As Turner and colleagues (2020, 589) note, "Landscapes must change. It is one of their fundamental characteristics, experienced every day at scales from diurnal rhythms, through the revolution of the seasons, to the passage of life and death." Elements on the landscape also change at different rates or tempos, contributing to the complex dynamics of these places at any given moment (Braudel 2023; de Certeau 1984; Gell 1992; Ingold 2011; Lucas 2005).

For the nonorganic elements examined here, processes of climate play a critical role in shaping the character of the landscape. The high, dry *altiplano* and high, abundant lake that we experience today is the result of geological and climatological processes that unfolded over very long time scales, hundreds of thousands of years, and even changes that have occurred over the relatively shorter 3,000-year period considered here. Geological and paleoclimatic datasets provide insights into the characteristics of the local region over this long span of time, especially highlighting its changes (Dincauze 2000; Rosen 2007). As will be elaborated, I quickly learned from the Taraco farmers that variations in rainfall and temperature experienced across the seasons fundamentally shape the nature and timing of agricultural work. This seasonal organization of daily life and its associated tasks seemed so important that I have chosen to organize the vignettes that begin each chapter by the seasons and activities of the agricultural calendar. So while I will consider how farming changed over generations of farmers, I will also consider what yearly and seasonal practices would have adjusted across these periods.

Plants and nonhuman animals also have their own rhythms and paces at which they change, develop, and interact with humans, particularly in the context of agriculture. As with the "nature-culture" dichotomy mentioned earlier, there have been great debates within anthropology and archaeology about whether the dynamics between humans and the environment through time are more evolutionary—shaped by biological processes such as natural selection (Boyd and Richerson 1988; Broughton and O'Connell 1999; Laland and O'Brien 2010)—or historical—shaped by human processes such as migration or trade (Balée 1998; Hodder and Hutson 2003; Ingold 2011). Landscapes, however, are fundamentally the outcome of both evolution and history, especially if we focus, as I do here, on plants. On one hand, humans intervened in the evolutionary process of natural selection by selecting for and promoting certain traits within plant and animal species, at first creating new domesticated species but then continuing to develop distinctive varieties (Rindos 1984; B. D. Smith et al. 2015). When certain species—maize, for example—were introduced to the region, experimentation was required to figure out the best way to grow this tropical crop in this cold, dry environment; thus, farmers eventually developed a variety of maize that grows and matures relatively quickly. As a result, the plant itself and the cob are quite small. It is nearly impossible, and I would say fruitless, to attempt to disentangle the historical from the evolutionary in this case as it is a product of both. Also, many of the "unintended consequences" of human behaviors, such as clearing land for fields, produce changes in the patterns of wild plant species. Some of these species flourish and other perish in the face of human disturbances (E. Anderson 1952; Bruno 2009). The life cycles and long-term patterns of both domesticated and wild species, and their responses, some might say their agency, to human activities are a central theme in this case study of multispecies resurgence (Hallam and Ingold 2016; Kimmerer 2013; McEwan 2022).

Although evolutionary processes such as climate change, natural selection, and gene flow contribute to the character of Taraco landscapes at any given time, I am most interested here in how such dynamics are experienced and acted upon by the human communities on the peninsula. For this reason, I do prioritize the term "history" regarding the temporal and interspecies dynamics of what is being read from the landscape. This leads to another key element of how landscapes can be defined and understood: they are not simply backdrops upon which humans act but are lived and experienced, constantly in a state of creation (Anshuetz, Wilshusen, and Scheick 2001, 158).

Lived and Grown

Landscapes are the ongoing creation of human and nonhuman actors. Crumley and others use the term "interaction" to describe the nature of these connections between nonhuman and human elements of landscape (Heckler 2009, 11). Interaction, however, can suggest some passivity or simply responses to a stimulus when, in reality, humans and nonhumans are actively engaging with, moving through, experiencing, and impacting each other on a daily basis. A term from phenomenology commonly invoked to describe this active engagement is to "dwell" (Heiddeger 1971). Ingold's (2011, 193) definition of landscape emphasizes this attribute: "the world as it is known to those that *dwell* therein, who inhabit its places and journey along the paths connecting them."

The notion of dwelling highlights the activities that create a landscape or, as Basso (1996, 143), referencing Albert Camus emphasizes, a *place* is something people *do*. Dwelling connects again with the first tenet that landscapes are material, they are created and experienced daily through tactile activities. This relates to social theories of practice, which understand cultural dispositions as those tangible things that are learned and lived through regular action, both habitual and purposeful (Barrett 1994; Bourdieu 1977; Giddens 1979; Pauketat

2001; Robb 2007). Thus, as Andrew Roddick (2013, 289) notes, dwelling "re-embeds particular technical practices into a wider lived landscape." The array of activities, or tasks, that take place across a landscape is what Ingold has termed a *taskscape*: "Just as the landscape is an array of related features, so—by analogy—the taskscape is an array of related activities" (Ingold 2011, 195). The taskscape framework has been used by archaeologists to examine a wide range of past activities (Rajala and Mills 2017; Roddick 2013; Walker 2012). There are many activities that have taken place and continue to do so across the Taraco landscape: fishing, herding, hunting, potting, building, organizing, worshiping, celebrating, and mourning. I build on Andrew Roddick's (2013) first steps to "develop an 'archaeology of inhabitation' for the Lake Titicaca basin." His work focused on embedding the technical practice of pottery production in the landscape, including links to agricultural practices. Here I elaborate on those. Agriculture involves a myriad of technical practices: preparing the soil, planting, tending, harvesting, processing, and, of course, cooking and eating (Walker 2011). These agricultural tasks were my main entryway into learning about Taraco farmers, as much of my ethnographic fieldwork was spent as a helper to the Quispe family and others who allowed me to accompany them. Furthermore, in the 74 interviews about the agricultural cycle that I conducted across four Taraco communities, Chiripa, San José, Santa Rosa, and Coa Collu, I quickly discovered that the farmers consistently described their agricultural year by talking me through the tasks that marked each season. For this reason, the opening vignettes also highlight these practices. Examining these particular agricultural activities and their material manifestations not only help us understand patterns present on the landscape today but provide an avenue for seeing and tracking them in the past.

Ingold (2011, 77, 86) argues that landscapes, particularly those inhabited by agriculturalists and pastoralists, are "grown" rather than made. Farming is not a mastery of humans over nature but a change in relationships. Take into consideration the abundance of potatoes and other tubers that grow on the Taraco Peninsula and across the Andes today. In the process of domestication, humans selected for traits in wild potatoes that made them more edible, such as less toxicity and larger tubers (Grun 1990; Hawkes 1990; Johns 1989). These traits, however, also made them more susceptible to damage by other organisms, such as nematodes, and environmental conditions, such as frosts, so it required humans to create specific conditions in which these new species could survive and flourish. This was brought to life for me one day when Alejandra declared, *"Bien he hecho papa"* or "I've done a good job making potatoes" after we had completed an afternoon of pulling weeds, piling up dirt around the base of the growing potato plants, and fixing the furrows running between each row. This whole process is called *th'aruña* in Aymara. This activity loosens the soil around the tubers so they have more space to grow and ensures that water reaches them without inundating them. Although we were months away from harvesting and seeing the final product of these efforts, Alejandra expressed how the work that goes into helping them grow is what makes a good potato. Therefore, an understanding of landscapes as places that are lived and grown can help us move from the patterns in lake levels, soil types, or plant species to how such activities would have shaped people's everyday experiences and understandings of their world. As Barrett (1994, 5) explains, a landscape approach moves us toward "an understanding of what the possibilities were of being human within those historical and material conditions."

While I examine tasks on their own terms and what they can reveal about past agricultural activities, they connect in important ways to other aspects of past Taraco livelihoods. These tasks were carried out in and upon social and political units, from members of a household harvesting their own field of potatoes to hundreds of people feasting on foods brought in from across the community. These interpersonal dynamics create another critical layer of understanding agricultural landscapes.

Social and Political

Landscapes are social and political. As Don Mitchell (1996, 33) observes, "Landscape structures social reality; it represents our relationships to the land and to social formations." The creation of agricultural landscapes is shaped by the social and political contexts in which they are embedded, as they are the direct result of people's labor. A plentiful harvest is as much the result of successful coordination of the human actors as it is the cooperation from the weather, soil, pests, plants, and animals. The relationships between agriculture and changes and characteristics of human social and political organization have long been a topic of anthropological interest (Graeber and Wengrow 2021; Wittfogel 1957). Around the world many (but not all) human communities that became dependent on domesticated plants and animals also saw transitions to more sedentary lives, larger population sizes, and increasingly complex ways of organizing and interacting with each other. Much debate has ensued about the causal relationships between social-political complexity and food production systems—which came first? Was there one driving force such as climate change, population pressure, coevolutionary entanglements, optimizing or aggrandizing human behaviors (M. N. Cohen 1977; Flannery 1969; Hayden 1990; Johnson and Earle 2000; Wittfogel 1956)? It is tempting to look at the final outcomes of hundreds of years of human-environmental interactions and tease out if there was a single factor driving the changes we observe, but a landscape approach moves us away from monocausal outcomes and shifts our focus to the practices and processes that produced changes in both agriculture and sociopolitical organization (Barrett 1994; Heckler 2009; Hirsch 1995; Robb 2007).

As John Robb (2007, 7) points out, "Social reality . . . is continuously generated through individual action—through ordinary actions whose proximate aim is to accomplish some specific task at hand." From the taskscape perspective, we can examine who is/was participating in agricultural activities and how they are/were organized at different scales (Gamble 1999; Roddick 2013; Walker 2011). We can also consider the products of those activities, particularly food, and examine how it was consumed, shared, and redistributed inside and outside the household (Appadurai 1981; Hastorf 2016; Logan 2020; Weismantel 1998). These considerations illuminate important dynamics and distinctions of social life such as age, gender, and status. The opening scene of this chapter highlights just a few that exist on the peninsula today: young and middle-aged men fishing, middle-aged and elderly women cooking and carrying out field maintenance, teenaged children tending to animals. Some of these tasks can be done alone, such as weeding or putting out grass/lake reeds for animals to eat. Big jobs such as planting not only require more than one person but get accomplished much more rapidly with many helping hands. While household units are usually the basis of these group efforts, they often involve additional neighbors and even relatives or friends from out of town and other communities. These are communal activities that not only accomplish an agricultural task but re-create and shape the social landscapes of Taraco life.

Many scholars have examined how power dynamics are inscribed onto physical spaces, molding how a place looks and feels and how individuals move through and experience it for generations (A. M. Bauer and Johansen 2011; A. M. Bauer and Kosiba 2016; Hu 2022; Jennings and Swenson 2018; Knapp and Ashmore 1999; A. T. Smith 2003; S. C. Smith 2016). There are political structures that influence who can do what; for example, there are quite strong rules around gendered activities. One of the most visible and dynamic elements of power that shape agricultural landscapes is where farming takes place. Farming requires space that is dedicated to the raising of plants and animals, and the regulations and negotiations of who plants and raises where is a fundamental political component of the landscape (Erickson 2000; Hastorf 2009; Kosiba 2018; Morrison 1995). For example, the layout of homes and fields today is not based on the optimal placement for productivity but rather a reflection of how land was divided up among families after the Bolivian Revolution in 1952 and the Agrarian Reform of 1953 (Klein 1993; Soriano 2017). As will be elaborated, access to the range of soil types is certainly part of the calculus of when and where to plant, as well as when and how long to fallow a field. Yet, as I learned in my interviews, for some families the length of fallow periods is not necessarily determined by the time the soil needs to recover but how much land they have available to cultivate. While some families have enough land to leave fields fallow for up to 20 years, some have so little they can only afford fallows of one or two years. This was a result of a political decision made over 60 years ago and how the land subsequently got divided up among siblings.

Where and to what scale agricultural tasks take place thus links us to the broader political landscape that is both shaped and created out of these practices and others. Considering the dynamics of agricultural production as well as food practices will shed light on the ways in which farming articulated with changes in sociopolitical structures across the Formative and Tiwanaku periods. I consider how agriculture articulated with the built environment (the location of fields, homes, monuments) and larger-scale, extra-household community gatherings and rituals. These, in turn, created new and different demands of the food production systems. Archaeologists in the region have long been interested in such political elements of the Titicaca Basin agricultural landscape, especially when it comes to one of its most unique features, raised fields, a topic that I will also address.

Meaningful

Entering through the materiality of agriculture, we can engage in the physical relationships that created a productive place in which generations of farmers could sustain themselves. Through these material practices we can also engage with some of the meaningful elements that are also part of landscapes. Keith Basso (1996, 109–10), describing Apache landscapes in Arizona, notes, "Represented and enacted—daily, monthly, seasonally, annually—places and their meanings are continually woven into the fabric of social life, anchoring it to features of the landscape and blanketing it with layers of significance that few can fail to appreciate." Thus, as tasks are carried out together, lessons are taught, not just about productivity but also life. These lessons are inscribed on these places.

This aspect of landscape allows us to engage with the idea of sustainability not just in an environmental sense but as a social one as well. The meaningful aspects of landscape often contain recipes for what a society believes is required to succeed and reproduce within their surroundings. According to Descola (1994, 3), "It is on this one condition that we can show how the social practice of nature hinges at one and the same time on the idea a society has of itself, the idea it has of its material environment, and the idea it has of intervention in that environment." While it is not possible to access all meanings of the landscape from past people, the material manifestations of how Taraco residents have interacted with the elements of soil, lake, animals, plants, and each other over generations reveals attitudes toward their relationships with the world and the ways in which they have been able to sustain their communities with both change and persistence.

EXPLORING TARACO AGRICULTURAL LANDSCAPES

I begin this exploration into the long-term development of Taraco agricultural landscapes, in chapter 2, with an overview of the cultural and political history of the peninsula's Indigenous communities beginning approximately 3,000 years ago. While I discuss the entire span of time up to the present, I elaborate on the early time periods that are the focus of my study: the Early Formative, Middle Formative, Late Formative, and Tiwanaku periods. I discuss major patterns in settlement, material culture, architecture, and sociopolitical dynamics based on data gathered from an archaeological survey and excavation at four sites by the Taraco Archaeological Project. In this overview I highlight the spatial characteristics of human settlements on the peninsula, including homes, community centers, and lands for farming and other productive activities. This also allows for an examination of how human interactions changed on the landscape as populations grew and new social and political dynamics emerged both on the peninsula and across the southern Lake Titicaca Basin. This framework sets the stage for discussing the elements of Taraco agricultural landscapes through time and space in the following chapters. While the chronological framework presented here is important for initiating this story, subsequent chapters will explore how different elements of the landscape have different temporalities, some of which correspond to social and political changes while others do not. This eventually requires a rethinking of some common narratives about the trajectory of human development in the Lake Titicaca Basin.

In chapter 3 I start with the initiation of the agricultural year when Taraco farmers begin to prepare their fields at the end of the dry season. I explore several inorganic elements of the Taraco Peninsula: topography, soil types, rainfall, and lake levels, and how their spatial and temporal variation influence agricultural landscapes. I consider how modern-day farmers plan the timing and distribution of their yearly agricultural activities in relation to these patterns. This informs a discussion about the character of Formative and Tiwanaku period land use for farming and herding and how inhabitants may have dealt with documented periods of lesser and greater rainfall by moving their activities across the landscape. This leads to an examination of raised fields, a technology that became particularly important during the Tiwanaku period and that developed, I will argue, out of Formative period farmers' experiences with shifting lake levels and soil manipulation.

Chapter 4 is the first of several chapters that highlight my primary source of information on Taraco landscapes: plants. This chapter begins with the planting of the annual harvest and an introduction to the domesticated plant species that contribute to the agricultural history of the area. While there are many species to consider, the primary actors visible in the archaeological record are chenopods (quinoa and *kañawa*) and tubers (potato and *oca*) as well as an introduced species, maize. I examine the broad trends in these species through the major Formative and Tiwanaku periods across four sites on the peninsula: Chiripa, Kala Uyuni, Sonaji, and Kumi Kipa. The history of these crop-actors is one of striking continuity, particularly in the cultivation of quinoa and tubers. There is also a trend of increasing crop diversity through time.

In chapter 5 we enter the rainy season and the work required to help crops grow. This involves an examination of the many noncrop species that dominate the archaeological plant record and that would have been important actors in shaping past landscapes. These plant species are responsive to human activities, including farming. Their changes through time indicate shifts in land use and other practices associated with smallholder agricultural intensification, particularly an increase in tilling the soil. Although many of these species might be considered "unwanted," as they present competition for crops, residents of the peninsula today also have many other uses for them, especially as animal fodder. The archaeobotanical evidence illustrates that these plants nourished past domesticated animal herds; thus, the patterns in these noncrop plant species also shed light on the pastoral elements of Taraco's ancient landscapes.

Chapter 6 begins to narrow the spatial and temporal scale of this study as I focus in on the processes and practices by which crops were transformed into food. This chapter begins with the harvest of the yearly crop and the processing required to store plants for future use. To consider such practices in the past, I look in greater detail at the plant remains from the site of Kala Uyuni. First, I introduce the archaeological evidence for how this community was established and transformed across each time period considered in this study. I then examine patterns in the density, diversity, and distribution of carbonized plant remains in different types of contexts, from living floors to garbage pits. These patterns reveal where plant-related activities, which were preserved through fire, took place. I focus specifically on evidence for the processing of crops, particularly quinoa, across time and space at Kala Uyuni.

In chapter 7 I turn to the transformation of plants and animals into meals at Kala Uyuni. The introductory vignette highlights the structure of daily and special-occasion meals prepared on the peninsula today. I then reconsider the list of archaeological plant and animal species as ingredients in meals taking on the roles of starches, proteins, relishes, and spices. Examination of specific contexts of food preparation, consumption, and disposal at different moments of Kala Uyuni's history illuminates patterns in both daily and special-occasion meals through time. Through the politics of food at Kala Uyuni, I consider how this community articulated with the social and political dynamics of the peninsula and the broader southern Lake Titicaca Basin.

In chapter 8 I weave back together the individual landscape elements of soil, water, animals, and plants to present a history of early Indigenous agriculture on the Taraco Peninsula. I synthesize these multiple lines of evidence by describing agricultural taskscapes and how they transformed through time. This inquiry prioritizes the patterns seen in plant and animal remains, which reveals continuities and ruptures in human life on the Taraco Peninsula that differ from the traditional cultural history described in chapter 2. This history reveals remarkable continuities in multispecies engagements and agricultural practices that enabled Indigenous communities on the Taraco Peninsula to manage fluctuations in local climate and significant transformations in sociopolitical configurations. This persistence involved not only profound knowledge of the nonhuman components of the landscape but meaningful engagements with them as well. I argue that Indigenous farmers of the Taraco Peninsula provide an important model of "resurgent communities" whose practices allow for human communities to endure in an area for long periods of time without exhausting the organic and nonorganic entities that they depend upon. While we cannot adopt these specific practices, we can look to cultivate those in our local places and support initiatives and policies that protect such livelihoods around the world.

2

Taraco Peninsula Communities

Space, Place, and Time

Today, the most common route to the communities on the Taraco Peninsula is by public minivan or bus. They leave from a bus terminal in the city of El Alto, the urban home to nearly 1 million people, who mostly originated from and still have connections to Indigenous rural communities. Whether it be small or large, drivers pack as many passengers as possible into their vehicles as well any number of goods being brought from the city to the countryside—including sacks of clothing and food and even live animals. The paved Pan-American Highway takes travelers west across the vast *altiplano* and into the Lake Titicaca Basin. To access the communities located along the southern shore of the small Lake Wiñaymarka, where the peninsula is located, the buses must leave the paved highway and travel the maintained dirt roads that circle the perimeter of the peninsula (figure 2.1).

All along the journey, one can see single-story homes scattered across the landscape, made of either adobe or brick and calamine roofs, although there are still a few homes that have traditional *totora* reed roofs. The homes usually have two or three rectangular buildings and an enclosed patio area. Several hectares (ha)[1] of fields and pasture separate one home from the next. Clusters of single- and multi-story buildings built around a paved or cobblestone plaza, usually marks the center of a town. The buses will stop anywhere along the road that a passenger requests, but they always make planned stops at these town centers.

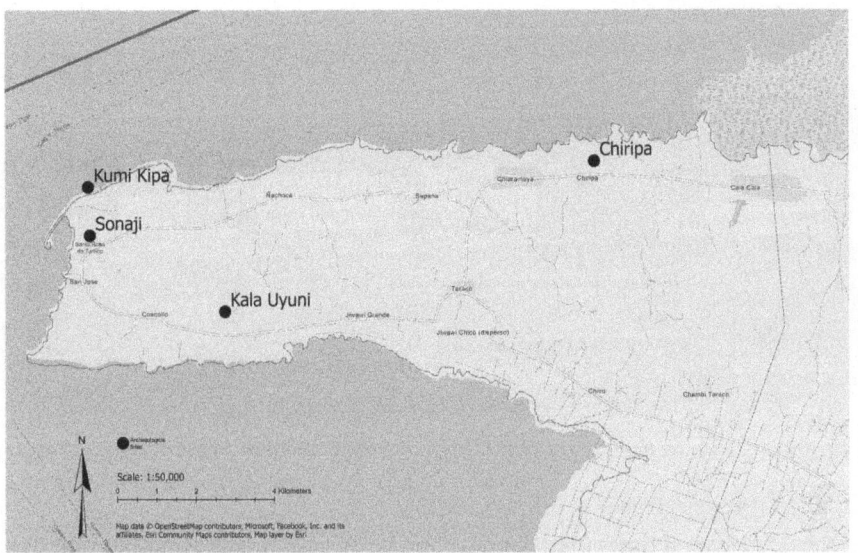

FIGURE 2.1. *Map of the Taraco Peninsula indicating the location of modern-day communities along the main road. Chiripa, Santa Rosa, San José, and Coa Collu participated in the ethnobotanical study. The four archaeological sites studied by TAP are also indicated.*

My first experience with this journey and the Taraco communities was in July 2000 when I traveled to the town of Chiripa to gather information from local farmers for my master's thesis about quinoa. Although I would later live in family homes during my visits to the peninsula, during this first trip I lived in a community building called the *sede social* (simply referred to as the *sede*) with four other North American graduate students who were there conducting excavations and artifact analysis for their PhD dissertations. The *sede* is an important communal building where meetings and other activities take place, and it is usually located in the center of town. Various natural and cultural features help Chiripa inhabitants establish this "center" (figure 2.2). While the current layout is in part due to the influence of hacienda-period architecture, Chiripa has been influenced by its ancient spatial organization. About 1300 BCE the first residents of Chiripa built several sunken enclosures to the north and south of where the *sede* is located today. Like the *sede*, these buildings were public spaces used for community gatherings and ceremonies (described in more detail below). About 600 BCE the community built a cluster of small ritual structures (named "Lower Houses" by archaeologist Alfred Kidder) just west of the modern-day *sede*. This architectural complex was then

FIGURE 2.2. *The community center of Chiripa as photographed in 2017.*

renovated several times over the next 600 years, resulting in a mound that has remained an important landmark even after its abandonment. Today Chiripa's "Montículo," or mound, is the most famous and visited archaeological site on the peninsula.

In the late 1800s, nearly 2,000 years after its construction, when families from the wealthy Bolivian mestizo aristocracy purchased and took ownership of the land of this community, transforming it into a hacienda, they took a cue from the ancient leaders and built their house just a few meters east of the mound (Soriano 2017). Over the course of about 50 years, the *hacendados* destroyed portions of the mound when they constructed storage buildings, animal pens, and perimeter walls to the south of the house and east of the mound as well as a tennis court north of the mound. Despite some significant damage, they left the mound largely intact and hosted several archaeologists in the early twentieth century who came there to excavate it. When ownership of the land was returned to the Indigenous residents several years after the 1952 revolution (Klein 2003; Mesa, Gisbert, and Gisbert 2003), much of the hacienda infrastructure was torn down, and community spaces such as a soccer field, school, houses for teachers, and the *sede* were built over the course of the next two centuries; yet the house was left intact.[2] This entire complex, ranging from ancient to modern architecture, now defines the center of modern-day Chiripa. The community as a whole is further defined by several natural and cultural features that emerged out of a long history of settler colonial processes.

The Chiripa center is roughly halfway between two river valleys that flank the eastern and western limits of the modern-day community and perhaps that of the past. Today the community is organized into two "sectors," the western sector is referred to as Ocorani,[3] and the eastern sector is referred to as Chiripa. Houses are relatively well dispersed throughout each side of the community but are primarily located on the gentle slopes between the highest peaks and lakeshore plain (Soriano 2017). The locations of these homes and privately held plots (known as *sayañas*) are based on the repatriation of lands to Indigenous residents during the 1953 agricultural reforms (Buechler 1969; Benton 1999; Carter and Mamani 1982; Flores 1955). Although some areas in the communities were designated as communal use (*aynokas*), mostly for grazing animals, each family was allotted land for their homes and fields.

Households typically have two to ten members. The larger families usually consist of a married couple, an elderly parent or parents, and several children. One or two of the children might also be married and live in the same house, but most people establish new residences once they begin to have children. The households with only a few residents, such as a middle-aged couple with one or two children or, increasingly common, two elderly adults, reflect the fact that many people now migrate to the city of El Alto, only about 80 km away. It is especially common for children to take up residence in the city once they finish high school, looking to further their education and obtain a job. Once they leave the countryside, they usually return intermittently to help with agricultural tasks, especially planting and harvesting, and for annual community parties. They may return to fulfill obligations such as serving in leadership roles, required of all landholding families.

While daily economic and subsistence activities take place in the homes and fields of individual families, community events take place in the center of town in various public spaces. Because the *sede* is not used every day (unlike the school or teachers' houses), it made sense for the archaeologists to occupy it as their residence and laboratory. It was not uncommon, however, to have nightly visitors from the community. Schoolchildren found us to be a huge source of entertainment and peered through windows and doors at any opportunity. The most regular visitors, however, were the community leaders known as *mallkus*. Although recently women have begun to occupy more positions of power and authority, historically these posts were held only by men. The positions rotate each year through the households of each community; although elections are held to determine the individuals for each post, the roster is based on a list of families and serving is obligatory. The *mallkus* organize the monthly community meetings and oversee various projects that are either generated by internal demand or brought to them through governmental and nongovernmental organizations aimed at improving development in the countryside. An archaeological project is also an opportunity for meetings and discussions. The community must approve the project and establish a rotation for working so that everyone gets a chance to earn a small salary by helping with the project. The visits of the *mallkus* were thus a way for them to ensure things were running smoothly.

While the local town government and *mallkus* handle most community decisions and projects, communities like Chiripa are also part of a larger governmental jurisdiction. Chiripa falls under the municipality of Taraco, the center of which is the town of Taraco, about 5 km southwest. The municipality has a mayor, who is elected every five years. The municipality has access to larger sums of money from the central government and is thus an important source of power and funds for town projects. In 2014 a project aimed at helping with tourism was the construction of a cement *puerta* or large entrance to the Chiripa Montículo, a modern monument that has fundamentally changed the experience of the site and town and reflects the political dynamics between town and municipality.

This brief description illustrates how the current community of Chiripa, which comprises a social and political center, dispersed households, and lands for agriculture and other activities, has been created out of a tumultuous history of local and global processes. As I will describe in further detail below, the other three communities that participated in both the ethnographic and archaeological research presented here, Coa Collu, Santa Rosa, and San José, formed through similar processes as those described for Chiripa. While this is important information for understanding the modern agricultural practices and landscapes presented here, it also provides a gateway to thinking about how past Taraco communities developed and transformed. As we can see from the more recent history of Chiripa, the distribution and character of homes, fields, and public spaces and buildings are greatly influenced by broader social and political factors. Although we do not have written records to define what types of sociopolitical organizations influenced the ancient Taraco communities, archaeologists can approximate what types of organizations existed based on patterns in settlement size, types of architecture, depositional histories of excavated sites, as well as trends in material culture such as ceramics and stonework. A regional analysis of archaeological findings provides insights into changes visible across broad spatial and temporal scales, which helps to contextualize what we can know about particular communities from the study of shorter time periods and at particular sites (figure 2.3).

Archaeologists use changes in material culture, especially ceramics, coupled with radiocarbon dating to create the temporal frameworks, or chronologies,

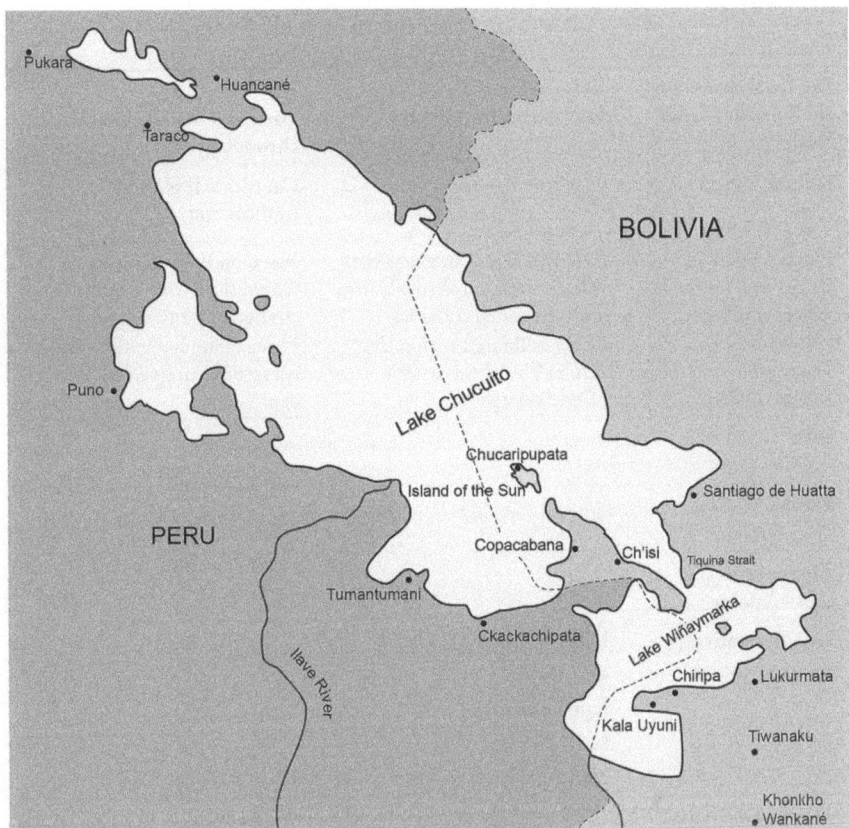

FIGURE 2.3. *Lake Titicaca, comprised of the larger Lake Chuquito and the smaller Lake Wiñaymarka, and archaeological sites mentioned in text.*

by which we define past culture-historic periods (Swenson and Roddick 2018). Although there is variation in these chronological schemas between countries and regions of the lake basin, there is some generally agreed-upon terminology and division of time periods (Hastorf 2005; Janusek 2003b; Stanish 2003). Here I use the chronology specific to the southern Lake Titicaca Basin where the Taraco Peninsula is located (Bruno et al. 2021) (table 2.1). This chronology is based on the most recent radiocarbon dates and calibrations, which have been refined using Bayesian statistical analysis, where possible. While I review the entire span of Taraco culture history here, I provide the most detailed information on the Formative and Tiwanaku periods, which are the focus of my research. The emphasis on these two periods is, in large part, a product of

TABLE 2.1. Archaeological chronology of the southern Lake Titicaca basin and Taraco Peninsula

Regional chronology for Southern Lake Basin	Refined South basin Late Formative chronology	Refined Chiripa Early and Middle Formative chronology
Janusek 2003; Hastorf 2008	Marsh et al. 2019	Capriles and Hastorf forthcoming
Based on sites in Katari and Tiwanaku valleys and Taraco Peninsula. Dates calibrated using IntCal curves	Based on Bayesian analysis of various sites across small basin with decorated ceramics. Dates calibrated with mixed IntCal/ShCal curve. 68% range of median date	Based on Bayesian analysis within the site of Chiripa using stratigraphy and ceramics. Dates calibrated with ShCal curve. 68% range of median date
Inca 1450–1532 CE		
Pacajes 1100–1450 CE		
Tiwanaku 500—1100 CE		
Late Formative 200 BCE–500 CE	Late Formative II 210–590 CE	
	Late Formative I 140–210 CE	
	Middle to Late Formative transition 250 BCE–140 CE	
Middle Formative 800–200 BCE		Middle Formative/Late Chiripa 725–226 BCE
Early Formative 1500–800 BCE		Early Formative II/Middle Chiripa 1026–725 BCE
		Early Formative I/Early Chiripa 1371–1026 BCE
Late Archaic 3000–1500 BCE		

the history of archaeology in the southern Lake Titicaca Basin. The site of Tiwanaku is considered one of the most important in Bolivia and has been the subject of investigation since the beginning of archaeology there (e.g., Bennett 1934; Posnansky 1945). The Montículo at Chiripa also attracted early researchers, particularly because it was recognized as a predecessor to Tiwanaku

(Bennett 1936; Kidder 1956; Portugal Ortiz 1992). Subsequently, more recent archaeological projects in this region of Bolivia have focused on understanding the dynamics of the Tiwanaku state itself as well as how it emerged from Formative period societies before it (Albarracin-Jordan 1996; Browman 1978a; 1978b; Hastorf 1999; Janusek 2008; Stanish 2003). This provides us with quite rich datasets upon which to understand this early culture history. Our archaeological knowledge of later time periods is more limited, particularly in the southern lake basin, and certainly deserve attention in the future. Although these periods are not the focus of this study, I include some description based on research in other regions and historical documents because they help to contextualize some of the practices of the modern-day Taraco inhabitants, which are important to the broader scope of this study.

In addition to the broad regional and temporal trends, specific developments that I examine at Chiripa, Kala Uyuni, Sonaji, and Kumi Kipa will illuminate other aspects of life in the region to complement the detail that will follow regarding agriculture. This chapter will set up discussions for broad and specific changes in the archaeological plant remains on the peninsula in the following chapters, which shed light on how agricultural landscapes articulated with the social and political dynamics of these early Taraco communities.

THE FIRST SETTLED COMMUNITIES: EARLY FORMATIVE PERIOD, 1500–800 BCE

The earliest evidence we have for human occupation of the Taraco Peninsula is in the Early Formative Period (1500–800 BCE). There were likely groups of hunter-gatherers that explored the peninsula earlier during what is known as the Archaic period,[4] 11,000–3500 BP (Aldenderfer 1989; Aldenderfer and Flores Blanco 2011; Haas et al. 2017; Haas and Llave 2015). Unfortunately, to date, archaeologists have not encountered any Archaic sites on the Taraco Peninsula, and they are scant in the broader southern basin (Bandy 2006, 87). The lack of Archaic archaeological sites may be attributed to the extremely cold and dry climate of this time (see chapter 3), which caused Lake Titicaca to be very shallow and saline (Aldenderfer and Flores Blanco 2011; Bandy 2001). In fact, the small Lake Wiñaymarka Basin, where the peninsula is located, was completely dry (Binford, Brenner, and Leyden 1996). Archaic hunter-gatherers seem to have spent most of their time in the more amenable environments of the northwestern region of the lake basin (Aldenderfer 1999; Aldenderfer and Flores Blanco 2011; Cipolla 2005; Craig et al. 2010; Haas and Llave 2015). Evidence suggests that these were highly mobile groups, and it is possible that they visited this southern region to collect specific resources near areas with some water. Unfortunately, these places are now submerged under modern-day Lake Titicaca (Bandy 2006; Erickson 2000). The general paucity of evidence for Archaic period sites, however, does suggest that it was not a particularly important place for humans until around 3,000 years ago (Marsh 2015). At this time, the relatively warmer and wetter climatic conditions that characterize the region to today—and the focus of chapter 3—became established.

The earliest archaeological sites on the peninsula, dating to about 1500 BCE, are the remains of small homesteads or hamlets, which were dispersed along the lakeshore and riverbanks (Bandy 2006; Bruno et al. 2021). The Early Formative hamlets of Taraco grew into one of the most populated regions in the basin at this time, yet were small enough so that households, fields, and grazing lands could be established throughout the peninsula without much competition. The presence of ceramics, stone hoes, and remains of domesticated plants and animals shows that these people were not hunter-gatherers but sedentary farmers and herders (Hastorf 1999).

The pottery that Early Formative Taraco inhabitants made was fairly simple, consisting primarily of different types of undecorated cooking and serving pots or *ollas* (L. Steadman 1999). These early communities also harvested the rich wild resources that the lake provided, such as fish, birds, and aquatic plants (Browman 1989; K. M. Moore, Steadman, and deFrance 1999; D. Steadman 1996; Whitehead 2006). Although most people likely lived full time on the peninsula, the presence of exotic materials such as obsidian and copper indicate that there was movement and/or exchange with areas outside of the basin as far as northern Chile and southern Peru (Browman 1998).

Early Formative deposits have been excavated at the sites of Kala Uyuni and Chiripa (Bandy 2007; Browman 1978b; Hastorf 1999). The earliest public architecture at Chiripa was a plaza built upon a natural terrace near a spring that overlooks the lake (Hastorf 2017). About 1000 BCE, people on the Taraco Peninsula began to demarcate important public spaces by building a specialized form of ceremonial architecture found across the Lake Titicaca Basin: the sunken court. As early as 1350 BCE (A. B. Cohen 2010), communities across the lake basin constructed these unique open spaces by first digging into the ground surface between 2 and 5 m deep. They used stones, mud bricks, and/or clay to erect the vertical walls and created smooth, clean surfaces with colorful yellow and red clays. They measured between 13 and 18 m wide but often had two shorter walls, creating a trapezoidal shape (Hastorf 2005; Janusek 2004c; Mohr-Chávez 1988). These buildings did not have roofs, indicating that the activities there involved observing the sky, very likely at night, from these semi-subterranean places (Hastorf 2017). At Kala Uyuni, above the Early Formative deposits on the hilltop of Achachi Coa Collu, residents built two sunken courts beginning around 1100 BCE (Bruno 2008; A. B. Cohen and Roddick 2007; Roddick, Bruno, and Hastorf 2014). Although these structures were simple, they represent gatherings of dispersed households in activities that were likely ritual in nature, yet were also settings where social and political ties could be forged and elaborated in early community landscape and place-making.

GROWING VILLAGES: MIDDLE FORMATIVE PERIOD, 800–200 BCE

The Taraco population continued to grow into the Middle Formative period, which spanned roughly 800 to 200 BCE. While small, isolated hamlets continued to exist throughout the basin and peninsula, many of them grew significantly, as estimated by sites on the surface measuring 5–10 ha (Bandy 2001). Such population growth within the limited space of the Taraco Peninsula required greater coordination among the residents to establish where homes, fields, grazing land, and even fishing areas could be established and utilized. It is possible that particular territories were established at this time, but communal land use was common in Indigenous communities in colonial and historic periods (Abercrombie 1998; Carter and Mamani 1982) and thus could have been an important form of land use in the past. This combination of growth and increased cooperation gave rise to the first villages: larger, more permanent settlements that included households and lands located within a defined area as well as communal spaces marked by the construction of more elaborate public architecture (Hastorf 2005; Janusek 2004c; Stanish 2003). Four such villages emerged on the Taraco Peninsula: Chiripa, Kala Uyuni, Janko Kala, and Yanapata (Bandy 2006).

Unfortunately, we have not been able to find much evidence of what Early or Middle Formative homes would have looked like. They were likely built of adobe and thatch, materials that do not withstand the test of time well. We do, however, find a great deal of garbage that accumulated through the activities associated with homes, fields, and pastures at both Chiripa and Kala Uyuni. These middens are rich in botanical, faunal, and lithic materials that have provided important insights into daily domestic activities (Bruno 2008; Browman 1998; Hastorf et al. 2022; K. M. Moore 1999; K. M. Moore, Steadman, and deFrance 1999; Whitehead 2006). Middle Formative villagers crafted pots and bowls for home use that were highly burnished or slipped with red paint and

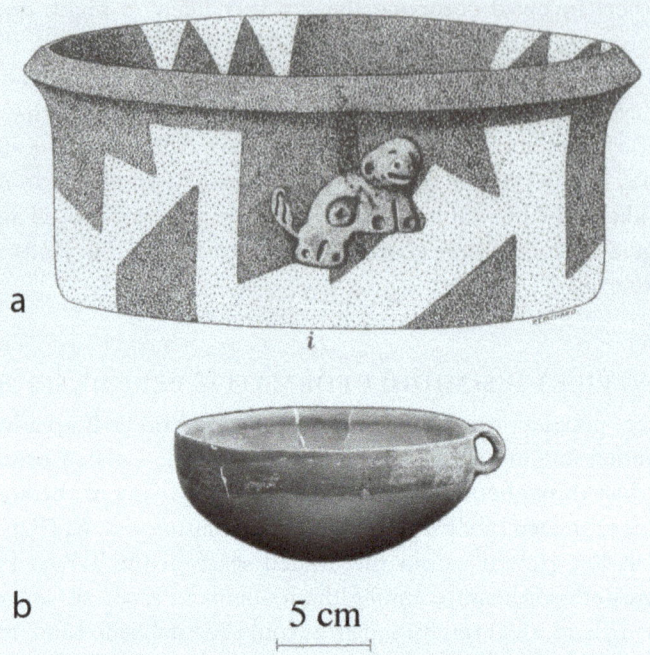

FIGURE 2.4. *Decorated ceramics from the Taraco Peninsula: (a) Middle Formative period, large cream-on-red bowl from Chiripa (Courtesy of the Division of Anthropology, American Museum of Natural History, cat. no. 41.1/3910, from Bennett 1936); (b) Late Formative period, red-rimmed/Kalasasaya bowls from Kala Uyuni (with permission from Andrew P. Roddick [2009]).*

were made from different combinations of clays and tempers than those their predecessors utilized (L. Steadman 1999, 2007). They also began to produce different types of vessels for public events and meals. The most common form was a large bowl (> 30 cm in diameter) that had a red slip with cream, black, or dark brown painted designs (Bennett 1936; Mohr 1966; L. Steadman 1999) (figure 2.4). Some vessels were incised or had modeled ridges, nobs, or zoomorphic designs. Some of the bowls have evidence of charring on the inside, suggesting they may have also been used as incense burners. In addition to vessels, people produced ceramic tubes with incised and modeled decoration, which archaeologists consider *trompos* or trumpets These decorated vessels are primarily associated with ritual architectural spaces constructed in each village (Roddick 2000; L. Steadman 2007).

FIGURE 2.5. *Stone monolith placed in the center of the Upper Court at KUAC and the "Lightning Stone" placed at the base of the monolith.*

The sunken court architecture that first appeared in the Early Formative became very widespread and elaborated during the Middle Formative period (Chávez and Mohr-Chávez 1975; Hastorf 2005; Levine 2020). At Chiripa the Choquehuanca sunken court continued to be used until about 800 BCE, when it was closed off and another, known as Llusco, was constructed about 80 m south (Hastorf 2017). At Kala Uyuni, on the hill of Achachi Coacoallu where the Early Formative burned features were found, two sunken courts were constructed, remodeled, and utilized for several centuries (A. B. Cohen and Roddick 2007; Roddick, Bruno, and Hastorf 2014). In the center of the Upper Court, archaeologists encountered a nearly 2 m tall sandstone monolith (figure 2.5). Among a fill of cobbles placed to stabilize the monolith was a stone with a *cross formée* engraved on the top and symmetrical serpentine pattern on the sides. The base was smooth and striated from use as a pestle. Similar stones are known around the basin and have been referred to as "Lightning Stones," but this is one of the only ones found in situ (Roddick and Janusek 2018).

Stone sculpture and stelae were important forms of expression in the lake basin starting in the Middle Formative period (Chávez and Mohr-Chávez 1975; Portugal Ortiz 1998; Roddick and Janusek 2018; Schaedel 1952; Stanish 2012; Valcárcel 1935). The earliest styles consist of zoomorphic figures such as snakes, frogs, and lizards, as well as shapes that are circular or wavy. Later the iconography becomes more detailed and includes human imagery. One of the most famous stelae is from Taraco, Peru (Chávez and Mohr-Chávez 1975). Each side of the large slab has a single human character with a T-shaped nose, round eyes, and a simple mouth. Each has arms crossed over the chest and other details that suggest that one represents a female and the other a male. This motif was also found on stelae from other sites in the basin, and Sergio and Karen Chávez (1975, 46) named the style "Yayamama," meaning "male-female" in Quechua. Bolivian archaeologists, particularly Max Portugal Ortiz (1998), also noted that many Formative period sculptures simply had two faces, not necessarily male and female, and so referred to the style using the Aymara "Pa-ajanu," meaning "two faces." This Yayamama/Pa-ajanu style also includes zoomorphic images, such as llamas, felines, raptors, and amphibians, geometric designs, but all with a more abstract, surreal design than that of the previous generation of sculpture.

Sunken courts were not the only type of public architecture to be constructed by Middle Formative communities, however. The famous Chiripa Montículo is the best-known example. Although a sunken court may have been at the center of the architectural complex since its inception (Bandy 1999), several other building types served as important spaces. Construction began around 600 BCE as a ground-level compound of rectangular buildings with simple cobble foundations and clay floors, which were rebuilt over several generations. As noted earlier, the archaeologist Alfred Kidder (1956) referred to them as the "Lower Houses." The term "house" is a bit misleading because there is no evidence of hearths or domestic trash to indicate that people lived in these buildings; rather they were spaces constructed for specialized purposes such as storage and possibly closed rituals and ceremonies (Hastorf 2003; 2017; Mohr-Chávez 1988). Residents at the site of Alto Pukara constructed similar structures on a terrace but without a sunken court (Beck 2004). Around 800 BCE Chiripa residents closed the lower buildings in a similar manner to the Achachi Coa Collu courts—with burnt offerings—and then built a mound with a fill of about 3 m (Bandy 1999; Browman 1978a; Kidder 1956). It is thought that they constructed a sunken court at the center, although it is difficult to know this because it was later remodeled and the earlier structure was not preserved. Around the perimeter of the mound they built 14 rectangular buildings, which Kidder (1956) called the "Upper Houses." These buildings were rectangular, approximately 10 m long and 5 m wide, with sliding doors. Along the interior walls they built narrow rectangular bins. These also were not "homes"; instead, they were used to store crops as well as very fine ceramics and gold. There are also several burials in and near the mound, including beneath the "house" floors (Machicado Murillo 2008). The use of this phase of the mound ended around 250 CE.

The developments in settlement patterns, site histories, ceramics, architecture, and art during the Middle Formative period reveal growing populations that expanded and elaborated local community gatherings, particularly at sunken courts, where ritual and political relations were forged and negotiated. Karen Mohr-Chávez (1988) suggested that the common occurrence of sunken courts, fine ceramics, and stones carved with the Yayamama (Pa-ajanu) iconography represented the spread of a shared religious tradition throughout the basin. She proposed that the individuals who coordinated the activities at places like the Chiripa mound "may have been involved in the administration of ritual and worship, and even production, distribution, and consumption, perhaps regulated by periodic ceremonies associated with the temples" (Mohr-Chávez 1988, 17). Through these rituals and religious ideology, she suggested that diverse groups throughout the basin were unified both ideologically and perhaps economically.

As populations expanded and specialization in ritual and political matters emerged, these places would be settings where disagreements could be settled, marriages and familial alliances could be arranged, and important members of previous generations could be remembered and revered. Matthew Bandy (2004; 2006) envisions that community tensions on the Taraco Peninsula were ameliorated at these important places, thus permitting a stable period of autonomous village formation during the Middle Formative period. While the four Taraco villages appear to have been autonomous, there may have been some competition among them. Charles Stanish (2003) and Abigail Levine (2012; 2020) also suggest a competitive scenario where early elites organized community members to construct these structures. In these scenarios competition could have been intensified by gaining control over the trade and display of exotic goods, which they "strategically redistributed in public ceremonial or commensal contexts" (Bandy 2001, 197). Christine Hastorf (2003; 2005; 2017) proposes a more grassroots organization and motivation for the construction and use of these public architectural spaces. Rather than a scenario where commoners are persuaded to participate in the construction of the structures by party-throwing elites or leaders, she argues for individual willingness to participate in the construction in order to connect with the ancestors and reify links with the community and its location on the landscape. She points out that many of these structures have burials associated with them and thus makes the argument that these are places where "ancestors" were remembered and venerated. Not only would such activities renew one's relationship with other members of the community and its territory, but rituals related to fertility and life would also ensure success in the agricultural season and the health of their animals. Hastorf's consideration of the role these buildings may have played in the agricultural landscape of the Middle Formative period is something that I aim to investigate in more detail here. In chapter 5 I will examine activity areas and the distribution of food remains across two main areas of Middle Formative activity at Kala Uyuni, Ayrampu Qontu, and Achachi Coa Collu. Consideration of how food production may have articulated with the activities in these areas, particularly the sunken courts, can shed light on the nature of social and political processes at this time.

EARLY POLITICAL CENTERS: LATE FORMATIVE PERIOD, 200 BCE–500 CE

Significant changes in material culture, architecture, settlement patterns, and sociopolitical organization occurred after 200 BCE, marking the beginning of what is referred to as the Late Formative period. Political centers that influenced people beyond their own villages, also referred to as multi-community polities, emerged throughout the lake basin at this time. These centers encompassed larger populations, built more elaborate ritual sectors, and developed new ceramic and artistic traditions, some of which had elements from the Middle Formative period while others were drastically different. In the northern lake basin in modern-day Peru, the site of Pukara is the best known and most studied of these centers (Franco Inojoso 1940; Klarich and Bustinza 2012; Mujica 1988; Stanish 2003; Kidder 1943). Work at sites such as Huancané (Plourde 2006), Taraco (Peru) (Levine et al. 2013), and Tumantumani (Stanish and Steadman 1994) on the western shore suggests that there were other centers vying for prominence, at times violently, in the region (Stanish 2003; Stanish and Levine 2011) (figure 2.3). In the southern lake basin political centers developed at Tiwanaku (Janusek 2004c; Marsh 2012b), Lukurmata (Bermann 1994; Janusek 2004c), Khonkho Wankané (Janusek 2018; S. C. Smith 2016), and Chucaripupata (B. Bauer and Stanish 2001; Seddon 1998; Stanish and Bauer 2004), while regions such as Santiago de Huatta appear to have remained more decentralized (Lémuz-Aguirre 2001).

Settlement data on the Taraco Peninsula indicates that there was a notable shift in the number and distribution of people. Three of the four largest Middle Formative villages declined in population (Chiripa, Janko Kala, and Alto Pukara) with only one, Kala Uyuni, growing significantly (Bandy 2001; 2004). Two other villages on the western tip of the peninsula, which had fairly small Middle Formative populations, rose to prominence, Sonaji and Kumi

Kipa. This cluster of Late Formative villages became the center of population growth and ritual activity, leading Bandy (2004) to propose that the western peninsula became a locus of political power, what he refers to as the Taraco Peninsula Polity. Although the surface remains of these villages cover large areas (12–15 ha), reflecting the broad horizontal extent of these settlements, excavations at these sites reveal an equally profound vertical depth, illuminating the complexities of growth and change during the Late Formative period (Bruno et al. 2006; Roddick, Bruno, and Hastorf 2014).

One of the most notable shifts from the Middle Formative to Late Formative was in the way people produced pottery. Paste recipes shifted to finer-grained clays with mica and other mineral tempers (Janusek 2003b; Lémuz-Aguirre 2001; Roddick 2009; L. Steadman 2007). Potters developed new sizes and shapes of pots and bowls and began to make jars (*vasjias*). Although the raw materials for constructing vessels became finer, decoration became simpler compared with the highly burnished and embellished Middle Formative finewares (Roddick and Hastorf 2010). There is an interesting absence in decorated ceramic production and use between the end of the Middle Formative period (250 BCE) and the Early Late Formative period (also referred to as Late Formative I) (120 CE) (Marsh et al. 2019). The most common decorative motif to emerge at this time was a simple red band painted along the rim of a beige-to-yellow vessel (Janusek 2003b; Marsh et al. 2019; Ponce Sangines 1993). Although this red rim occurs on finely made jars and pots (*ollas*), the most common form is a small, delicate bowl (figure 2.4). The timing and presence of Kalasasaya[5] red-rimmed vessels varies across the southern basin, but they are very common at Taraco Peninsula sites through the end of the Late Formative II (420 CE) (Marsh et al. 2019; Roddick 2009). Another type of decoration that appears around 120 CE is zonal incision, with incised designs on a beige-to-yellow base with red, black, or white paint of geometric shapes (Janusek 2003b; Ponce Sangines 1993; Roddick 2009; L. Steadman 2007). On the Taraco Peninsula and across the southern basin, this style is less common, especially compared with the red-rimmed vessels, but was found in small quantities at Kala Uyuni, Sonaji, and Kumi Kipa (Roddick 2009). This style also seems to be shorter-lived than the red-rim, declining around 240 CE (Marsh et al. 2019). At the end of the Late Formative period, around 420 CE, a new style develops, referred to as Qeya[6] (Janusek 2003b; Marsh et al. 2019; Ponce Sangines 1981; Wallace 1950). This style is marked by painted black-on-red geometric designs as well as anthropomorphic and zoomorphic designs. There are also new vessel types, including deep, scalloped bowls (*sahumadores*) and jars with flat bases and wide, flaring rims (*escudillas*). This style is quite rare across the basin, but some vessel fragments were recovered at Kala Uyuni, Sonaji, and Kumi Kipa on the peninsula (Roddick 2009).

There is both continuity and change in Late Formative public and ritual architectural forms. The sunken court continues to be an important feature across the basin, appearing in new architectural complexes at sites such as Pukara, Taraco (Peru), Khonkho Wankané, Lukurmata, and Tiwanaku, among others (Hastorf 2005; Levine 2020). In contrast, they do not appear to be particularly important on the Taraco Peninsula at this time. In fact, there appears to be an overt abandonment of them. The court at Chiripa may have continued to be in use (we cannot know because later modification during the Tiwanaku period destroyed such evidence), but it was not a particularly influential place during the Late Formative when population and politics appear to have shifted to the west (Bandy 2001; 2004). At Kala Uyuni the residents closed the sunken courts of Achachi Coa Collu, burning and burying their floors, walls, and powerful stones by approximately 200 CE (A. B. Cohen and Roddick 2007; Roddick, Bruno, and Hastorf 2014). While it is likely that this place was remembered and revered, new traditions were established down the hill, where the new population center was established by approximately 20 CE.

During this period at Kala Uyuni, as well as at Sonaji, central sectors were demarcated by prominent earthen platforms oriented toward the lake, measuring nearly 50 m × 50 m in area (Bandy 2007; Hastorf et al. 2005). Elevated and terraced platforms were also constructed at other Late Formative political centers, such as the "Qalasasaya/Kalasasaya" areas of Pukara and Tiwanaku. While the lake and streams cut into the hillsides to help create these terraces, excavations reveal that generations of occupants built these areas up, resulting in the prominent platforms we see today (Bruno et al. 2006; Roddick, Bruno, and Hastorf 2014). Rather than subterranean spaces for public gatherings, platforms, often with yellow clay surfaces, created large and open spaces for gatherings. As will be discussed in more detail in chapter 6, the platform at Kala Uyuni was built up over a series of four occupations, several of which included architectural complexes distinctive from those we have seen at other sites. The most elaborate of these phases included oval-shaped buildings that had thick walls, which we have termed "chambers." They had an opening toward the west, possibly facing a larger, open plaza. They were eventually closed, and the area was reworked in what appears to be a more residential sector. The reconfiguring of these sites may have corresponded to the shifting political dynamic on the western peninsula across the Late Formative period.

To date, we have not encountered any carved stelae or portable carved stone (aside from tools) that can be attributed to the Late Formative period at any of the Taraco Peninsula sites. This could simply be a matter of (bad) luck, despite fairly extensive excavations at several sites. Alternatively, if we consider the apparent abandonment of sunken courts, the lack of such objects could also reflect a rejection of the previous "Yayamama/Pa-ajanu" religious traditions that utilized carved stone as a means of expressing and engaging with the supernatural or possibly an object of authority. This certainly was not the case at other prominent Late Formative centers in the southern Titicaca Basin, particularly at Tiwanaku and Khonkho Wankané, where production and use of carved stone objects continued and became quite sophisticated (Roddick and Janusek 2018; Stanish 2012). In the Late Formative stone iconography, there is a shift away from more naturalistic imagery to more detailed, geometric, and stylized imagery. There are still some similar human motifs that derive from the Yayamama/Pa-ajanu tradition, such as complete individuals who are front-facing with large eyes and wearing belts and headbands (Hastorf 2005). Human heads without bodies also become more common, some of them possibly depicting living individuals or important ancestors, such as the tenon heads found in the Tiwanaku sunken court, but some may also be decapitated heads (D. Y. Arnold and Hastorf 2008; Hastorf 2005). Animals continue to be represented while some are more lifelike, such as camelids; others are more mythical or supernatural and appear to be flying (Janusek 2004c). At Khonkho Wankané, Janusek (2004b, 147) describes a combination of human and animal motifs on monoliths depicting "a single anthropomorphic being with facial decoration or ornaments, arms crossed over the chest (left over right), and associated zoomorphic mythical images."

This new imagery, while developing out of earlier styles, reflects changes in belief systems related to religion and politics, particularly as leaders in these various political centers may have been attempting to differentiate themselves (Janusek 2004c). It is also worth mentioning that in the northern basin, particularly at Pukara, decorated ceramics became a primary medium by which ritualistic and political messages were conveyed. Using an incised polychrome style, Pukara potters incorporated red, black, and white paint to create images of felines and llamas, supernatural beings, dismembered heads, humans holding axes, and decapitated human heads (Chávez 1992; E. Franquemont 1986; Rowe and Brandel 1969). Important figures, both male and female, who are front-facing and holding their arms out to their sides with objects such as staffs, leashes holding camelids, and even tenon heads, first appear in the lake basin on Pukara pottery. Hastorf (2005, 89) describes this as "more aggressive power imagery," suggesting a shift away from the communal, ancestor-oriented gatherings and political dynamics of the Middle Formative period.

These Late Formative political centers appear to have developed greater influence over surrounding populations compared with the Middle Formative village centers, and it appears that some individuals or groups began to wield greater, disproportionate power and influence than previously existed (Bandy 2006; Hastorf 2005; Janusek 2004c; Stanish 2003). The nature and source of power among each polity seems to have varied on some common themes as we find diversity in how monumental centers were constructed, how material culture such as serving wares and stonework were crafted and deployed, and the degree to which physical violence or aggression may have been utilized or at least threatened. While there is some evidence for small-scale warfare or physical aggression in the northern lake basin (Levine 2012; Stanish and Levine 2011), the success of other political centers appears to be rooted in the ability to manage elements of the economy, particularly trade via camelid caravanning and agriculture, as well as success in hosting rituals and potentially feasts where the religious prowess and generosity of local leaders would be on display (Janusek 2018; Lémuz-Aguirre 2001; Marsh 2012b; S. C. Smith 2016).

Bandy (2001, 2006) argues that trade and redistribution of nonlocal goods underwrote the influence of the "Taraco Peninsula Polity" and that leaders at the centers of Kala Uyuni, Sonaji, and Kumi Kipa appear to have shared and shifted influence during this time. In general, little consideration has been given to the potential contribution of agricultural production and intensification in the emergence of these Late Formative polities. This could be due to the fact that many scholars viewed raised field agriculture, which will be discussed in more detail in chapter 3, as the primary indicator of "intensive" agriculture, which has primarily been attributed to the Tiwanaku period (Bruno 2014a). In addition to investigating the role that food played in the gatherings taking place in the Kala Uyuni chamber architecture, I will also consider the work and coordination involved in agricultural production on the peninsula during the Late Formative and what role it might have played in the dynamics of polity formation there.

The Taraco Peninsula Polity shared some characteristics with other Late Formative polities, particularly in the southern Basin, such as expanded monumental architecture with the construction of raised platforms as well as the manufacture and use of red-rimmed and incised vessels and later some Qeya wares. Yet the lack of powerful and supernatural imagery on stonework or pottery suggests that political influence for local leaders was rooted in distinct ideals and strategies. Several scholars suggest that while each of the regional polities only controlled the local communities, they likely interacted with each other and may have been in competition as well (Bandy 2006; Janusek 2004c;

Stanish 2003). It was out of this regional dynamic that the region's first state, Tiwanaku, emerged in approximately 500 CE.

NEIGHBORS OF THE STATE AND CITY: TIWANAKU PERIOD, 500–1100 CE

As significant as the changes appeared to be on the Taraco Peninsula between the Middle and Late Formative periods, an entirely and perhaps even more profoundly different social and political shift occurred in the next chapter of its history. Throughout the entire Formative period, Taraco Peninsula political and ritual leaders came from within their own communities and villages, although the dynamic shifted from village to village. As the Late Formative polities of Kala Uyuni, Sonaji, and Kumi Kipa negotiated their local dominance, the leaders emerging in the Tiwanaku political center, just 20 km to the southeast, created new forms of material culture, architecture, stone sculpture, and ritual that would translate to a highly influential political and ideological entity that eventually encompassed all of the Late Formative centers around the lake. Tiwanaku's influence would then extend to parts of the larger south-central Andes, becoming the region's first state (Albarracin-Jordan 1996; Janusek 2008; Kolata 1993; Ponce Sangines 1981).

There is scant evidence for Early or Middle Formative occupation at Tiwanaku. Marsh (2012a) argues for the founding of Tiwanaku in the Late Formative period around 110 CE. This village had a sunken court and associated monoliths in the Yayamama/Pa-ajanu style. This court was later elaborated with the addition of tenoned heads and remained part of the monumental core where larger buildings were constructed around it (Vranich 2009). As described earlier, much of the data that helped to define Late Formative ceramic styles derived from excavations of the earliest levels below the Kalasasaya temple (Ponce Sangines 1993).

The Tiwanaku people converted the modest Formative village and polity into an impressive ceremonial center with a series of monuments made of earth and massive carved stone originating from quarries across the lake basin (Browman 1978b; Janusek et al. 2013). Over several generations, the Tiwanaku constructed the major monuments of the Kalasasaya platform, the Akapana platform mound, and the Puma Punku platform as well as other smaller plazas and temples such as the Chunchukala and Kerikala (Escalante Moscoso 1997; Janusek 2008; Kolata 2003b; Nair and Protzen 2013; Vranich 1999, 2009). Tiwanaku leaders transformed Late Formative ideological traditions into a new, highly influential religion that was at the heart of their ability to garner widespread regional political and economic control (Albarracin-Jordan 1996; Janusek 2008; Kolata 2003a; Ponce Sangines 1981). The ideology was certainly communicated via verbal and performative acts, which we no longer have access to, but aspects of it were conveyed via artistic media of stonework, ceramics, and textiles.[7] The Tiwanaku further developed the art of stone carving and engraving that emerged in the Formative period. In addition to carefully shaped stones used in the site's architecture, immense stones were shaped into monoliths, lintels, and doorways that were intricately engraved with images of humanlike deities, animals, and other beings that were likely central to the people's religion (Nair and Protzen 2013). The most prominent deity is a front-facing anthropomorphic being with a rayed headdress and arms extended to the side holding two staffs, commonly known as the Staff God. This individual is often flanked by human and birdlike attendants standing in profile with a staff (W. H. Isbell and Knobloch 2006). The most famous portrayal of this assemblage was carved onto the Gateway of the Sun but is seen on other stones and on textiles. The largest monoliths were carved into individuals holding paraphernalia in each hand, a drinking vessel (*keru*) and a snuff tablet (Janusek 2020). These "Presentation Monoliths" appear to be serving or consuming alcoholic maize beer (*chicha*) and hallucinogenic plants, elements likely central to the rituals and transformations conducting by the Tiwanaku religious and political leaders. While some of these traditions may have been practiced in exclusive locations, such as in rooms atop the Akapana with only people who had access to the most intimate ceremonies, rituals were also conducted in more open spaces. Areas such as the Kalasasaya and Puma Punku could hold a large number of people, and there is evidence for massive feasts in and around this impressive and elaborate ceremonial center. The immense quantity of sheet middens and large garbage pits encountered around the city have also led Janusek (2013) and others to suggest that feasting and rituals took place everywhere across the city. Not only did these events attract visitors during special occasions, but a large, permanent population established itself into what is now considered one of the earliest urban centers in the high Andes.

While local households that were established in the Late Formative period may have grown in number and size, the greatest population growth derived from people migrating from other regions both near and far. Distinctive residential sectors, or barrios, were established both within the ceremonial center and surrounding it (Couture 2002; Janusek 2003a, 2005; Kolata 2003b). The elite rulers and ritual specialists of Tiwanaku lived closest to the central monuments, just west of the Akapana, at the Putuni palace (Couture 2004; Couture and Sampeck 2003). At least five distinct barrios have been identified surrounding the center (Couture 1993; Janusek 2004a; Rivera Casanovas 2003). Household archaeology at Tiwanaku has provided a rich understanding of urban life and daily practice there. Although there is evidence for a diversity of lifeways that people brought to Tiwanaku from their homelands, such as ceramics and foods, many adopted practices that contributed to a Tiwanaku identity. For example, housing compounds were built with a similar orientation and construction style. They also began depositing garbage in a similar way. While extensive sheet middens have been encountered in these residential areas, the most ubiquitous feature are large pits, often with amorphous shapes that may have initially been dug for construction (mud brick) and were filled with refuse from daily and special-occasion activities (Couture 1993; Janusek 2013). While this may seem like a minor detail, large garbage pits have become one of the ways in which archaeologists identify Tiwanaku occupations both in the city and outside of it.

Tiwanaku not only became *the place* to be but also developed a material culture that was used in the city center and became an important element of its influence elsewhere. While this included new textile fashions (Conklin 2013; Oakland 1986), Tiwanaku's new ceramic styles spread widely and have been preserved well in the archaeological record. By 590 CE in the southern lake basin, there were notable changes in ceramic styles from the Late Formative period (Marsh et al. 2019). Tiwanaku ceramics are characterized by a fine paste, thin but durable walls, a reddish-yellow base color, and burnished red slip. Painted over this red base were designs of black, yellow, white, and even pink (Alconini Mujica 1995; Bennett 1934; Janusek 2003b; Ponce Sangines 1981). Some designs were geometric, but many included scenes of humans, animals, and supernatural beings. Molding was also used to create vessels with incredibly realistic figures of animals and human faces. Forms that first emerged in the Late Formative (Qeya) period, such as the *sahumador* and *escudilla*, became more elaborate and common. As with earlier periods, there was a common bowl form (referred to as *tazón*), that measured slightly larger than the red-rimmed bowls and with angular walls. Perhaps the most iconic vessel associated with Tiwanaku was a tall drinking goblet, referred to as a *keru*. There are a few examples of proto-*kerus* that date to the Late Formative period at the Putuni in Tiwanaku and even at Kala Uyuni, but the Tiwanaku artisans refined the form, making the walls thinner and often including a modeled band or figure along the rim. The vessels produced at Tiwanaku were found throughout the city from temples to house middens. Although there are many markers of Tiwanaku influence, its ceramics are one of the most diagnostic features of the state's reach beyond the city.

Hand in hand with its ideological influence, the Tiwanaku people built upon, and transformed in novel ways, the well-established Titicaca Basin economic bases of agriculture, pastoralism, and trade. They increased agricultural production by building expansive systems of raised fields throughout the lake basin, a topic that I will address in more detail in chapter 3 (Bandy 2013; Erickson 1996; Kolata and Ortloff 1996; Seddon 1994a; Stanish 1994). They also obtained nonlocal goods, including maize, precious stones, salt, and hallucinogenic plants through trade and exchange via camelid caravans (Browman 1978b; Nuñez and Dillehay 1979; S. C. Smith 2016). Camelid herds were managed by the state not only for transport of goods via trade but for their wool, meat, and dung, an important fuel and fertilizer in the treeless *altiplano* (Bruno and Hastorf 2016; Janusek 2013). As Janusek (2004c, 150) notes, Tiwanaku was able to garner greater influence over the other Late Formative polities through "its ability to incorporate diversity through the creation of a flexible, elegant cosmology and a range of prestigious goods and practices that gave each group good material and ideological reasons for being part of its overarching culture, network, and polity."

While the archaeology of Tiwanaku itself has helped us define many aspects of this early state, sites outside of the center have revealed the unique nature of its statecraft and degrees of control, which was by no means homogenous and in many ways distinctive from other states that would emerge in the Andes (Vranich and Stanish 2013). Tiwanaku established strong links with two temperate regions outside of the lake basin, likely to increase its inhabitants' access to maize. Sites in the Moquegua Valley of southern Peru show that people from Tiwanaku itself moved there and created settlements that reflected their direction relationship with the center. For example, at the site of Omo 10, residents constructed a sunken court, residential sector, and cemetery similar to what is found in the highlands (Baitzel 2018; Goldstein 1993a, 1993b, 1998). There appears to have been very little interaction with the Indigenous inhabitants of the valley. In the temperate Andean valley of Cochabamba, Bolivia, the relationship to the highland populations appears more indirect but still quite influential. Tiwanaku-produced ceramics spread to the region, and local variations of the style developed (K. Anderson 2013; Higueras-Hare 1996). There were likely *altiplano* people living among the local populations, but the settlements in the area appear to be more of a mixture of local culture and adopted Tiwanaku elements. At sites such as Piñami, residents constructed a mound and appear to have been partaking in Tiwanaku-style religious and feasting ceremonies (K. Anderson 2013). Additionally, there is evidence for inhabitants from Cochabamba settling in Tiwanaku itself in the neighborhood of

Ch'iji Jawira (Rivera Casanovas 2003). Finally, in San Pedro de Atacama in Chile, there are only isolated finds of objects and burials of individuals with high-quality Tiwanaku paraphernalia, particularly snuff tablets (Berenguer Rodriguez 1998). The political and demographic influence there was minimal, but there may have been important individual relationships established through trade and interactions perhaps specifically around the religious use of hallucinogenic plants (Torres 1995; 2001; Torres and Conklin 1995). Overall, the Tiwanaku influence across the broader south-central Andes appears to be patchy, yet strategic in gaining greater access to important goods, particularly maize and hallucinogenic plants, and primarily ideological and religious in nature. This is in contrast to the Wari state that developed during the same period (also referred to as the Middle Horizon) in the central Andes. Wari settlements outside of its capitol, Huari in Ayacucho, Peru, appear to be more carefully planned and organized around a specific set of architectural elements for both residential and ritual architecture (W. Isbell and McEwan 1991; Jennings 2010; Williams 2013). There was a clear elite class with material culture and practices carefully replicated outside of the center as well as efforts to influence local populations through a combination of force, feasting, ritual activity, and even craft production (Biwer et al. 2022; Nash 2019). Although Wari and Tiwanaku appear to share some of the same belief systems—the front-facing god and attendants are found in the iconography of both states as well as rituals that involved the consumption of *chicha* and hallucinogens—they had contrasting approaches to their influence outside of their heartlands (W. H. Isbell and Knobloch 2006).

The Tiwanaku state appears to have had the greatest influence over communities in the Lake Titicaca Basin. Across the basin Late Formative communities eventually adopted Tiwanaku material culture, as evidenced by wide use of the redwares (Marsh et al. 2019). Tiwanaku's influence derived not necessarily from forceful colonization or conquest but from its unique and highly attractive religious activities as well as its ability to coordinate and possibly redistribute agricultural and trade goods across the basin (Bandy 2013; Janusek 2008; 2013; Stanish 2003). Despite the widely adopted material culture, the nature of Tiwanaku's influence over local economies and social practices varied. The community of Lukurmata, located on the shore of the southern lake basin and just east of the Taraco Peninsula sites, affiliated directly with Tiwanaku leadership and has been interpreted as its "second city" (Bermann 1994; Janusek 1994; Kolata 1989). The community constructed a monumental core with a platform mound and sunken court. There is evidence of elite residences with a Tiwanaku ceramic style that had a local flare (Janusek 2002). Residential settlements, which grew from the Formative period population, clustered along the shoreline and appear to be specifically overseeing and managing one of the largest expanses of raised fields utilized during this period (Janusek and Kolata 2004). Meanwhile, at one of the largest and elaborate Late Formative polities at Khonkho Wankané, the Tiwanaku influence appears to have dampened construction and expansion there, with several of the monuments becoming abandoned. Yet this likely remained an important region for camelid herding and node of caravans and exchange (Janusek 2018; S. C. Smith 2016).

The relationship with sites on the Taraco Peninsula is less clear and until recently has not been a focus for researchers there. Bandy (2001; 2006) notes a decline in population at the end of the Late Formative period, or Late Formative II, and he attributes this to the initial rise and influence of Tiwanaku in the valley around 300 CE. He argues that residents of the Taraco Peninsula migrated to the Tiwanaku center, attracted to its "hospitality," including influential religious and feasting practices (Bandy 2006; 2013). Yet there is relative continuity in population size and settlement patterns from what he defines as the Late Formative II into the Tiwanaku phase. Bandy's survey data suggest that Kala Uyuni, Sonaji, and Kumi Kipa continued to be some of the largest sites on the peninsula during the Tiwanaku period, but places like Chiripa also appear to have witnessed a resurgence. A surface survey indicates that the population at Chiripa grew again during the Tiwanaku period. The mound underwent some significant reconstructions, specifically the sunken court within the mound, suggesting that it became an important ritual site for the Tiwanaku people (Bennett 1936; Browman 1978a). The Late Formative II population decline may, in fact, be a misreading of the ceramic styles that defined it and what is found on the surface during the survey. Excavations appear to provide a better understanding of this transition and the impact that Tiwanaku had on Taraco populations.

In terms of settlement, there appears to be great continuity at Kala Uyuni, Sonaji, and Kumi Kipa, where we find deep deposits of Tiwanaku habitation overlying the Late Formative settlements. The horizontal deposits appear to be occupation zones that were disturbed and reworked by later farming activities. At Sonaji excavators encountered the remains of a Tiwanaku adobe structure, and at all three sites we found Tiwanaku burials with complete vessels and other fine goods (Hastorf et al. 2005). The most notable features left by the Tiwanaku people at these sites were abundant and, in some cases enormous, garbage pits. At Sonaji, in only a 6 × 6 m excavated area we encountered 22 Tiwanaku period pits (Bruno et al. 2006), and I will discuss several large pits at Kala Uyuni. As a result, TAP excavated a good deal of Tiwanaku period refuse, which provides insights into foodways, agricultural and pastoral activities, and other local daily practices during this time. Aside from a small cluster of raised fields near Chiripa, the lack of large expanses of raised fields on the Taraco Peninsula have led most scholars to conclude that the Tiwanaku state had little impact on agricultural production here (Bandy 2001; 2013; Janusek 2008). No one has made this argument directly, but an inference of these statements is that agriculture may have "de-intensified" in areas that were outside of the raised field producing areas in communities such as Kala Uyuni. The wealth of data presented by the organically rich Tiwanaku pits provides an opportunity to examine whether there were notable changes in agricultural production during this period. Additionally, Janusek (2013) suggests that the ubiquitous refuse pits found surrounding the site of Tiwanaku itself may not only be the result of daily activities but feasts and rituals that were central to Tiwanaku's appeal. The Taraco pits could also potentially represent such activities taking place in this "provincial" community and provide further insights into the influence of the state on the peninsula.

Tiwanaku's influence finally began to wane around 1100 CE, and its demise appears to be due to a variety of intersecting factors (Janusek 2008). The role of climate change has been a prominent explanation for its decline, particularly the claim that a drought curbed the production of raised fields (T. E. Arnold et al. 2021; Kolata et al. 2000; Ortloff and Kolata 1993). While it is possible disruptions or changes in production could have played a role in the state's collapse, other processes were likely unfolding that impacted the ritual and political leaders' ability to also manage these changes. There is evidence that the Tiwanaku elite became more exclusive and disconnected from the general population. The later phases of Tiwanaku residential architecture and ceramics suggest greater differences between the haves and have-nots (Couture 2004; Janusek 2008). By approximately 1150 CE, the city had declined in population, many of the important monuments were ritually closed off, and the state ceased to exist (Kolata 1993; Manzanilla and Woodward 1990).

DECENTRALIZATION AND ANDEAN CONQUEST: LATE INTERMEDIATE PERIOD AND LATE HORIZON 1100–1532 CE

After the fall of the Tiwanaku state, the population throughout the Lake Titicaca Basin split into smaller groups that formed independent kingdoms referred to as *señoríos* in Spanish (Stanish 2003). The southern Lake Titicaca Basin was part of the *señorío* called Pacajes. This seems to have been a relatively contentious time in the region, and throughout the Andes, as people abandoned their homes and villages located in lower-lying valleys near the lakeshore and moved to fortified hilltop enclaves, known as *pukaras*. While this shift in residence could reflect a shift away from agriculture and toward pastoralism, the defensive nature of these settlements suggests it had more to do with political disputes and warfare (Arkush 2006). In fact, studies of terraces of the *pukara* settlement at the hilltop site of Ayaviri, Peru, suggests continued successful production of tubers and quinoa (B. S. Langlie 2016). Bandy's survey (2001, 236) indicated that during the Late Intermediate period the Taraco Peninsula population remained high but that the Formative and Tiwanaku villages were abandoned and new settlements were established. We unfortunately have not yet excavated any sites from this period, and this would be an important future endeavor. As will be discussed in chapter 3, however, the raised fields in Chiripa continued to be used into the Late Intermediate period, providing some intriguing insights into land use and agriculture during this period.

The *señoríos* were powerful groups that controlled the productive Lake Titicaca Basin. It took two attempts for the Inca Empire to successfully conquer them between 1450 and 1475 CE (Klein 2003; La Barre 1948; Tschopik 1963). In order to better control the rebellious groups around the lake, the Inca relocated many people, often entire villages, to other regions of the empire (La Barre 1948, 28). The Inca also integrated the remaining populations into their regional economic network that involved two types of tribute (Rowe 1963). One form of tribute, called *m'ita*, was paid in labor: able-bodied men had to go work building roads, mining, and farming for the Inca. There was also a payment in goods such as crops and wool. Bandy (2001, 248–49) notes that on the Taraco Peninsula there is a shift in settlement toward the lakeshore and more agriculturally productive lands. This could potentially reflect pressure on local populations to produce goods for the Inca Empire.

SPANISH CONQUEST, *COMUNIDADES INDÍGENAS*, AND HACIENDAS: COLONIAL AND REPUBLIC PERIODS 1532–1952 CE

When the Spanish arrived in the lake basin in 1532, they encountered the populations around the lake and throughout the Andes laboring and producing for the Inca Empire and quickly inserted themselves as the benefactors of this system (La Barre 1948; Rowe 1963; Tschopik 1963). Although these local populations had been affected by Inca colonization, the Spanish colonization had a particularly drastic impact on local demography. New diseases caused many deaths, but also many people were sent to work in the silver mines of Potosí and perished there (Cole 1985; Klein 2003). The Spanish also claimed ownership over the newly discovered lands and redistributed them to Spanish governors in what were called *encomiendas*. The Indigenous people living on these lands thus became serfs of the new landowners and had to produce for themselves and the new owners (Klein 2003; Mesa, Gisbert, and Gisbert 2003). There is some indication that a colonial period hacienda was established near Chiripa, but not much evidence is available on where it was or how it impacted local populations (Soriano 2017).

In many areas the local populations were very dispersed and had agricultural lands spread throughout many different areas. In the late sixteenth century Viceroy Francisco de Toledo reorganized the Spanish colonies to gain better control of the Indigenous populations, particularly for taxation (Abercrombie 1998; Mesa, Gisbert, and Gisbert 2003). Based on Mediterranean farming communities, he wanted people to live in permanent, settled villages with access to "fixed and contiguous" agricultural lands. This was the origin of what are now known as *comunidades indígenas* or rural Indian communities, many of which still have the same names today (Albó and Barnadas 1985). Toledo also introduced the *reducciones*, which involved constructing new towns complete with a plaza, church, and government buildings and forced families to build their houses near this central location. The town of Taraco was founded at this time and likely drew in people from the surrounding area (Flores 1955). Historical documents indicate that there was a dramatic population decline across the lake basin during this period, attributed to the impact of both disease and displacement (Klein 2003). Interestingly, Bandy and Janusek's (2005) analysis of archaeological settlement patterns on the Taraco Peninsula and Tiwanaku Valley suggests that populations there may have fared better than historical documents indicate. They document many sites across the region during this time, although, as seen in previous eras, their locations shift. Bandy and Janusek suggest that this may reflect people purposefully moving to escape exploitation, as only persons labeled as *originarios* (locals) versus *forasteros* (outsiders) were obliged to participate in the labor tax. Some may have traveled to distant areas to escape taxation, but the settlement patterns suggest more local shifts.

In addition to the demographic impacts on local communities and agricultural production, the Spanish conquest had a very significant effect on the character of farming across the Americas but also locally (Crosby 2003; Tapia Vargas 1994). The Spanish introduced Eurasian crops such as barley, wheat, and fava beans; these were also accompanied by new wild species, such as the weedy mustard. They also introduced new domesticated animals, including pigs, cows, sheep, and goats. With cows and bulls also came a new technology, the plow. As will be illustrated in the ethnographic vignettes of the following chapters, these introductions have become essential to the agricultural landscapes of the Taraco Peninsula today.

Bolivia obtained independence in 1825, and lands were once again redistributed to the non-Indigenous elite and ruling classes. In many ways, this change may have had the greatest impact on Taraco communities than any previous colonization. In the 1860s the government required that individuals, even rural farmers, purchase titles to the land that they worked (Benton 1999; Buechler 1969). While some Indigenous groups bought back their land (Abercrombie 1998; Burke 1971; Klein 1993), the vast majority could not, and this opened the doors to redistribution of land: wealthy, urban Bolivians purchased large areas of land around the lake and in the *altiplano*. These lands were called haciendas, and the Indigenous people living in the purchased areas were required to labor in the fields and pasturelands of the landlords in a form of peonage. They were given small plots of land, but often in less productive areas, to cultivate for themselves (Buechler 1969; Buechler and Buechler 1971). Then Bolivian president Ismael Montes purchased all of the lands west of the town of Taraco, including the areas of Kala Uyuni, Sonaji, and Kumi Kipa, some of which were taken by force (Flores 1955). As discussed in the introduction, the lands surrounding the site of Chiripa has various landowners, the last of which was the Iturralde family (Soriano 2017). This period profoundly impacted agricultural production on the peninsula in ways that continue into the present. This system dissolved after the Bolivian Revolution of 1952 (Albó and Barnadas 1985; Mesa, Gisbert, and Gisbert 2003). Along with the implementation of universal education and suffrage, the Agrarian Reform of 1953 redistributed the hacienda lands to Indigenous populations of the highlands. This reform formalized the landholdings of the Indigenous communities that we pass along the road today and are the focus of the ethnographic research conducted here (Benton 1999; Carter and Mamani 1982).

This chapter provides an introduction to what we have learned through the archaeological record of the Taraco Peninsula communities that have existed through its nearly 3,000-year history. As Roddick (2009) has discussed, this is a typical meta-narrative that archaeologists deploy to synthesize and write about the major events and transitions of these communities as well as broad trends in their cultural, social, and political character, based primarily on trends in settlement, architecture, and ceramics. While I utilize this spatiotemporal framework to organize the initial exploration of the datasets that provide insights into past agricultural activities, I also explore the distinctive tempos and rhythms of other processes, such as climate, plant and animal life cycles, agricultural activities, and even food practices that created the landscapes and taskscapes of the Taraco Peninsula through time. The organization of the book starts with the widest spatial and temporal scales, those of earth and climate processes, and moves toward more refined and specific scales of humans, plants, and animals. Each scale offers important insights into the multiple components that operate and intersect in the long-term history of Taraco agricultural landscapes.

3

Field Preparation

Earth, Water, and Variability

On a crisp, clear day in late August, after all of the morning tasks had been completed, the Quipse family and I headed down to the lakeshore with picks and the large wooden *yunta*, a long (2–3 m) wooden post that has a hook-shaped plow at one end to which a metal blade will be attached (figure 3.1). *Yunta* literally means "a pair of bulls," but it is used to refer to the whole plow system that was introduced to the region by the Spanish and was still widely used in the early 2000s when I conducted my fieldwork (Tapia Vargas 1994, 39). Julio had on loan his neighbors' bulls for the day, and with the plow mounted, our job was to "move the earth" or *qhulltayxasina* in Aymara, which means to prepare this parcel of land to be planted in a few weeks. Once the plow was mounted, Julio began at one edge of where the field would be located and used a whip and hollers to encourage the bulls to move forward. He lowered the plow into the ground, and it turned over large chunks of earth with mats of plants attached. Once at the end of the desired field length, he lifted the plow out of the ground and maneuvered the bulls about 180 degrees to make another pass. This was very physical work, and it is traditionally adult men who conduct the plowing (Carter and Mamani 1982), but one of Julia's daughters, Alejandra, commented to me that women could do it too.

After Julio made several passes, Alejandra, Marta, Valentina, and I entered the field and began the process of breaking up the clods of earth, a task called *k'uphaña*

FIGURE 3.1. *Planting a field with a* yunta *in San José, Bolivia.*

in Aymara. We each whacked the earth with wooden sticks and *chuntillas*, or picks. The *chuntilla* is another common agricultural tool today. It has a metal pick head, which is usually purchased at the market, with one pointed end and one flat end. It comes in a variety of sizes, with the smaller, narrow picks preferred for weeding and harvesting tubers, and larger, wider picks for breaking up soil clods. A wooden handle, usually made from a local *Eucalyptus* tree, is attached. As the soil gave way to our blows, we grabbed handfuls of plant stalks to pull them loose and shook them a few times to remove the adhering soil. We then tossed the plants into little piles accumulating along the side of the field. Once these dried, they would be burned and tilled back into the soil before planting.

While we did today's plowing with a *yunta*, the family had also been saving money to hire a tractor for plowing a field in the next week that had been fallowed for over five years and was located on a clay-rich soil that was dry and compact. The tractor would take less than an hour to complete the work, worth about 60 to 75 bolivianos (about 10 US dollars). In conversations with farmers in 2022, it seemed nearly everyone hires a tractor to plow their fields. The price had come down, as each community now owned one as well as the municipality, so it is more accessible. The *yunta*, which was so common across the landscape in the early 2000s, is now used only by the poorest inhabitants or in very steep slopes that are not accessible to tractors.

FIGURE 3.2. *Planting a field with a* chaquitaclla *depicted by Guaman Poma de Ayala (1615).*

Prior to the Spanish conquest, and until recently in some very rural areas of Peru and Bolivia, Andean farmers did this work with the *chaquitaclla*, or Andean foot plow (Morlon et al. 1996) (figure 3.2). These are long, thick wooden poles with a pointed end or an attached stone blade. The digging end is called the *q'orana*. There is a platform just above the blade for the foot. For preparing the fields and planting, rows of men thrust the blade into the ground with the weight of their bodies and lift up the soil. This can be a very energetic activity because men literally jump to get more force into the blade as it enters the soil. Stone and wooden clod breakers also existed in the pre-Hispanic Andes.

This process of *qhulltayxasina*—plowing, breaking up dirt clods, and removing the vegetation—is done one or two more times before the field is ready to be planted. The number of times depends on the type of soil in the field and how long it has been fallowed. Today's work was relatively easy because it was

FIGURE 3.3. *Distribution of planting zones on the Taraco Peninsula.*

done in a field close to the lakeshore, and the soils had been moistened by the receding shoreline. In areas farther from the lake, farmers will wait until there is a rain shower to loosen up the soil.

Another reason we began preparing a lakeshore field first is that as the rains begin to fall with more frequency into November and December, the lake will begin to rise again and consume the lakeshore fields beginning in February. Thus, these crops need to be grown and harvested early. Because these are the first areas to be cultivated in the year, the lands along the lakeshore are called *milli*, which translates to "first potato" (figure 3.3).

During a break, while we snacked on bread, fruit, and cups of soda pop, Julio exclaimed to me that he much prefers the *qhulltayxasina* in the *milli* because there aren't any rocks. He explained that the soils here were *ch'iara laq'a*, or black earth, similar to the colloquial use of "soil" in English to mean organically rich, loose earth that is good for growing plants. The fields higher up the hill are *k'ala laq'a* (some also used the term *ch'ata*) because they have a lot of rocks (*k'ala*), rounded cobbles ranging from 3 cm to 10 cm in diameter. Large piles of cobbles off to the sides of fields illustrate the effort of generations of farmers trying to move them; yet it is impossible to remove them all, so the plowing, planting, and harvesting continues despite the intruding stones. Ximena, however, notes that even though the soils on the hillside can be rocky, the soil is *ch'alla*, or sandy, which is good for potatoes and other tubers.[1] She indicates with her hands how large the tubers can grow in that loose soil. In the denser, clay-rich soils at lower elevations, she explains, water accumulates and can rot the underground tubers. For that reason, she must perform *th'aruña*, fixing the furrows and mounding up the dirt around the tubers (described in chapter 4) while the plants grow during the rainy season. I asked them if they could plant only certain crops in certain soils, and they said no. They plant all of their crops across all areas, but they do so at different times.[2] They begin with the *milli* fields, which are already moist from the lake. As the rains become more frequent, they prepare the fields in the *pampa*, or lower-elevation plains, and then the *laderas*, or hillsides. The fields at the top of the hill (*cerro*; *q'ullu* in Aymara) are planted last and possibly not at all if there is not enough rain[3] (figure 3.3) (Bruno 2011).

After our short break, we returned to plowing, breaking up dirt clods, and removing vegetation. We finished in about two hours, just before it was time to start bringing the animals back to their corrals and serving them their evening meal of lake plants.

In 74 interviews with Taraco farmers, nearly all of them described the agricultural cycle as starting with this process of *qhulltayxasina* in August or September. Once the fields are prepared, then the planting begins as the rains increase in October and November. The crops grow throughout the rainy season and get harvested when it ends from April to June. They are then processed during the dry season from July to August. As the Quispe family explained, this cycle begins earliest on the lakeshore and latest on the hilltops. Unlike other regions of the Andes (Denevan 2001; Guillet 1987), there is little use of irrigation systems in the Lake Titicaca Basin. On the Taraco Peninsula one of the hacienda owners and a former Bolivian president, Ismael Montes, had constructed an irrigation system that pumped lake water to fields in several communities on the western edge of the peninsula, including San José, Santa Rosa, and Coa Collu. It was dismantled after the agrarian reforms of 1953. Thus, Taraco and most Titicaca Basin farmers rely entirely upon seasonal rains to water their crops. The timing of the rains as well as the distribution and water retention qualities of the soils profoundly shape the timing and rhythm of agricultural work and land use on the Taraco Peninsula (Bruno 2011).

The seasons are quite regular, but there is annual variation: sometimes the rains come earlier, sometimes they come later, sometimes they are heavy, sometimes they are light. Depending on the circumstances, the farmers will adjust the timing of field preparation and especially planting: if there is not enough water, the crops will not grow. Andean farmers have several ways to observe, predict, and prepare for this variation. Some observe the brightness and position of the Pleiades in June. If the farmers find the Pleiades stars to be dim and/or fewer in number, they predict that it will be a dry year and set tuber planting back several weeks (Orlove, Chiang, and Cane 2000; 2002). Although I did not witness this practice on the Taraco Peninsula, my family did listen carefully to the Aymara-language radio news each night for the weather forecast. They even purchased the yearly farmer's almanac, available for only one boliviano in the town market and on the streets of El Alto. They read the small paper booklet for predictions about the year's weather patterns. They also employed rituals to prevent any particularly bad weather, including hail and frost. In San José I was told that local shamans known as *yatiris* collected donations and carried out offerings to prevent hail from damaging the coming year's crops. In ethnographic interviews about landscapes conducted in Chiripa between 2017 and 2018, we learned about a circuit of offerings that the *yatiris* and local authorities must perform each year at important locations throughout the community. If there is a hailstorm or other calamitous weather event, these individuals are blamed for not conducting the rituals properly!

Some years are especially difficult. For example, when I returned in 2016, the rains were not good that season, and people reported less than stellar harvests. In my interviews I did not ask specific questions related to periods of drought or flooding, but I noted comments made about periods of distress. Experiences with severe droughts in the 1960s, 1980s, and 1990s have been recorded by other observers, and they include significant declines in crop and fish harvest, as well as loss of animal herds (Vicente-Serrano et al. 2015; Zubieta et al. 2021). As will be discussed in more detail in later chapters, there are particular plants and forms of storage that can be utilized when crop harvests are low. In our 2018–2019 interviews we collected several stories from individuals in Chiripa who described how in the past the lake dropped so low it was possible to walk across the exposed plain to the neighboring islands. Subsequent studies of trends in rainfall suggest that I was conducting my dissertation research during relatively dry period for the basin (Vicente-Serrano et al. 2015; Zubieta et al. 2021); yet there were not any noticeable food shortages in the communities in which I worked. While there was a lot of conversation about the status of the weather, the Taraco farmers were prepared to start work as the rains dictated, do their best to protect the crops as they grew, and, even with some losses due to a range of unfortunate circumstances (hail, frost, rogue animals), they harvested enough food to keep the family fed, sell some in the market, and save seed for the following year. These are practices that have developed over generations of living on the peninsula and learning how best to make it productive.

In this chapter, I explore the nonorganic actors, the Earth's processes, that gave rise to the geological and climatological characteristics seen today, and I discuss how they have varied in the past on the Taraco Peninsula and broader lake basin. Andean ethnography has long acknowledged that nonorganic elements of the Earth are dynamic, animate actors in Indigenous livelihoods (Allen 1988; Bastien 1985; Cadena 2015; Gose 1994; 2018). Mountains, peaks, and glaciers are often referred to as powerful male entities, *apus*, that are invoked in offerings and called upon for protection and guidance. Quarried and carved stones, including monoliths, still are thought to become animate and to cause storms and earthquakes, if disturbed (Janusek 2020; Janusek et al. 2013). The soil that people live upon and cultivate is female, *Pachamama* (Earth Mother), frequently acknowledged, and offered drink. Her permission is sought before planting by pouring some of a shared carbonated beverage onto the soil so that she too can imbibe. While the particular meanings and associations of these entities have transformed over time, especially in the face of European colonialism and the imposition of Christianity (Allen 1988; Gose 2018; Kosiba 2020), it is certain that the Earth and its climatic processes have been important actors in Taraco's agricultural history. Here I examine the dynamics of the local topography, soils, rainfall patterns, and lake level. My focus for this chapter is less on the meaningful aspects of these elements and more on the ways in which they shape the character and timing of agriculture.

The time scales for these Earth processes are unique compared with some of the other chronologies discussed in this book. In many cases, the rates of change are much longer, such as those shaping topography and general climatic patterns. Others are much shorter, including yearly rainfall and lake level shifts. The tempos of these changes are important because there is a long history of archaeologists comparing cultural and climatological changes in the Lake Titicaca Basin and striving to make causal correlations between them (T. E. Arnold et al. 2021; Binford et al. 1997; Ortloff and Kolata 1993; Posnansky 1945). Indeed, the Lake Titicaca Basin is not only a relatively extreme environment in which to live—at very high elevation with a dry, cold climate—but also a quite variable one on short- and long-term temporal scales. These variables have profoundly shaped the character and trajectory of human history here, but as my colleagues and I have argued elsewhere (Bruno et al. 2021;

Erickson 1999; Marsh et al. 2021), a particular drought or dry period was not solely responsible for complete cultural change; rather, the systems of production that developed here appear to be adapted to frequent changes.

In this chapter, I review the characteristics of soil and water that contributed to past agricultural landscapes of the Taraco Peninsula. Paleoclimatic datasets not only provide information about past rainfall but also shed light on dynamics of the lake level through time. Shifts in lake level shaped the availability of land for farming and herding. Considering how Taraco farmers today utilize the water retention qualities of different soils to manage variable rainfall, I consider how past farmers may have interacted with these dynamics to sustain their fields and herds across frequent climatic shifts. This exploration of soil and water also provides an opportunity to consider an innovative wetland farming practice that is no longer in use: raised fields. There has been much debate about the origin and subsequent disappearance of this unique technology, and I argue that a consideration of lake level changes, particularly the gradual increase of the lake across the Formative and into the Tiwanaku period might explain one of the reasons they became particularly important after the eighth century CE.

EARTH: TOPOGRAPHY AND SOILS

As previous descriptions of moving up and down from hill to lakeshore illustrate, the Taraco Peninsula is a gently sloping mountain range with peaks around 4,100 m a.s.l. and plains meeting Lake Titicaca at about 3,810 m a.s.l. There is a more moderate slope to the shore along the northern peninsula (4%–8% gradient) and a steeper one (20%–40% gradient) along the south.

The various soil characteristics described by local farmers are the products of geomorphological processes (IGM 1994). The underlying formations, a rocky one known as the Taraco Formation and a clay-rich one known as the Kollu Kollu Formation, were uplifted at some point. Erosion aided by gravity and water as well as rising and falling lake levels have contributed to the sediments at the base of the hills and plains. The rocky soils, *k'ala laq'a* and *ch'ata*, at the top of the hills derive from the Taraco Formation, quartzite cobbles that were deposited 5 million years ago during the Pliocene (Argollo et al. 1996, 60) (figure 3.3). The rocky hilltops appear to be the least settled areas of the peninsula today and even in the past (Bandy 2001). While some maps claim the hilltops are not cultivated (IGM 1991), there are fields there today. Some important sites, however, are located on these points, including the Middle Formative Achachi Coa Collu ceremonial center.

The loose sandy soils, or *ch'alla*, along the base of the slopes are colluvial deposits of the eroding Taraco Formation. In some areas at this elevation, thick deposits of clay are exposed. These are clays, known as *k'ink'u*, formed deep in geological time, probably in the mid-Miocene between 18.3 and 16.6 million years ago (Argollo et al. 1996, 69). These clays were particularly important for pottery production (Bandy 2001; Roddick 2009) and mud bricks, but large, eroded exposures are also farmed.

The looser, silty sediments, known as *laq'a*, are common on the lower slopes and lakeshore and were deposited primarily by actions of the rising and falling lake levels during the Pleistocene (Wirrmann, Mourguiart, and de Almeida 1990; Wirrmann, Ybert, and Mourguiart 1992). Today Lake Titicaca rises and falls with the seasons, continuing to deposit lacustrine sediments along the lakeshore and constantly reconfiguring the shoreline.

In addition to the lake's contributions to the peninsula topography, small rivers and streams cut through these various sediments, dissecting the slopes and creating small valleys that today often serve as community boundaries. The elevated areas between these cuts create terraces that have the good *ch'alla* soil for farming and provide level surfaces for settlements. As seen at sites like Kala Uyuni and Sonaji, while settlement started on these natural terraces, they became higher and larger through human activity. Today both sites are very productive agricultural fields.

For farmers, working the soil to create the conditions for growth of their crops is a fundamental practice that shapes their yearly activities and relationship with the Earth. As described in the opening vignette, preparing the fields for planting starts the agricultural year. Moving and manipulating soil is a hallmark of smallholder agricultural intensification around the world (Bruno 2014a; Netting 1993). The archaeological record provides some indications of the history of soil manipulation on the Taraco Peninsula and southern lake basin. Unfortunately, wood does not preserve in this environment, so we have no record of wooden implements, such as *chaquitacllas*. Fortunately, the stone components of digging tools preserve well, and stone hoes are common in the archaeological record. These are relatively flat stones that are longer than wide, usually with side notches where they would have been hafted to a wooden handle. While some stone implements were likely used in the Early Formative period, stone hoes, made of andesite and quartzite, become very common in the Middle Formative period both on the Taraco Peninsula and other southern basin sites (Bandy 2001; Hastorf et al. 2022; Janusek and Kolata 2004; Seddon 1994b). While these implements could certainly have been used for all digging needs, other archaeological evidence, particularly plant remains (see chapter

5), suggest that agricultural soil manipulation increased across the Formative periods, particularly for tubers, which require excavation to both plant and harvest (Bruno 2014a). Furthermore, Seddon (1994b, 66) made an interesting observation of the tools he studied: "The *chakitaclla*, when used for field preparation, is thrust into the ground and then used to pry up large sections of earth. This would put stress along the vertical (or proximal-distal) aspects of the *q'orana*, which could easily result in fractures from one lateral edge to the other, the most common type of fracture seen on the hoes and adzes."

Other potential digging implements include antler and bone. In a Late Formative context at Lukurmata, Bermann (1994, 114) encountered a deer antler with "heave-wear" similar to ethnographically documented tools for harvesting potatoes. He also encountered grinding stones and hoes. Amanda Logan (2006, 57) identified a possible tuber starch grain on a llama mandible scraper from a Late Formative I context from Sonaji.

Relict field systems are another indication that ancient farmers were turning over the earth for agricultural purposes and utilizing soils and sediments in creative ways (Denevan 2001). Although other areas of the lake basin have terraces and sunken gardens known as *q'ochas* (Craig et al. 2011; Erickson 2000; Flores Ochoa 1987), there are no remnants of these technologies on the Taraco Peninsula. There are, however, raised fields. In the 1960s archaeologists encountered approximately 82,000 ha of relict raised fields in valleys throughout the Lake Titicaca Basin (C. T. Smith, Denevan, and Hamilton 1968). At least three clusters of raised fields have been identified at Chiripa (Bandy 2001; Graffam 1990). These systems consisted of long, elevated beds separated by broad canals of water. They were built in low-lying areas along the lakeshore or near springs and streams that flood seasonally or year-round. These systems were not in use at the time of European contact, so archaeologists have played a key role in bringing information about this ancient farming technology to light through both study and rehabilitation (Erickson 1988b, 1996; Graffam 1992; Kolata 1991; Kolata and Ortloff 1996; Ortloff and Kolata 1989; Stanish 1994, 2006). Studies have revealed the many benefits of raised fields. There is a ready source of fertilizer and water for the crops from the canals, and the warming effects of the water in the canals help protect the crops from frost damage. While these early experimental projects touted the greater productivity of the raised field compared with dryland fields, Matthew Bandy (2005) has argued that over time they would have developed some of the same limitations on production (soil depletion, nematodes) as dryland fields but that the microclimate of these inundated fields would have allowed farmers to plant earlier, thus extending the overall growing season.

While this technology involves a good deal of soil manipulation to create the beds, its more fundamental function is to manage water that floods these areas. Before delving into this practice further, it is useful to first understand the variables of climate, particularly rainfall, that shape the timing and distribution of water in the region.

WATER: CLIMATE, RAINFALL, AND LAKE LEVELS

The agricultural cycle follows the austral seasons with a colder, dry winter from June to September and a warmer, rainy summer from October to March. The Lake Titicaca Basin receives from 500 to 900 mm of precipitation per year with approximately 80 percent of it occurring in the summer (Roche et al. 1992, 68). The rainy season in the lake basin occurs when the Intertropical Convection Zone (ITCZ) shifts south and hovers over the Amazon Basin (Montes de Oca 1995). The moisture is brought from the Amazon by way of the "Bolivian High," which pushes the moisture over the eastern Andean slopes and into the *altiplano* (Lenters and Cook 1997). In the winter, cool westerly winds from the Pacific weaken the Bolivian High, displacing it to the northeast and creating drier conditions in these months (Garreaud 1999; Vuille 1999).

The high elevation and general weather patterns make the lake region relatively cold with mean annual temperatures between 8°C and 10°C (Boulange and Aquize 1981; Roche et al. 1992). In the winter it is common for evening temperatures to drop below freezing, with an average of 45 days of frost per year (Vacher, Brasier de Thuy, and Liberman 1992). These lake basin temperatures are on average 2°C warmer than the surrounding *altiplano* and produce nearly 200 frost-free days per year. This is thanks to the warming effects of Lake Titicaca. The two basins together measure 8,562 km^2 with a maximum depth of 284 m. This immense and deep lake absorbs the sun's radiation, heating the water temperature to between 10°C and 14°C and "continuously giving out heat to its surroundings" (Roche et al. 1992, 70). Thus, the combination of relatively rich soils, abundant summer rainfall, and warmer temperatures makes the Lake Titicaca Basin one of the most agriculturally productive regions of the *altiplano*.

The lake itself fluctuates with the seasons, particularly in the small, shallow basin of Lake Wiñaymarka, where the peninsula is located. The large northern basin, referred to as Lago Chuquito, is 7,132 km^2 in size, and has a mean depth of 100 m, the maximum depth being about 284 m. The smaller southern basin, Lago Wiñaymarka, is approximately 1,470 km^2 and has a mean depth of 10 m, the maximum depth being 41 m. The two basins are connected by the Strait of

Tiquina, which is about 850 m wide and has a sill about 35 m below the modern lake level (Vacher, Brasier de Thuy, and Liberman 1992). When the lake is high enough, it drains out to the Desaguadero River to the south, whose sill is about 5 m below the modern lake level at 3,804 m. The mean modern lake level today is 3,810 m.

The balance of water inputs and outputs determines the lake level. Runoff from rivers draining the surrounding mountain ranges accounts for 53 percent of yearly input, while rainfall accounts for 47 percent (Roche et al. 1992). Although rainfall contributes a bit less than runoff, it is more variable and therefore has a greater influence on total yearly input. For outputs, outflow to Rio Desaguadero only accounts for 9 percent of water loss, while evaporation accounts for 91 percent. Given the relative importance of precipitation and evaporation, the balance between these two variables is the greatest determinant of lake level (Roche et al. 1992).

As the Taraco farmers' designation and use of the *milli* planting zone reflects, seasonal lake level shifts make the land along its shores available for cultivation between the months of August and February. The small lake drops due to high evaporation during the sunny and dry winter months. Depending on the area, the seasonal rise and fall of the lakeshore can be quite dramatic, averaging around 10 m in some places on the peninsula but with a recorded average around the lake of about 0.7 m (Abbott et al. 1997; Baker et al. 2001; 2005; Roche et al. 1992). As the rains and runoff increase in the rainy season, the lake fills up again, reaching its peak around April (Roche et al. 1992).

While farmers are accustomed to these seasonal fluctuations, there have been times in recorded history when multiple years of drought have caused the lake to drop below its normal levels, even instances of abundant rain when it has risen higher (Roche et al. 1992, 79; fig. 10). The families I have met over the years have not experienced such drastic changes, but they know of accounts from their parents and grandparents of the lake being so low that they could walk to the islands north of Chiripa. Clark Erickson studied the response of farmers in Huatta, Peru, to droughts in the 1890s and 1940s; he found that while drought certainly caused stresses and shortages, farmers clamored to cultivate the exposed lake beds. According to Erickson (1999, 637), "A drop of 1 m can expose 200,000 ha of previously submerged lakebed." Abbott and colleagues (1997, 178) also describe areas around Lago Wiñaymarka that were low from 1995 to 1996 and that were "quickly colonized and used for agricultural purposes."

Paleoclimatic studies of the small lake basin suggest that there were even greater fluctuations in lake level in the past. Studies that use a range of proxies help to reconstruct when the lake was high or low, which is also an indication of greater or lesser rainfall (Abbott et al. 1997; Baker et al. 2005; Cross et al. 2000; Guédron et al. 2023; Rigsby, Baker, and Aldenderfer 2003; Seltzer et al. 1998; Weide et al. 2017). Prior to the human occupations described here, but certainly when hunter-gather populations were living in the *altiplano*, during the mid-Holocene (~8,500–4,500 years ago), the Lago Chuquito level was nearly 100 m lower than it is today. It was so low that the small Wiñaymarka basin was almost completely dry except for the deep Chua subbasin. Additionally, the connection with the larger lake via the Strait of Tiquina was lost (Baker et al. 2001; Cross et al. 2001). Around 2450 BCE, precipitation increased, and lake levels rose again, reconnecting the two basins and filling in the smaller Wiñaymarka basin.

Diatom studies show that between 2000 BCE and 700 CE, saline species predominated the record, suggesting that the lake was on the average lower than it is today (Weide et al. 2017). The predominance of freshwater species was not established until around 700 CE, which is just a few hundred years after the Tiwanaku state was founded. While there appears to be another dry episode around 1120 CE, just after the fall of the Tiwanaku state, the lake levels rise again around 1270 CE, establishing the lake levels we are familiar with today. Thus, it appears that although there were fluctuations between wetter and drier years across the Formative and Tiwanaku periods, the lake was overall lower than it is today and its level increased through time (Guédron et al. 2023; Weide et al. 2017).

Here I consider how this broader context of regularly shifting lake level and relatively drier climatic conditions would have shaped the long-term development of farming on the Taraco Peninsula across the Formative and Tiwanaku periods. What is clear from the continuous archaeological record over a 2,000-year period on the Taraco Peninsula, particularly at sites like Kala Uyuni and Chiripa, is that droughts never caused complete abandonment of the region. In fact, the period in which there does seem to be a slight gap in production of decorated pottery between 250 BCE and 100 CE (which some could interpret as a kind of population hiatus), the diatom assemblage suggests that the lake was relatively higher (Bruno et al. 2021; Marsh et al. 2019). Periods of low lake level, or drought, also do not seem to correspond with the major sociopolitical shifts detected across these time periods. Instead, such fluctuations appear to be experienced by people *within* each of these phases. Thus, it appears that Formative and Tiwanaku period residents of the Taraco Peninsula and the greater southern Lake Titicaca Basin experienced regular changes in both rainfall and shifts in the landscape itself, sometimes with a lake that was relatively higher and sometimes with exposed lake beds and open plains.

The flexible agricultural land use that is practiced today, which takes into account water retention qualities of soils as well as annual precipitation patterns, likely developed out of these long-lived experiences (Bruno 2011; Bruno et al. 2021). As farmers today observe and plan their planting schedules around fluctuations in rain and lake levels on a seasonal basis, this logic could have been applied to these larger-scale shifts. In drier periods farmers may have had to follow the receding lakeshore, as this land would have continued to be moist and fertile even during droughts (Vacher, Brasier de Thuy, and Liberman 1992, 516). Even with reduced rainfall, the hillslopes would have continued to be productive, particularly in places where natural springs might provide some additional water to nearby fields. Where the Taraco and Kollu Kollu Formations meet, there are many springs (Argollo et al. 1996, 60). They are particularly common along the northern flank of the peninsula. These springs provide fresh water and are managed today by cleaning out the vegetation and even digging deeper into the soil to create larger pools. These springs were likely very important water sources for early Taraco inhabitants, and many archaeological sites are located near them, including Chiripa (Bandy 2001; Hastorf 2017). In 2016 we mapped several water features in the community of Chiripa, and while we did not encounter large irrigation systems that drain this water to distance fields, we documented smaller canals that drain to fields from the springs. Such water movement may have occurred in the past, but documenting the age of these features is difficult (figure 3.4).

The only areas that may have been abandoned during dry periods were the rocky hilltops that require greater rainfall to be productive. The plains where the lakeshore previously existed may have become difficult to cultivate without extra plowing, but perhaps they became especially good grazing areas for camelid herds. Identifying exactly where ancient farmers located their fields is difficult archaeologically, but taking into account the dynamic land use visible today, particularly within the constraints of historic land ownership, we can imagine how ancient famers might have taken advantage of changes in rainfall and the land itself.

What happened, however, when rainfall increased and the lakeshore began to rise, consuming the lands that had been exposed for farming and herding? What would be the options for these populations? They could follow a reverse course, moving fields back up slope and into the flat, grassy areas as the lake level rose. They may have also been able to reclaim this land by constructing raised fields.

FIGURE 3.4. *Aerial image of Chiripa indicating mapped canals (linear features) diverting water from springs to fields. The two clusters of points indicate areas of ancient raised fields mapped by TAP. Gray Graffam (1992) conducted excavations in the westernmost area of the fields.*

LAKE LEVELS AND RAISED FIELD AGRICULTURE

This broader perspective on ancient lake levels and soil types provides insights into the development and role of the raised field systems. Several scholars have estimated the origins of these systems. Dating of such field systems can be difficult; nonetheless, these researchers have employed various techniques to provide a broad temporal framework for the timing of raised field use in the lake basin. Albeit limited, there is evidence that raised fields were first used in the Formative period beginning as early as about 1400 BCE. The only early direct date we have on fields themselves is from Clark Erickson (1988a), who obtained a thermoluminescence date of 1310 ± 660 BCE on ceramics found in raised fields in Huatta, Peru. Other archaeologists have used the presence of Middle and Late Formative period ceramics on the surface of raised fields to argue that they were first built and used at this time. Charles Stanish asserts that this technology was important in the Juli-Pomata region during the Middle Formative period based on that fact that 41 percent of sites from this time are located within one kilometer of relict raised fields (Stanish 2003; Stanish et al. 1997).

Gray Graffam (1990) studied a small pocket of raised fields (< 1 ha) in Chiripa (figure 3.4). He was not able to obtain direct radiocarbon dates, but based on his interpretations of a complex aqueduct system, he argued that they may have been built and managed as early as the Late Formative period but were most important during the Tiwanaku period. He identified an incised "Tiwanaku III greyware *keru*" in a gravel stratum beneath the fields. With our improved Late Formative ceramic database this Qeya-style vessel could indicate early field construction at the end of the Late Formative period (Marsh et al. 2019). Based on surface ceramics, Matthew Bandy (2001, 42, 226) associates these fields with the Tiwanaku period occupation. In 2013 we reexamined a long profile of one Graffam's excavation trenches and took sediment samples for dating as well as micromorphological analysis. The area is very wet, and we were unable to reach the base of the field systems due to water infiltration and so could not date the earliest deposits. While we obtained one date that falls in the Tiwanaku period (658–777 CE), five dates that we obtained from a clearly identified buried paleosol came back quite late, all between 1400 and 1450 CE, well into the Late Intermediate period/Inca period.

The majority of direct radiocarbon dates of raised fields come from the Pampa Koani at the northeastern end of the Taraco Peninsula. The Wila Jawira project obtained 25 radiocarbon dates from mollusk shells and carbon taken from contexts of raised field construction and abandonment (Janusek and Kolata 2003, table 2). Fourteen of them correspond to the Tiwanaku period (approximately

600–1100 CE). Survey data support the radiocarbon results, as there were many sites in the Pampa Koani during the Tiwanaku periods (Kolata 1986). While Janusek and Kolata (2004) agree that people may have practiced some raised field agriculture in the Middle Formative period, they did not find direct evidence of it. The increase in raised field construction happens to correspond with the increase in freshwater diatom species at around 700 CE. So it could be that part of the efforts of the Tiwanaku state was to reclaim lost production lands in the shallow areas of the basin as lake levels rose during this period.

Some scholars have argued that climate change, a drought around 1100 CE, resulted in the collapse of the Tiwanaku field systems and subsequently the state (T. E. Arnold et al. 2021; Binford et al. 1997; Ortloff and Kolata 1993). While their use likely contracted, they did not completely disappear until later, and the reasons were likely more political than environmental. Graffam (1990; 1992) studied mound sites associated with raised fields in the Pampa Koani, and six of them dated to the Pacajes period (1100–1450 CE). He therefore argued that they continued to be used and managed by kin-based groups after the fall of the Tiwanaku state. Janusek and Kolata (2004, 419) believe that some of these dates might be related to abandonment rather than use. The very late dates we obtained from Graffam's Chiripa raised-field excavations, however, support their use into later periods. It seems reasonable that these fields would have still been of use to farmers at this time. As rainfall increased and the lake continued to rise (Guédron et al. 2023), it would have permanently flooded fields that were lower in the *pampa*.

The decline of their use is best attributed to changes that came with subsequent colonists. It is possible that the Inca modified these production systems, with their emphasis on terracing; however, the arrival of Spanish colonists and the later haciendas more profoundly disrupted these farming systems. In the 1980s and 1990s several development projects in Bolivia and Peru tried to rehabilitate raised field farming in the lake basin. While there was initially successful production, none of the projects lasted beyond the first years of activity, and the fields were abandoned again. The failure of these rehabilitation projects seems to be due, in part, to the large amount of labor required to maintain the fields (Swartely 2002). European colonization and reorganization resulted in not only smaller and/or more dispersed rural populations, but also new labor demands locally and in the cities seem to have diverted energy away from large-scale agricultural works such as raised fields. The productivity of these fields simply did not outweigh the labor required to maintain them. Dryland agriculture, however, which has also supported these populations for generations, continues to thrive (Bruno 2014a).

In this chapter, I have explored the interactions with local topography, soils, climate, and water that shaped the temporalities of farming, particularly the timing of soil preparation and planting, as well as the spatial dimension of where fields are located and how that may have shifted through time. The shifting schedules and land use that Taraco farmers developed in association with the Earth's processes of climate, soil, and water variables helped them to create conditions for nourishing and growing several domesticated plant species, to which we now turn.

4

Planting

Growing Domesticated Plants

A few weeks after we prepared the *milli* field, we returned to plant the seeds that, with favorable conditions, would provide food for humans and animals the rest of the year. The rainy season would begin soon, and the process of planting the prepared fields begins with the *milli*. Although this literally means "first potato," other crops were planted this year following a rotation. The previous year, this field was planted with a mixture of the Andean tubers *oca*, *isañu*, and a couple of rows of maize (table 4.1). The year before that, it was planted with several varieties of potato. This year we were planting *habas* (fava beans) and some oats along the edges. Julio once again set up the *yunta*, the steer-driven plow, to create furrows running the length of the field about 1–2 m apart. As Julio drove the plow forward, Alejandra, Marta, and I followed behind, placing a couple of dried beans, saved from the previous year's harvest, into the furrow at about every 50 cm (see figure 3.1). At the edge of the field Julio would turn the plow around and carefully run it alongside where the beans had been planted. This pushed the soil over the seeds and created a new furrow alongside the now-planted row. This pattern was repeated across the whole field until it was completely planted. Then Alejandra and Marta grabbed a sack of oat seeds and scattered handfuls of them in the furrows along the edge of the field, and Julio made one more pass with the *yunta* along the edges to bury the oat seeds.[1]

A few weeks later, after the first rainfall of the season, we planted a field with potato seed further up the

TABLE 4.1. Crop species grown on the Taraco Peninsula

	Species Name	Common Name(s), Spanish/Aymara	Common Name(s), English
Tubers			
	Solanum tuberosum L.*	papa/chuqi, imilla	potato
	Oxalis tuberosa Molina*	oca/apilla	oca
	Trapaeolum tuberosum Ruíz and Pav.*	isañu	isañu
	Ullucus tuberosa Caldas*	papa lisa/ullucu	papa lisa
Legumes			
	Lupinus mutabilis Hook*	tarwi	lupine
	Vicia faba L.	haba	fava bean
	Pisum sativum L.	arveja	pea
Grain/Seed			
	Chenopodium quinoa Willd.*	quinua/jhupa	quinoa
	Zea mays L.*	maíz/tonko	maize, corn
	Hordeum vulgare L.	cebada/qhach'u	barley
	Avena sativa L.	avena	oats
	Triticum sativum L.	trigo	wheat

*Indicates pre-Columbian cultigen.

hillside in the *ch'alla* soil. This field had been left fallow the past two years. As with the *haba* field, Julio created the planting furrow with the *yunta*, and the women followed behind, carefully placing the potato seeds. Unlike any other crop, the potatoes were also planted with a handful of sheep dung. Before planting, we visited the corral where the sheep spend their nights and where a good meter-deep layer of their droppings had accumulated over the past year. We shoveled loads of dung into a wheelbarrow and brought it down to the field. The young son, Nicolas, would then fill a sack full of dung and follow behind those of us planting the potatoes. According to the Taraco famers and farmers throughout the Andes, potatoes need the most nutrients to grow; thus they are the first crop planted after a fallow period and always planted with fertilizer (Orlove and Godoy 1986). Farmers throughout the region use animal fertilizer, traditionally camelid dung, to augment soil nutrients and fertility, especially for potato production (Winterhalder, Larsen, and Thomas 1974).

Today sheep or camelid dung is the most common form of fertilizer, but some farmers do use synthetic, chemical fertilizers rather than that produced by their own livestock. These products were uncommon in the early 2000s, possibly because of the cost, but several farmers told me that the potatoes do not taste as good with the chemical fertilizers. As with the *habas*, once the tubers and dung were placed in the furrow, Julio would pass the plow alongside to cover them and create the drainage furrow, which is particularly important for the underground crops.

In general, planting occurs in a short window between February and April, roughly following the schedule of field preparation discussed in the previous chapter and dependent on the rain. The fields closest to the lake are planted first, and those up on the hill, last. During my stay in 2004 the rains were delayed, and so planting occurred mostly in March. The number of fields that a family maintained depended on many factors; primarily how much land the family received as a result of the 1953 Agrarian Reform and how it has been subsequently divided up among the children. Most families seemed to have about 10 fields, but some has as few as 4 and a few had up to 30. It was also very common for families to pool their resources, such as seed, labor, and tools, and plant a few rows of the crop for each family in a single field (see chapter 8).

Each family also planted a diverse range of crops across their different fields. To learn more about the crop rotation and fallow sequences on the peninsula, I conducted 17 "field history" interviews. We would visit each field in a given area, map the fields with a GPS, and ask the farmer to recount what had been planted over the course of three or four years as well as the length of any fallow (Bruno 2011). At minimum, a family would plant the food crops potatoes, *oca*, *habas*, and some combination of maize and/or quinoa. They would also plant food for their animals, primarily barley and oats, and some wheat. I found there to be a very consistent pattern that is also found in other communities across the Lake Titicaca Basin and Andes (Bruno 2011; Orlove and Godoy 1986). Potatoes are always planted first, then the other Andean tubers, especially *oca*, in the second year, then fava beans, and finally a cereal. Crops such as peas, maize, and quinoa usually get intercropped with the fava beans and even *oca* or *isañu* are planted before fava beans in the rotation. Several varieties of potatoes are planted, and it is quite common to see mixed fields of Andean tubers, maize, and quinoa. This sequence is followed by a fallow period, which is typically between 5 and 10 years, although there is variation on each end depending on the amount of land owned by a family. Each of a family's fields is at a different point in the rotation, so each year the full range of crops is planted. This not only provides a diverse suite of foods to eat but also ensures that some part of the harvest will be successful. Each crop or field faces a range of risks—from drought, frost, or hail to infestations of pests. Having a range of different crops, planted across the different microenvironments of the peninsula, reduces the risk of complete failure, a strategy quite opposite an industrialized agricultural model of monoculture but common among subsistence farmers around the world (Altieri and Toledo 2011; da Cunha 2017; Netting 1993).

In this chapter, I examine the domesticated plants that were the foundation of Taraco Peninsula farming systems. Today Taraco farmers have selected a diverse mixture of crops that have their origins in the Andes, Mexico, and Eurasia. We know that the Eurasian crops—fava beans, wheat, barley, and oats—were introduced upon the arrival of the Spanish. They have become very successful, important crops in the region and on the peninsula (Tapia Vargas 1994). The crops that have a deeper history are the various tubers, a legume called *tarwi*, quinoa, *kañawa*, and maize. Our understanding of these crop histories is dependent not only on their uses in the past but their ability to survive in the archaeological record and be recovered. Before delving into these histories, I first describe the processes by which plants preserve in the archaeological record in this region and the ways in which archaeobotanists study their patterns. I then turn to the specific histories of each crop and their contributions to the agricultural landscapes of the peninsula. This exploration reveals the prominence of quinoa and tubers across Taraco's early agricultural history as well as the appearance of *kañawa* and maize.

THE ARCHAEOLOGY OF PLANTS

The study of archaeological plant remains, archaeobotany or paleoethnobotany, provides the means for understanding the role of these plants in the past. This study builds on a strong tradition of archaeobotanical research on the Taraco Peninsula. One of the first studies of archaeological plant remains to be conducted in the Andes by Margaret Towle (1961) included plants recovered from the site of Chiripa by Wendell Bennett in the early 1930s. When David Browman excavated at Chiripa in the 1970s, his was one of the first archaeological projects in the Andes to employ water flotation to recover carbonized plant remains, also referred to as macrobotanical remains. He and Clark Erickson, then an undergraduate student, analyzed these remains (Browman 1989; Erickson 1976). When archaeobotanist Christine Hastorf began the Taraco Archaeological Project, it included opportunities for several theses based on the plant remains from four different sites: Chiripa, Kala Uyuni, Sonaji, and

Kumi Kipa (see figure 2.1). William Whitehead (2007), BrieAnna Langlie (2008), and I (Bruno 2008) analyzed the macrobotanical remains. Amanda Logan (2006) and Sophie Reilly (2017) analyzed microbotanical plant remains, particularly phytoliths and starch grains. While I draw on all of these studies, the analysis here focuses on results from 786 macrobotanical samples: 192 from the Early Formative period, 384 from the Middle Formative, 153 from the Late Formative, and 57 from the Tiwanaku period. Because TAP focused primarily on the Formative, we have many more samples from that period. Furthermore, the focus of that project for many years was on the Middle Formative period, particularly at the site of Chiripa, resulting in a particularly large sample from that time. Fortunately, there is also published data on archaeobotanical research at the site of Tiwanaku that we can compare with our records for that period. These samples all derive from a range of contexts that include garbage middens, activity areas, surfaces, and structures.

Before delving into the patterns of the ancient plant remains, it is first necessary to understand the processes by which they get deposited and preserved as well as the fragments we observe. All of these remains are leftovers and scraps of what were once living plants that likely became meals for humans and animals or were transformed into baskets, buildings, and matting. We do not see the actual meals or baskets but rather what was accidentally spilled and eventually thrown away. On very rare occasions, such as the bins of the Montículo "Houses," we find plants where they may have been stored or used.

The Taraco climate cycles of wetness and dryness aids in breaking down organic materials such as plants; thus they must be converted to a stable state in order to be preserved. The most common process of preservation is carbonization. Thankfully, fire was used for many activities in the past, from heating a house to cooking and firing ceramics. People also frequently burned their garbage. For this reason, the archaeological record of the Taraco Peninsula is quite rich in carbonized plant remains, and we can recover high quantities of them through flotation. TAP takes a 10 L soil sample from each excavated context (sometimes less if the context is small). The soil is processed with water, and the light, carbonized fragments "float" up and are separated, dried, and ready for examination under a microscope (Pearsall 2015).

Because food plants can get burned during cooking or in their disposal, we luckily do encounter them; although not in the exact frequencies with which they were actually consumed (Dennell 1976). I will make some comparisons of abundance using the measure of density (number of seeds/fragments per liter of soil) of different plants, such as quinoa versus potato (Popper 1988). These differences, however, are more likely associated with the type of context in which they were found (in a kitchen midden versus a clean floor) and the very nature of the plant itself (hundreds of tiny seeds versus a large starchy tuber) rather than their overall relevance to diet. To gain a sense of relative importance, I rely on a measure that is less dependent on quantity and preservation biases, known as ubiquity. This is the percentage that indicates the presence of the species. For example, if we examine 100 samples and wood is encountered in 98 of them, wood's ubiquity is 98 percent. It does not matter how many fragments of wood are present, just whether it is present or not.

The most common plants we encounter are those that were regularly in contact with fire, intentionally and unintentionally. As will be elaborated in chapter 5, the *altiplano* is quite sparse in trees, so while wood is common, present in 87 percent of the samples, it is much less common than seeds, which are present in *all* of the samples. Before the introduction of gas stoves, the most important source of fuel for people living on the Taraco Peninsula and the broader *altiplano* was camelid dung (Winterhalder, Larsen, and Thomas 1974). Llamas and alpacas provided important resources: not only wool, meat, and transport but also daily droppings that could be used to fertilize fields and fuel the fires. Dung is used in many regions of the world as an important fuel and is the source of many seeds in the archaeobotanical record (Browman 1989; N. F. Miller and Smart 1984). Hastorf and Wright (1998) examined the contents of modern camelid and sheep dung from areas surrounding the site of Tiwanaku and encountered many of the seeds species we find archaeologically, including food plants like quinoa! Hastorf and I examined the range of species found in macrobotanical samples between the Taraco Peninsula and Tiwanaku, and the evidence suggests that the Taraco camelids were eating locally on the peninsula across a variety of ecological zones (Bruno and Hastorf 2016). Thus, the burning of camelid dung provided an excellent record of the Taraco botanical landscape through time. It also reminds us of the important interconnections forged between humans, plants, and animals. This chapter focuses on the crop plants in this record, and we will return to the others in the next.

The macrobotanical record is further complemented with additional botanical and chemical analyses. TAP also collects smaller soil samples and residues from artifacts that can then be processed for microbotanical remains, particularly phytoliths and starch grains. These tiny plant cells experience different processes of preservation and in some cases provide better records of species like maize and tubers (Pearsall 2015). Finally, as humans consume these plants, their chemical (isotopic) signatures are absorbed and preserved in human bone. Melanie Miller has studied the patterns in isotopes from human remains as well as cooking residues found on pots, providing direct insight into what plants (and animals) were being consumed over time. Through these multiple lines of evidence, a dynamic history of Taraco crops emerges.

CROP HISTORIES

Understanding when and where the Andean crops were domesticated is a major field of study, but it is not the focus here. Given the high diversity of quinoa, potatoes, and *oca* species encountered in the Lake Titicaca Basin in modern times, botanists have long hypothesized that they were domesticated in this region (Cardenas 1989; Heiser 1979; Leon 1964; Ugent 1970; Vavilov and Löve 1992). Phylogenetic research on these species, however, has not entirely supported this hypothesis, placing the domestication of some of these crops outside of the basin: quinoa in the eastern Andean slopes or plains of Argentina, Uruguay, and Paraguay (Jarvis et al. 2017; Wilson 1990) and *oca* on the eastern slopes of the Andes (Emshwiller 2006). Potatoes may have been domesticated in south-central Peru just north of the Titicaca Basin (Spooner 2005; Sukhotu and Hosaka 2006); thus, it is likely that a mosaic of Archaic hunter-gatherers began the process of domesticating these plants in regions not far from the lake basin, although this story is far from complete. It does appear that once these species were domesticated, they eventually impacted the lifestyles of the Archaic hunter-gatherers, who were once quite mobile, and people began to settle more permanently on the landscape (chapter 2). While the initial processes of domestication may have occurred elsewhere, people began to settle on the Taraco Peninsula with the onset of warmer, wetter condition around 3500 BP (1500 BCE). Here they continued to experiment and create new varieties of these crops, which not only thrived in the face of varying weather conditions and threats from pests but also served a variety of culinary traditions utilized inside and outside the household, resulting in the great diversity of species seen today (Bruno 2014b). Here I focus on the two most enduring groups of crops, chenopods and tubers, and then turn to a species introduced from Mesoamerica and adapted to South American environments, maize. While some of their culinary qualities are mentioned, particularly in relation to their preservation, the role of these plants in food contexts is discussed further in chapter 7.

Unfortunately, we have little evidence for the presence of the Andean domesticated species *tarwi* (*Lupinus mutabilis*) in the archaeological record. While there are a few larger-sized legume fragments, we cannot positively identify them as *tarwi*. Today *tarwi* is commonly planted along the borders of a field of other crops, with occasional full fields. In my time there I did not see it incorporated into a meal, but it can be boiled or toasted. Most people described *tarwi*'s importance as medicine and an as insecticide for their crops. They soak the beans in water before cooking, and this water can be consumed for pulmonary problems. One interviewee told me that the bean could be ground into a powder and placed in the soil with potatoes to kill pests. The borders of *tarwi* also protect the fields from wandering livestock. The lack of *tarwi* in the archaeological record could be due to poor preservation of legumes, or it is also possible this was not a particularly important crop during the Formative and Tiwanaku periods. While being very nutritious plants, high in protein and fiber, legumes are also very important in maintaining soil quality in agricultural fields because they have bacteria on their roots that replenish nitrogen in the soil. It is no accident that fava beans are some of the last crops to appear in the agricultural cycle today, as they help the soil recover after being depleted from the other crops. It is possible that *tarwi* could have been used in a similar fashion in the past, but we do not currently have any manner of assessing this. The long-term history of *tarwi* is an area open to future research.

Chenopods: Quinoa and *Kañawa*

Since the late 1990s the Andean crop quinoa (*Chenopodium quinoa* L.) has become an increasingly popular food globally (Bazile, Jacobsen, and Verniau 2016). Although quinoa is today the most widely known domesticated species of this genus, there is another Andean species, *Chenopodium pallidicaule*, called *kañawa* in Aymara and *cañihua* in Quechua, and a Mexican species, *C. berlandieri* ssp. *nuttalliae*, with two varieties known as *huauzontle* and *chia* (Aellen and Just 1943). Archaeologists have also discovered that there was a domesticated chenopod cultivated in eastern North America during the Late Archaic and Woodland periods (~1800 BCE–1400 CE). It had either fallen out of use or was overlooked by early explorers in North America and thus was lost to history until recently (Fritz et al. 2017). Thus, *Chenopodium* can be considered one of the most important food taxa in the Americas.

While central Peru and the southern Bolivian *altiplano* have experienced a boom of quinoa production supporting its popularity abroad (Kerssen 2015; Laguna 2011; Ofstehage 2012; Seligmann 2023), on the Taraco Peninsula you will be hard-pressed to find it in daily home meals or growing in one of the hundreds of fields. Today Taraco farmers grow it only in limited amounts. Of the 17 field interviews I conducted in 2003–2004, only five households had planted quinoa in the past three years. In the interviews about the agricultural cycle, most farmers mentioned quinoa when describing the general crop rotation, but it was usually along with maize or fava beans. Seligmann (2023, 80) reports that in Huanoquite, Peru, Indigenous Quechua farmers describe maize and quinoa as having a "kinship" and that they should be planted together because maize protects the quinoa from predation by birds and too many weeds growing around it.

Quinoa was only an occasional food in the household I resided in, and it was never served to me when I visited other families on the peninsula. I most frequently ate quinoa when visiting the nearby town of Tiwanaku, about 20 km southeast of the peninsula. The Tiwanaku family I visited grew quinoa annually, and they also produced the lesser-known chenopod *kañawa*. *Kañawa* is not well known outside of the Andes, but it is a significant crop to Indigenous farmers because it is highly nutritious and is particularly resistant to frost, drought, salt, and pests (IPGRI, PROINPA, and IFAD 2005; National Research Council 1989; Rodriguez et al. 2020). It is not grown by Taraco farmers today, but it is by their neighbors in communities away from the lake. These farmers cannot grow crops such as fava beans and maize, which require the warmer, wetter conditions along the lakeshore, so it is possible that *kañawa* adds an important element to the yearly cycle. Today quinoa and its relative, *kañawa*, are much more prevalent in Tiwanaku and other regions of the Andes than on the Taraco Peninsula; this was not the case in the past.

Chenopods through Time

Chenopods constitute one of the densest and most ubiquitous plant categories in the archaeobotanical record of the Taraco Peninsula and elsewhere in the Lake Titicaca Basin. Taken together, chenopods appeared in 98 percent of all samples examined. Why is this so? Part of the answer lies in the traits of the plant and its fruit, a small but abundant seed or achene. One single plant can produce thousands of seeds. In fact, the Aymara have a song dedicated to the plant that is known as *waranq waranqa*, which means "thousands of thousands" (D. Arnold, Aruquipa, and de Yapita 1992)! In the processing and preparation of quinoa for food (described in chapter 5), the seeds often scatter, becoming embedded in kitchen floors, burned in the hearth fire, and tossed into the garbage. The seed itself is also very favorable to preservation. The dense endosperm is surrounded by a curved embryo and encapsulated by a seed coat, or testa, and a papery layer called the pericarp (Bruno 2006). The pericarp, and often the testa, are removed as people process the seeds for consumption (López, Capparelli, and Nielsen 2011). When boiled or burned, the endosperm expands or "puffs" and the seed coat can be lost, but the overall shape and size remain intact, allowing us to at least identify the seed as a chenopod and often differentiate the species based on the characteristics of the seed coat (López, Bruno, and Planella 2015). Although its characteristics help the chenopods to be well represented in the archaeological record, their consistency and regularity through time also suggest that chenopods were very important crops to the people of the Taraco Peninsula.

To date, we have been able to regularly identify four types of chenopods: domesticated quinoa, wild *quinoa negra*, domesticated *kañawa*, and wild *kañawa*. There are also many seeds that lack a seed coat and other distinctive traits that allow us to designate one of the four listed above. The most common in this category are relatively large (> 0.71 mm) and have seed shape (truncate) that is prevalent in domesticated quinoa (Bruno 2006). In an ethnographic study of traditional quinoa preparation in southern Bolivia, López and colleagues (López, Bruno, and Planella 2015) found that toasting and light grinding of the seeds prior to boiling results in the loss of the pericarp and testa; thus, it is likely the category of "no testa truncate" seed reflects grains that were exposed to cooking. For this reason, I have included them in the "quinoa" category for analysis. The ability to identify these different species and track how they vary through time and space provides incredible insight into their roles in the past. While nearly all of the samples studied by the TAP team contained some form of *Chenopodium* seeds, detailed sorting was not carried out in the earlier years of analysis. The data in table 4.2 come from 364 samples for which we identified each type of chenopod to understand their trends through time.

Domesticated quinoa seeds appear in 86 percent of all samples through time; while there are some slight shifts, this is a pattern of continuity. When we compare the ubiquities of chenopods from Taraco to those studied at the site of Tiwanaku by Melanie Wright, Christine Hastorf, and Heidi Lennstrom (2003), we find a similar pattern of continuity and importance. *Chenopodium* seeds (> 1.18 mm in size, most likely to be quinoa) are present in over 90 percent of the Late Formative (N=25) and Tiwanaku (N=171) samples. Overall, quinoa appears to have been one of the most prominent crops on the Taraco Peninsula through time.

We have only recently begun to document the history of *kañawa* (Bruno 2023; Bruno, Pinto, and Rojas 2018). For many years, it was either lumped in with quinoa or estimated based on the presence of smaller-seeded chenopods (< 0.5 mm) in samples. Using both light and scanning microscopy, we can now positively identify both the crop and its wild counterpart, known in the region as *illama*, in our samples. Unlike quinoa, *kañawa* does not appear in the Taraco archaeological record until the Late Formative period and in very small quantities compared with quinoa. It increases in the Tiwanaku period.

TABLE 4.2. Ubiquity of *Chenopodium* types through time

Period	Quinoa	Quinoa negra	Kañawa	Illama
Early Formative (N=71)	93%	79%	0%	39%
Middle Formative (N=87)	93%	77%	0%	79%
Late Formative (N=149)	98%	85%	2%	93%
Tiwanaku (N=57)	91%	81%	7%	77%

Mabel Ramos and I have also examined *Chenopodium* samples from the Mollo Kontu sector at Tiwanaku and identified *kañawa* there. These data suggest that *kañawa* was a crop that came into the southern Titicaca Basin farming systems relatively late (Bruno 2023). Such a scenario was proposed by ethnobotanist Daniel Gade (1970), who hypothesized that *kañawa* was a secondary crop domesticated by farmers who noticed the wild species growing in potato and quinoa fields, having perhaps survived poor harvests due to frost or drought. We might hypothesize that the domestication process was taking place with the wild populations present during the Late Formative period and that the crop began to be formally cultivated in the Tiwanaku period.

Aymara farmers today also recognize and interact with the wild chenopods, particularly *quinoa negra*, as they are common "weeds" in the fields of all their crops (see chapter 5). Despite many years of plant collection on the Taraco Peninsula, we have not found it growing there. This suggests that the wild *kañawa* plant has mostly disappeared from the peninsula, but it still grows in other areas around the Lake Titicaca Basin (Rojas et al. 2010). Taraco farmers are very familiar with the wild quinoa species, *quinoa negra*, and I observed that they often let these individual plants grow to maturity. Several farmers report that this plant has been important in times of scarcity and that its leaves and seeds can be eaten (Bruno 2008; C. Franquemont et al. 1990). People even collect the mature seeds and store them. So, while we can interpret the "wild" chenopods as species not directly cultivated by humans, they are a regular part of the agricultural landscape and can even serve as a food (Hastorf and Bruno 2020). I discuss the patterns in these species in greater detail in chapter 5.

Tubers

Today farmers on the Taraco Peninsula and in the broader Titicaca region cultivate a variety of indigenous, tuber-producing species, which make up the bulk of the year's annual crop production. North Americans are very familiar with the potato (table 4.1), as it forms a staple of cuisines around the world.

TABLE 4.3. Ubiquity of tuber remains and maize through time

	Early Formative (N=192)	Middle Formative (N=384)	Late Formative (N=153)	Tiwanaku (N=57)
Parenchyma	76%	72%	92%	93%
Solanum sp.	0%	1%	16%	26%
Oxalis sp.	0%	4%	17%	39%
Maize	0%	0%	1%	11%

A North American consumer, however, would be surprised by the diversity of colors, shapes, and sizes of potatoes that Taraco inhabitants grow and eat. I recorded at least five different potato varieties being cultivated by the farmers on the Taraco Peninsula in 2004. The common Aymara word for potato is *chuqi*, but the round, colorful varieties have individual names that indicate their color (red, white, black) and are usually combined with the term *imilla*, which means "young girl" (D. Arnold and de Yapita 1996). For example, *wila imilla* is a red potato. The other most common tuber grown on the peninsula is *oca* or *apilla* in Aymara. There are two sweet varieties that are distinguished by color: *q'ellu apilla*, the yellow *oca*, and *qheni apilli*, which means "best" and is usually red. There is also a bitter variety called *chuchulla*, which is used exclusively for making *kaya*, or freeze-dried *oca*. They are a deep, pinkish-yellow color and have a very waxy, shiny surface. Potatoes and *oca* are planted each year, and in the year that I conducted my research, they represented about 80 percent of the harvested crops. Farmers plant the two other tubers, *ullucu* and *isañu*, in much smaller quantities, usually just a few rows within *oca* or potato fields.

While tubers are the foundation of the yearly harvest and daily meals of Taraco families (see chapter 7), their presence in the archaeological record is more enigmatic than that of the chenopods. What could confidently be identified as tubers were found in 10 percent of all samples; more generic parenchyma, storage tissue from what are likely to be tubers, was found in 78 percent of samples (table 4.3). Why does this seem lower than expected? First, the watery, fleshy tubers with very thin cellular walls do not preserve as well archaeologically (Wright, Hastorf, and Lennstrom 2003, 388). Furthermore, people eat the entire tuber, so their chances of entering and surviving in the archaeological record are diminished. We very rarely encounter entire tubers. During TAP's 2004 excavations at Sonaji, a local Indigenous worker was sifting through the excavated soil of a garbage pit and encountered a black, rounded object. Being a farmer herself, she said, "Look, a potato," and handed it to the dig supervisor, who happened to be Christine Hastorf. Suddenly, Christine erupted in jubilation because in 15 years of excavating on the Taraco Peninsula and supervising an archaeobotanical lab that had examined hundreds of plant samples, she had never encountered an entire tuber. In her mind, this was the most precious and valuable find of a lifetime. She went around to all of the archaeologists and local participants exclaiming, "THIS is gold! THIS is gold!" As archaeologists around the world can attest, it is very common to be asked if you are looking for or have encountered gold. In our minds, this ancient potato (or possibly a freeze-dried *chuño*) was gold! While our project found only one whole potato, excavations of the Chiripa Upper Houses by Wendell Bennett recovered whole carbonized potatoes, *oca*, and *ullucu* (Browman 1989, 149; Towle 1961, 84). At the site of Ch'isi on the western shore of the lake, Lee (1997, 7) reports identifying remains of *chuño* and *oca*.

Tubers through Time

What we most commonly find in the archaeobotanical record representing the category of tubers are fragments of parenchyma. Other plants and plant parts produce parenchyma, including *totora* reeds, maize, and beans, but their structure is distinct. In this study we consider only fragments of parenchyma that are larger than 1 mm. Thus, we consider the presence of parenchyma to be a good general indicator of the presence of tubers. Using parenchyma as one proxy for the presence of cultivated tubers, we find a ubiquity of 72 percent and 78 percent, respectively, in the Early and Middle Formative periods, increasing to 92 percent and 93 percent, respectively, in the Late Formative and Tiwanaku periods (table 4.2).

Two of the most important tuber-producing genera, *Solanum* sp. (potatoes) and *Oxalis* sp. (*oca*) also produce identifiable seeds that we can track through time. These seeds would not have been consumed (potato seeds are poisonous to humans!) but likely made their way into the record through camelid dung. I observed that farmers would often feed their animals the leafy stalks of harvested tubers. Additionally, wild varieties of these two species also grow on the landscape and are consumed by grazing animals. The seeds of wild and domesticated potato and *oca* are indistinguishable; therefore, we are tracking not just the presence of crops but all of these species on the landscape. Interestingly, we find an increase in ubiquity of both types of seeds through time (table 4.2). Neither is present in the Early Formative samples, and both first appear in low ubiquities (1%–4%) in the Middle Formative period. *Solanum* sp. seeds increase to 16 percent in the Late Formative and 26 percent in the Tiwanaku periods, while *Oxalis* sp. increases to 17 percent in the Late Formative and 39 percent in Tiwanaku periods.

If we take the parenchyma and seed data together, there seems to be a fairly clear trend that the presence of tuber-bearing species increased through time on the Taraco Peninsula, beginning in the Late Formative period. As I will explore in chapter 5, there is also increased evidence for the tools and types of work that were likely associated with tuber production, particularly digging.

Maize

Today maize is a regular part of the agricultural repertoire on the Taraco Peninsula; yet it is the only crop discussed here that was introduced from outside of the Andes. Maize is a tropical plant, adapted to warm conditions, whose domestication from the wild grass teosinte (*Zea mays* ssp. *parviglumis*) began in the Río Balsas Valley of Mexico approximately 8000 BCE (Matsuoka et al. 2002). An early version of domesticated maize arrived in northwestern South America possibly as early as 6000 BCE and was selected by local farmers to grow in its diverse environments, including the Andes (Grobman et al. 2012; Kistler et al. 2018). The shores of Lake Titicaca are one of the few places maize can be grown in the cold, dry *altiplano* (Ramírez et al. 1960). Farmers on the peninsula plant it each year in areas protected from frost and low temperatures. It is often intercropped with fava beans or quinoa, but many farmers grow entire fields of maize. They cultivate the *altiplano* maize variety, which has a short cob and eight to ten rows of kernels. The grains range in color from yellow, red, and purple to variegated mixtures of these. The grains are small and pointed (figure 4.1). The maize produced each year is for household consumption and not for sale, as is common for potatoes.

There are many ways to detect maize in the archaeological record. Macrobotanical remains such as fragments of the cob and kernels tend to preserve well when the plant is commonly grown and utilized. These remains are more elusive when the crop is being introduced into a region and perhaps only parts of it (such as the kernels) or small quantities are being brought in through trade and exchange. In this context microbotanical remains such as phytoliths and starch grains, small, durable cells produced by the plant that get deposited in soil or embedded in artifacts, are helpful in detecting maize's presence. Finally, maize is detectable in human stable isotopes because it has a distinctive photosynthetic pathway than other edible plants in the area. Maize is a C_4 plant, whereas quinoa and tubers are C_3 plants. Thus, the presence of maize in a diet can be detected by the isotopic signatures in human bone.

FIGURE 4.1. *The* altiplano *maize variety.*

Maize through Time

There are no macrobotanical remains of maize in the Taraco Peninsula samples from the Early and Middle Formative periods. In the Late Formative period we found only a couple of fragments of kernels from the site of Kala Uyuni (1% ubiquity) (table 4.2). There is, however, microbotanical evidence for maize in the earliest periods. Amanda Logan (2006) identified maize phytoliths and starch grains from Middle Formative period soil samples and artifacts from Chiripa and Kala Uyuni. Maize microfossils are also common in Late Formative soil samples and ceramic vessels from Kala Uyuni and Kumi Kipa (Logan, Hastorf, and Pearsall 2012; Reilly 2017). Finally, the human stable isotopes from the Formative period reflect a diet dominant in C_3 plants, quinoa and tubers, with hints of higher maize consumption by some individuals in the Late Formative period (M. J. Miller et al. 2021) (also see chapter 7).

The presence of maize increases in both the macrobotanical and isotopic record during the Tiwanaku period on the peninsula. While still low compared with other crops, the occurrence of maize fragments in the macrobotanical samples on the peninsula increases to 11 percent. The signature of maize also increases in human stable isotopes but is still comparatively low compared with other individuals in the Lake Titicaca Basin region at the time, particularly at Tiwanaku itself (Berryman 2010; M. J. Miller et al. 2021). At Tiwanaku maize macrobotanical remains are more common, in general, but also show an increase through time. They occur in 20 percent of the samples in the Late Formative, increasing to 38 percent in the Tiwanaku period (Wright, Hastorf, and Lennstrom 2003).

The scant evidence of maize during the Formative period on the Taraco Peninsula suggests that it was not cultivated there but brought in through trade or long-distance travel by locals. Its increase in the Tiwanaku period suggests this may have been a time when people began to experiment with growing it locally, particularly if it began to take on a larger role in meals and events associated with the activities of the Tiwanaku state. Its role as food, and most likely an ingredient in alcoholic beverages, will be discussed further in chapter 7.

CROPSCAPES

Examining trends in the botanical evidence, we can add to the landscape the primary crops that were raised by the earliest Taraco Peninsula farmers and examine changes and continuities through time (figure 4.2). From the earliest occupations of the Early and Middle Formative periods, quinoa and tubers, most certainly potatoes and *oca*, but possibly others, appear to be the principal cultigens fostered in the area. While there are some minor fluctuations, this pair of crop types, chenopods and tubers, persisted through the Late Formative period and into the Tiwanaku period. The importance of tubers increases through time. Rather than imagining that these crops replaced quinoa, however, we might think of them as adding to the productive ability of the farmers on this landscape. This additional production may have enabled the human population growth that is detected in the archaeological record across the Formative period. While we cannot see crop rotations and the layout of particular plots, as we do today, we might imagine multi-cropped mixtures of quinoa and tubers. This perhaps evolved into a rotation where one crop followed the other year after year as farmers experimented with planting not only two types of crops but different varieties of them. As they noticed the characteristics of the crops and their responses to different soil types and rainfall regimes, new varieties and even species, such as *kañawa*, were created. There certainly is much varietal diversity that is hidden by carbonization and fragmentation, but the persistence and continuity of these two categories of domesticated plants is striking. The introduction of a new domesticated

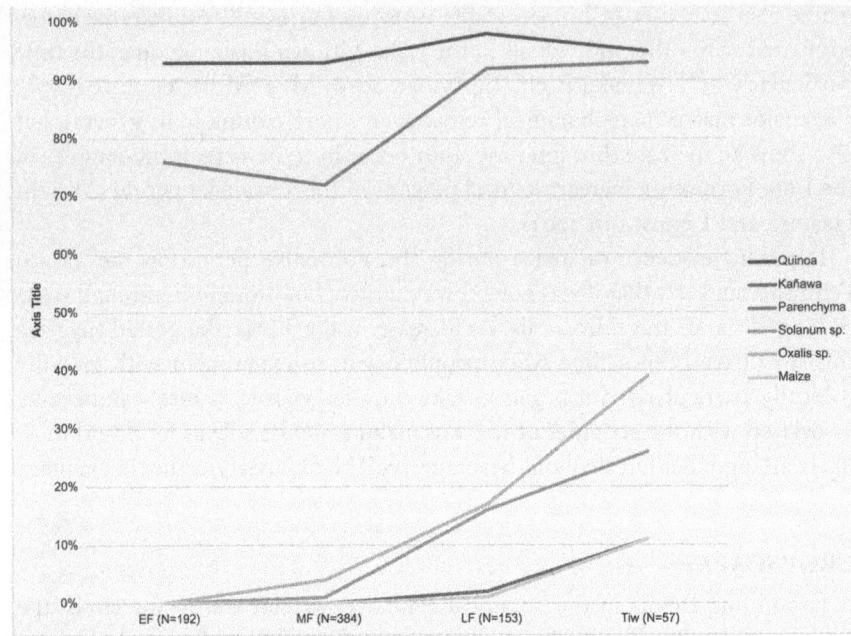

FIGURE 4.2. *Ubiquity of crop plants through time.*

plant, maize, did not displace the importance of chenopods and tubers. On the Taraco Peninsula the human isotope data strongly complement the archaeobotanical record in that the signature of maize consumption remains low, even into the Tiwanaku period, when we know the crop was at the height of its popularity in the urban and ritual center just 20 km away. In the city itself, chenopods and tubers provided the daily sustenance for most of the population (Wright, Hastorf, and Lennstrom 2003).

With this understanding of the crop-actors that were part of the early Taraco agricultural landscapes, we can think about their interactions with other elements of the environment. If we consider landscapes to be "grown," farming is more than putting a domesticated seed in the ground and hoping it produces. Farmers must create the ideal conditions for plants to grow, and this is a dynamic process that depends on other elements, the soils and weather, as elaborated on in the previous chapter, but also other species living on the landscape. Thankfully, the archaeobotanical record is rich in information about the noncrop plant species that grew on the peninsula, and they provide surprising insights into the creation of the agricultural landscape.

5

Tending

Wild Plants and Domesticated Animals

As the rainy months progressed, all of the fields had now been planted, with green shoots emerging from the soil, developing full leaves and flowers. As described in the opening vignette of chapter 1, Alejandra's work shifted to ensuring that she could "make" good potatoes and other crops by returning to the field and removing as many threats as possible. On a clear March morning I accompanied Alejandra to a blooming potato field with a small pick (*chuntilla*) and a few woven blankets to complete the *th'aruña*. Along each row of crops, we used the pick to pull up various species of nondomesticated plants that might interfere with the growth of the potatoes. Alejandra deftly plucked out these plants and tossed them to the side of the field where they were collected into a pile (figure 5.1). She would then take the loosened soil and mound it up around the potato plant to ensure that there was plenty of room for the tubers to grow beneath the soil. Finally, we fixed the furrow between the rows of crops, creating canals that would ensure that any heavy rainfall would produce the needed moisture for growth but not puddle and possibly inundate the tubers, causing them to rot. There was even one occasion where Julio brought out the *yunta* and carefully drove the plow through the furrows, pulling up intrusive plants but also turning over the black, fertile soil. Alejandra followed behind and made sure to replace any turned-up small tubers and then mounded the earth up around the growing potato and *oca* plants. This left a clear and deep canal between the crop rows.

https://doi.org/10.5876/9781646426133.c005

FIGURE 5.1. Th'aruña. *Using a* chuntilla *to remove a mustard plant from a growing fava bean field.*

At this stage in the process people who use pesticides spray the growing crops. This is a common practice today. One of the products used on the potato crops is an insecticide called KARATE (produced by the US company Syngenta Crop Protection, Inc.). Farmers either rent or purchase sprayers and do the spraying themselves. It does seem to be effective as one farmer commented that he had much higher yields in the sprayed fields than in one he did not spray. I also heard about the technique of using *tarwi* water as an insecticide but never witnessed it myself.

We carried out *th'aruña* once and sometimes twice in each field. Despite this effort, many wild plants still thrived in the fields, and by the end of the growing season there were many plants growing alongside the crops and out across the landscape in general. To learn more about these plants, their local names and potential uses, I carried out an ethnobotanical collection resulting in a field reference collection that contained 63 specimens (Martin 1995). I collected about 20 of these informally during walks with local residents. I retrieved the majority of them, however, during a systematic plant collection in February 2004 (Bruno 2008). Assisting me was a collection team consisting of three Bolivian university students and local Aymara consultants. We aimed to collect at least three examples of each species encountered in 22 plots measuring

5 × 5 m along transects that extended from the lakeshore to the hilltop in the communities of Chiripa, Coa Collu, and San José. Because we did not want to disturb growing fields, the collections were primarily in fallowed fields and grazing areas. As will be discussed further below, many of these plants also grew in fields. The *th'aruña* work was occasionally held up by my querying Alejandra the names of the plants we were plucking out of the ground! In a similar fashion, as we collected the plants, we would ask the local consultant the names and uses of each. We then dried and pressed the specimens. One copy of them went to the Herbario Nacional de Bolivia, where they were identified and given their Linnean, scientific names. Their seeds and other parts that could be found archaeologically entered our archaeobotanical comparative collections. Finally, we created a "field herbarium" of 55 plants (Bruno 2008). I completed 31 additional interviews and asked the participants to look at each specimen and, if known, provided its name and use. Although the plants sometimes looked different dried and pressed, most people were able to recognize them and provided names in Aymara and Spanish, and nearly every plant had at least one use. These interviews not only helped me identify these plants archaeologically but also revealed that these noncrop plant species are incredibly important actors in the Taraco agricultural landscapes.

Uses of these plants included as medicines, herbs used in cooking, and steeped in hot water for warm drinks. By far the most common use (60% of responses), however, was *"para chancho"* (for the pig) or *"para los animales"* (for the animals). Even if the name was unknown, the plant would often be recognized as something the sheep liked to eat (Bruno and Hastorf 2016).

As for the wild plants that Alejandra and I removed from the potato field, they were gathered up in blankets and then carried over to the cows to eat after our work was completed. During the growing season animals are carefully kept away from the fields. It is not unusual, however, for one to accidentally escape and eat part of someone's field. The owner of the animal is then held responsible for compensating the farmer for the loss. These animals are fed throughout the year through various methods. The wheat and barley cultivated each year is dried and fed to herds, particularly in the winter months. Additionally, people harvest the lush *totora* reeds and other aquatic plants in the lake to feed their animals. Finally, as the ethnobotanical interviews revealed, the wild plants growing across the landscape provide another important source of food for domesticated animals as they are grazed from lakeshore to hilltops.

As has been documented in other smallholder communities, the care and maintenance of domesticated animals often goes hand in hand with sustainable farming practices (Netting 1993). Animals contribute to overall agro-biodiversity and in important ways to productive crops. As already described in chapter 4, animal dung is a critical fertilizer in *altiplano* fields, particularly for potatoes. While the dung is collected in pens and placed with seed, it also gets deposited in the soils as animals graze in newly harvested or fallowed fields. This organically rich material gets integrated into the soils that will eventually be planted. This multispecies entanglement creates an environment in which these "wild" plant species thrive. While we might view them as "undomesticated" plants, their life cycles are closely wedded to human productive activities and as a result provide an important proxy for them in the past.

In this chapter, I examine the noncrop plant species that contributed to past landscapes. Their patterns and life cycles are intimately linked to the activities of humans, domesticated plants and animals, and the nonorganic elements of the environment such as rainfall and soil types. This exploration reveals increases and decreases of these species through time. I use two terms in this discussion, "wild" and "weedy," neither of which is straightforward. "Wild" implies something untouched or unaffected by humans, but as will become apparent, this is not necessarily the case. I include trees, woody shrubs, cacti, and several aquatic species under this category, as they tend to be less directly managed by humans, but they are certainly utilized and impacted by human activity. "Weedy" plants are herbaceous species that are well adapted to disturbed environments and are most closely linked to agricultural and pastoral activities. While the English term "weed" and the Spanish term *malas hierbas* ("bad plants"!) have very negative connotations, these plants play an important role in the history of these landscapes. As described above, work is often needed to remove them, and they might be considered unwanted growing alongside crops, but they also have many other uses (Bentley et al. 2005). In fact, there is no such negative Aymara term to encompass these plants; they are often just referred to by their names or as an herb (*ali*) or grass (*qura*). These wild and weedy plant-actors provide some of the most important insights into past agricultural activities. While tree and cactus populations appear to have experienced some declines due to human pressure, weedy species thrive and diversify as part of growing agricultural landscapes. Together these plants shed light on the colors, textures, and even aromas of the past Taraco landscapes.

WILD AND WEEDY PLANT HISTORIES

All human societies from hunter-gatherers to city-dwellers impact the ecology of local plant life (e.g., Baleé 1994; Fowler 1996; Tsing 2015). Currently a good deal of attention is being placed on the negative impacts that humans have had on the diversity of Earth's plant and animal species as population growth, destruction of habitats, and global warming are causing alarmingly high rates of extinction (e.g., Chew 2001; Kolbert 2014). There are well-documented instances in which past human societies caused declines in plants species, particularly trees, through deforestation (e.g., Beresford-Jones 2011; Hughes 2011; N. F. Miller 1985). While it may seem from such cases that humans inevitably cause species depletion, ethnobotanical and agroecological studies of foraging and nonindustrial, smallholder farming communities show that they actually *increase* the number of plant species in their environments (Baleé 1994; da Cunha 2017; Nabhan et al. 1982). For example, a group of biologists and anthropologists led by Gary Nabhan (Naban et al. 1982) compared the diversity of plant species at two different locations in same region of the Sonora Desert. One location, Quitovac, was a pond oasis in northern Mexico that still had Indigenous farmers working and living on the land. The other location, Quitobaquito, just 50 km to the north in the state of Arizona, was formerly an Indigenous settlement that was closed off to create part of the Organ Pipe Cactus National Monument. Botanical surveys in both areas revealed that the inhabited Quitovac area had 76 *more* plant species than the uncultivated area Quitobaquito. They attributed this difference to the various activities of the Indigenous farmers. In addition to 17 cultivated crop and tree species, 59 wild and weedy plant species adapted to disturbed habitats occupied the tilled fields, areas of small-scale burning, and along living fencerows.

Many activities associated with farming, particularly clearing, burning, digging, and even water management, are, ecologically, considered to be "disturbances." While such practices can result in the loss of some species, they also, often unintentionally, create spaces for other species to flourish. These plants are often referred to as "weeds," a term that projects a negative connotation; yet ecologically it simply means a plant that is adapted to disturbed environments (E. Anderson 1952; de Wet and Harlan 1975; Harlan and de Wet 1965). They serve as a proxy for the ecological conditions in which they are growing, which is influenced by the nonbiological elements of the landscape, such as climate, soil types, and elevation, as well as the human activities that they are responding to, particularly associated with farming and herding. I gathered information about ecology and uses of the plant taxa through the ethnobotanical collections as well as from several published studies of other farming communities in Bolivia and the Andes, which inform my interpretation of their patterns in the archaeobotanical record. As Nabhan and colleagues did in the Sonora desert, I document the diversity of noncrop plant species in the archaeological record through time to measure the impact of Taraco societies on the botanical landscape (Lepofsky and Lertzman 2005; Popper 1988).

Plant Communities of the Present

Before delving into the ancient plant record, it is helpful to examine current plant ecology of the peninsula and the landscape of the wider southern Titicaca Basin. The dry, cold climate of the Andean *altiplano* supports a relatively low density of plant species compared with the warm, humid tropics of the nearby Amazon Basin. Nonetheless, it is home to a diversity of species adapted to such conditions—numerous grasses, herbs, shrubs, and a few unique tree species. This ecological zone is referred to in classic ecological treaties as the *puna*, or mountain grasslands (Troll 1968; Weberbauer 1945). Lake Titicaca itself and the microclimate it creates supports additional terrestrial species of grasses and sedges as well as many aquatic species. This more temperate ecological zone is also referred to as the *suni* (Pulgar Vidal 1972). The Taraco Peninsula falls within both of these broader zones, but local botanical studies provide a more detailed picture of its floral ecology (Bruno 2008; Loza de la Cruz 1998). Based on the botanical collection and survey that my team carried out on the peninsula, the sunflower family, Asteraceae, was the richest, with 29 species encountered (26% of the total collection), followed by 14 different grass species (Poaceae, 12%), 10 legume species (Fabaceae, 9%), and 5 species from the mustard family (Brassicaceae, 4.5%). Although the majority of the species we recorded are native to the Americas (66%) and specific to the Andes (31.2%), 15.2 percent of the collection contains species from Eurasia and 1.8 percent from Africa (Brack Egg 1999; Bruno 2008, table 5.4; Loza de la Cruz 1998; USDA, NRCS 2007). Many of these species are particularly pervasive; for example, the carpet of green grass growing on the paths leading to the lakeshore is the African species, *Pennisetum clandestinum* Chiov., locally called *chixi*. While it is good for pasture, it is very aggressive and invades agricultural fields as well. It has an expansive root system that is difficult to remove during weeding and in field preparation.

Plant communities do vary across the Taraco landscape. Vegetation, particularly grasses and herbs, grows most densely near the lake and other water sources such as springs and becomes sparser on the rockier, thinner soils of the *laderas* and *cerro*, which support a variety of shrubs, bunch grasses, and cacti. Although the overall density of plants increases with greater soil moisture toward the lake, most wild species on the peninsula are not correlated with any particular soil types or ecological zone (Bruno and Hastorf 2016; Loza de la Cruz 1998). Loza de la Cruz (1998, 83–84) has hypothesized that the homogeneity of plant species found in Indigenous Bolivian lake communities is due to animal grazing, which helps disperse plant seeds across the landscape.

The only wild species that can be specifically attributed to a particular ecological zone are those adapted to aquatic environments. At the margins of springs, streams, and near the lakeshore we find clusters of water-loving species of the Cyperaceae family, commonly known as sedges. The lake itself supports dense and economically important plant communities. Tall, dense stands of *totora* reeds (*Schoenoplectus californicus*) occupy the first 5 to 10 m of the lakeshore, comprising 30 percent of lake vegetative cover in the small lake (Iltis and Mourguiart 1992, 244). These reeds were traditionally used to make boats, thatch roofs, and baskets (Levieil and Orlove 1992). The *totora* reed beds are highly managed, being cut on a regular basis and also replanted. Today they are also cut to feed cattle and sheep, and there is some debate about whether they were used to feed camelids in the past (Bonavia 2008). Growing submerged in the water are several species, *Potamogeton* sp. and *Ruppia* sp., which are also harvested to feed livestock.

Plant Communities of the Past

Pollen studies from lake cores provide a broad perspective of what the past botanical landscape would have looked like at the end of the Pleistocene into the late Holocene. They correspond with the broader climatic changes discussed in chapter 3 as well as with the impact that human populations had on the landscape. During the extremely dry mid-Holocene (approximately 8000–3100 BP), vegetation in the area was similar to today's dry *puna* or *puna brava* in the southern *altiplano* (Graf 1981). An increase in Cyperaceae pollen around 3400 BP corresponds with documented wetter conditions at this time as well as indications of increased human presence. Paduano et al. (2003) and Binford, Brenner, and Leyden (1996) find the highest percentages of Amaranthaceae (the quinoa and amaranth family) pollen after 2000 BP. While this may reflect increased disturbance of the landscape, it may also indicate the presence of cultivated quinoa. Other species adapted to open-ground environments also increase, including asterids, grasses, *Plantago*, *Evolvulus*, and Malvaceae (Graf 1981, 364; Paduano et al. 2003, 273–74).

While the palynological studies show broad trends between long periods of time, they do not detect changes on a smaller time scale. The archaeobotanical record of noncultivated plants provides insights into local vegetation patterns and their relationships to the local environment and human activities across the landscape through time.

WOOD: TREES AND WOODY SHRUBS

Today the *altiplano*, including the Taraco Peninsula, is a grassland with only small pockets of trees. The most common tree on the peninsula is the introduced *Eucalyptus*, which was planted near houses and along roads by the haciendas in the nineteenth and twentieth centuries. There are also small groves of introduced pine trees as well as the native Andean species *Buddleja* sp. (*quishwara*) and *Polylepis* spp. (*keñua*). All of the native tree species are known sources of fuel today (Ansión 1986; Cardenas 1989) and were in the past (Hastorf, Whitehead, and Johannessen 2005; Johannessen and Hastorf 1990).

There has been some debate about how the Andean *altiplano* came to be relatively treeless. Pollen studies indicate a greater presence of several species, including *Polylepis/Aceane*, *Podocarpus*, *Alnus*, and *Hedyosmum* as well as higher densities of charcoal in lake cores during the mid-Holocene, a period of colder, drier conditions (Graf 1981; Hanselman et al. 2005; Paduano et al. 2003; Valencia et al. 2018). *Polylepis* pollen steadily declines in the Lake Titicaca Basin starting around 3,000 years ago but becomes quite sparse around 1,000 years ago (Kessler and Driesch 1993; Valencia et al. 2018). These trees are especially adapted to wetter, muddy microclimates, which may have naturally decreased in the late Holocene but could also be related to changes in human use of the landscape, particularly increased agriculture and grazing (Bush 2020).

The Taraco archaeobotanical remains provide some revealing patterns in wood use through time. Although dung was likely the primary source of fuel, the archaeobotanical record shows that wood was used as well. Wood ubiquity generally increases through time with a decline in the Middle Formative period (table 5.1). The much lower ubiquity of the Middle Formative period may simply reflect a much wider range of contexts in the samples, particularly floor areas or places where there was not a lot of burning (see chapter 6 for variation in plant density by types of contexts). There does, however, seem to be more wood fuel use in the later time periods. At Tiwanaku there is a similar trend of increasing ubiquity of wood in samples with about 80 percent ubiquity in the Late Formative to 90–93 percent in the later Tiwanaku periods (Wright, Hastorf, and Lennstrom 2003). These patterns might suggest more intensive wood use in the Late Formative and Tiwanaku periods. Does this mean that there was more wood available in the landscape later in time? Or were people gaining access to wood through exchange and trade with more forested regions? Unfortunately, we do not yet have anatomical studies of the wood samples to determine which types of trees were being used. A study of bird species from the site of Chiripa, however, does suggest that *Polylepis* habitats existed in the area during the Early and Middle Formative periods (D. Steadman 1996). The

TABLE 5.1. Ubiquity of woody plant species through time

	Early Formative (N=192)	Middle Formative (N=384)	Late Formative (N=153)	Tiwanaku (N=57)
Wood	91%	80%	99%	96%
T. cristatum	0%	0%	1%	23%

Titicaca Basin pollen record of *Polylepis* suggests that there might, in fact, have been fewer local tree species (Valencia et al. 2018) and that the increased burning of wood during these later periods possibly contributed to deforestation. This is a pattern seen across the Nasca periods (approximately 100–550 CE) on the southern coast of Peru, where *Prosopis* sp. trees were more intensively used and resulted in a loss of those forests and related ecologies (Beresford-Jones 2011).

There are also several woody shrub species on the peninsula that are commonly used as fuel: *Tetraglochin cristatum* (Britton) Rothm., *Adesmia spinosissima* Meyen., and *Baccharis* sp. Again, analysis of charcoal could help identify some of these species. Fortunately, *Tetraglochin cristatum* produces a diagnostic seed, which first appears in the archaeobotanical record during the Late Formative period and increases in ubiquity in the Tiwanaku period from 1 percent to 23 percent (table 5.1). This is a spiny bush that grows on the rocky hillsides and in noncultivated areas of the Taraco Peninsula (Pestalozzi Schmid and Nina 1998). It is referred to as *kayña*, *añawaya*, and *ch'aphi* (which is a general descriptor for spiny plants). This may be another indication of tree clearing and wood fuel use in later periods. An ethnobotanical study of flora in Indigenous fields in a southern region of Bolivia by Pestalozzi Schmid and Nina (1998, 180) noted that these bushes often occupy heavily grazed areas as the animals do not eat them, and they can thrive with the removal of other vegetation, such as grasses. This species could be indicative of such activities on the peninsula through time, which will be discussed in more detail below.

TERRESTRIAL, HERBACEOUS PLANTS

As mentioned above, seeds from herbaceous species far outnumber any other plant category in the Taraco archaeobotanical record. Again, this is likely due to the burning of camelid dug for fuel, introducing the plants these animals grazed on year-round into the archaeological record. All of the species we encounter in large numbers are endemic to the peninsula and nearby *altiplano*. We, therefore, can rule out that camelids that had been grazing

TABLE 5.2. Ubiquity of common herbaceous wild taxa in order of discussion

	Early Formative (N=192)	Middle Formative (N=384)	Late Formative (N=153)	Tiwanaku (N=57)
Poaceae	97%	91%	100%	96%
Malvaceae Type 1	99%	90%	96%	91%
Malvaceae Type 2	0%	1%	4%	9%
Amaranthus sp.	13%	6%	58%	70%
C. pallidicaule var. *pampalasta*	(N=71) 39%	(N=87) 79%	(N=149) 93%	(N=57) 77%
Trifolium amabile	59%	63%	97%	91%
Verbena sp. Type 1	32%	40%	91%	86%
Verbena sp. Type 2	0%	0%	10%	28%
Galium sp.	28%	21%	21%	19%
Relbunium sp.	41%	40%	86%	77%
Sisyrinchium sp.	2%	6%	82%	79%
Brassicaceae Type 1	20%	11%	34%	40%
Brassicaceae Type 2	5%	6%	71%	74%
Asteraceae	6%	6%	14%	26%

in distant areas were introducing nonlocal plants at a level we could detect (Bruno and Hastorf 2016). Table 5.2 lists the most common species encountered in the sample chosen for this analysis, and figure 5.2 illustrates their ubiquity through time. I begin with the most common species and end with those that are less abundant but provide insight into human plant and land use. As will become apparent, many of these species first appear in the earliest periods but increase in ubiquity through time.

As would be expected for the *puna* environment, grasses (Poaceae) dominate the Taraco archaeobotanical assemblage with over 90 percent ubiquity across all time periods (table 5.2). There are several different types of grasses in the archaeological assemblages, but they have not been identified in the analysis because doing so would be very time consuming given the high seed densities in the samples. Several are recognizable as *Stipa* sp., *Festuca* sp., and others present on the landscape today but not sorted out in this analysis. A more detailed analysis of species through time might reveal changes in local ecology, but for our purposes the grasses simply reflect the dominant grassland ecology of the peninsula.

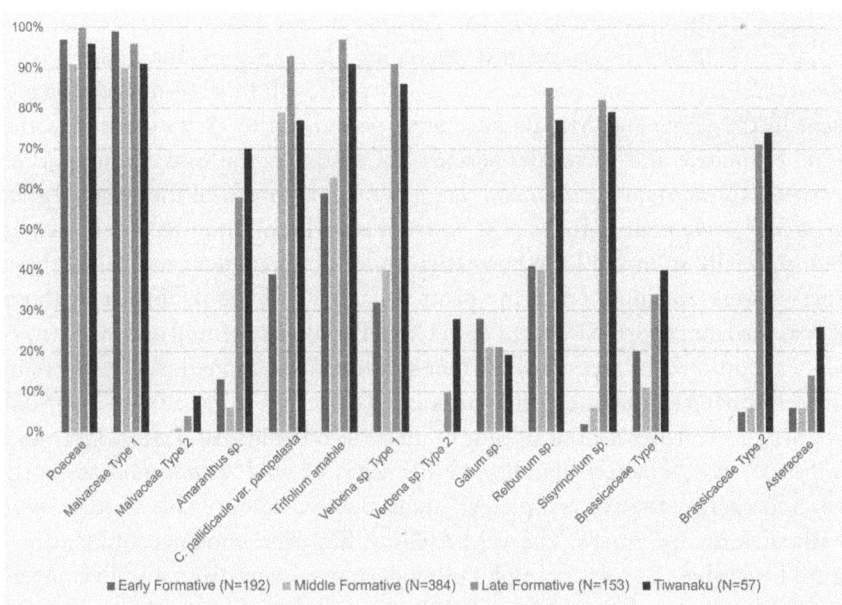

FIGURE 5.2. *Ubiquity of common wild taxa in order of discussion.*

The next most common wild plant family is Malvaceae, or mallows. The most common mallow seed type (Type 1) could belong to a number of local species, including *Tarasa tenella* or *Urocarpidium* sp. This is the most common type and has a ubiquity of over 90 percent across all periods. A larger seed type with a spiky seed coat (Malvaceae Type 2) first appears in samples from the Middle and Late Formative periods (1% and 4% ubiquity, respectively) and increases substantially in the Tiwanaku period (9% ubiquity). It resembles the seeds of a species common on the peninsula today *Urocarpidium shepardae* (I. M. Johnst.) Krapov. (= *Urocarpidium echinatum* [C. Presl] Krapov. and Fryxell) (Zuloaga and Morrone 1999, 2:842). Although mallows generally appear in open, grassland environments, they are commonly recognized agricultural weeds (C. Franquemont et al. 1990, 85; Pestalozzi Schmid and Nina 1998, 56, 170) and are particularly adapted to highly fertile soils. I observed *U. shepardae*, called *amkaraya* by Taraco residents, in growing fields but very frequently in recently fallowed fields, especially ones where animals were left to graze. Some species of mallow are known to thrive in eutrophic, or nutrient-enriched, environments often created by animal manure (Pestalozzi Schmid and Nina 1998, 56)

TENDING 99

There are two species within the Amaranthaceae family that I classify as wild/weedy in our Taraco context (excluding *quinoa negra*). The first is a wild *Amaranthus* species that increases in ubiquity through time, from about 10 percent in the Early and Middle Formative periods up to 58–70 percent in the Late Formative and Tiwanaku periods. The second is the wild counterpart of *kañawa, Chenopodium pallidicaule* var. *pampalasta*, known in the wider region as *illama* or *illamancus* (Rojas et al. 2010). It is fairly common across all periods but especially so in the Late Formative period. Interestingly, neither of these species were encountered in my plant collections of the peninsula or those across the lake reported by Loza de la Cruz. Pestalozzi Schmid and Nina (1998, 114) encountered *A. peruvianus* farther south and mentioned that it grows in areas fertilized by manure or human waste. Brack Egg (1999, 27) lists two wild species that can grow at the altitude of the Taraco Peninsula: *A. hybridus* L. and *A. peruvianus* (Schauer) Standley. While seeds of wild *Amaranthus* are fairly common across the Americas, TAP archaeobotanists were able to identify it without local specimens. The wild *kañawa*, however, remained unidentified until I was able to access examples of modern specimens from a Bolivian seed bank (Bruno 2008; Bruno, Pinto, and Rojas 2018). The absence of these species on the modern landscape speaks to some of the important changes that have occurred across the landscape over this long span of time (see chapter 8).

There are a number of species that are present in lower ubiquities in the Early and Middle Formative period samples but show significant increases in the Late Formative and Tiwanaku periods (table 5.2; figure 5.2). These species are not only adapted to the open, grassland ecology but are particularly indicative of agricultural and pastoral activities.

Trifolium amabile is an American clover that is common on the peninsula today, referred to as *layu-layu*, and is encountered across the Andes (Zuloaga and Morrone 1999, 2:734). On the peninsula and in other Bolivian Indigenous communities it is recognized as an agricultural weed and thrives in tilled and fallowed fields (C. Franquemont et al. 1990, 82; Loza de la Cruz 1998; Pestalozzi Schmid and Nina 1998, 55). As a legume, clovers are nitrogen-fixing plants, so although not purposefully planted by farmers in this region today, these species would contribute to the maintenance of soil fertility.

There are several species of the verbena genus and family (Verbenaceae) growing across the Titicaca Basin landscape today. I collected *Verbena* cf. *bangiana* Moldenke, which has a small seed, and *Verbena microphylla* Kunth (= *Glandularia microphylla* Kunth) (Zuloaga and Morrone 1999, 2:1165), which has a larger seed. In the archaeological assemblage we most commonly find small seeds like those of *V. bangiana* and other species in the genus, and they become more ubiquitous through time. A second type of verbena, possibly *V. microphylla*, first appears in the Late Formative (11% ubiquity) and Tiwanaku (28% ubiquity) samples. We found these verbenas growing across the landscape from uncultivated hillsides to fallowed fields. Taraco residents did not seem to recognize these plants as much as others and often referred to them simply as *pastos*, which means "grass." They are plants that their animals graze upon.

There are two species within the bedstraw family (Rubiaceae): *Galium* sp. and *Relbunium* sp. *Galium* sp. occurred at about 20 percent ubiquity across all time periods, while *Reblunium* sp. increases through time. I collected *Relbunium ciliatum* (Ruiz and Pav.) Hemsl, and Loza de la Cruz (1998) collected a species he identified tentatively as *Relbunium* cf. *richardianum* (Gill ex Hook and Am.) Hicken.[1] Yet it was not a species that residents were currently very familiar with aside from an herb that their animals ate. Hastorf and Wright (1998, 1) found *Relbunium* seeds in dung from camelids living near Tiwanaku. They suggest that perhaps camelids prefer this species, for it was not common in the landscape but very common in the dung (Hastorf and Wright 1998, 221). Additionally, Loza de la Cruz (1998, 53) found *Relbunium* cf. *richardianum* growing in hilltop fallows, which are common grazing areas. Importantly, however, *Galium* and *Relbunium* are well-known dye plants across the Andes (Brack Egg 1999, 219; Wallert and Boytner 1996, 857) and likely served this purpose in the past. Current residents of Taraco still weave wool blankets but use bright synthetic dyes purchased in the market, which likely explains the loss of knowledge about the name and use of this plant today.

Sisrynchium sp. is a species of the iris (Iridaceae) family. I collected modern specimens of *Sisrynchium chilense* Hook, and the most common name for this small herb was *aykayka*. On the peninsula and in other regions, species of *Sisrynchium* are recognized as a medicine but also fodder for animals (Loza de la Cruz 1998, 41, 81; Pestalozzi Schmid and Nina 1998, 195). Like *Verbena*, it grows across the landscape, including in agricultural fields.

Species of the mustard family (Brassicaceae) are very common on the landscape today, particularly species introduced from Eurasia, including *Coronopus didymus* (L.) Sm (= *Lepidium didymium* L.) (Zuloaga and Morrone 1999, 1:394), which locals refer to as *mostaza*, the Spanish word for mustard. While these Eurasian species dominate the landscape today (chapter 1), the archaeobotanical record suggests Andean species of this family were quite common in the past. The most well-known Andean brassica, called *maca* (*Lepidium meyenii* Walpers) is cultivated, and its medicinal properties are today recognized globally (Quirós and Cárdenas 1997). There are also wild, native species of *Lepidium* sp. that have similar-looking seeds, which we classify as Type 1. These are present in relatively low densities and ubiquities in the Taraco samples; while it is possible that they may derive from cultivated tubers, we have not been able to identify the tubers in our samples, and it is not a species that is cultivated in the region today. We, therefore, assume that these are wild seeds. The most common seed, which we refer to as Brassicaceae Type 2, is similar morphologically to the European *Coronopus didymus* and is abundant in the archaeological record. There is an Andean species, which I have not encountered on the peninsula today. Taraco famers, as well as those of other Indigenous Bolivian communities, recognized wild mustards as common in fertile soils of agricultural fields and pasture areas (Pestalozzi Schmid and Nina 1998, 144–45). It is also widely cited as a medicine for humans but toxic to animals (Brack Egg 1999, 289; C. Franquemont et al. 1990, 64; Loza de la Cruz 1998, 47–50). Given that its pattern in the archaeological record is similar to that of other fodder species, showing an increase through time, the Andean species must not have been toxic to camelids and likely arrived through the burning of dung.

The sunflower (Asteraceae) family is one of the most diverse on the peninsula today; yet it fairly sparse in the archaeological record (table 5.2). Although most of the species we collected are endemic to the region, it is possible that these species came to dominate only in more recent times. Pollen records do suggest a decrease in asterids around 3000–1500 BP (roughly correspondent with the Formative period), with a spike again around 750 BP (Hanselman et al. 2005). Their low presence may also reflect that these species are less amenable to archaeological preservation. They produce very thin, oily seeds that might easily be destroyed by fire. Despite their low occurrence overall, like the other wild species, they increase in ubiquity through time.

CACTI

Another important plant family that presents an interesting trend is that of the cactus (Cactaceae) (table 5.3). Small, cushion cacti are quite common on the Taraco landscape today, particularly in very rocky areas. I collected three species: *Maihueniopsis* cf. *boliviana* (Salm-Dyck) Kiesling, *Opuntia soehrensii* Britt. and Rose, and *Rebutia* sp. We can positively identify the seeds of all three of the species, although the seeds of *Rebutia* are also similar to those of other cacti in the Cactoideae subfamily, including *Trichocereus pachanol* Britt. and Rose, the hallucinogenic San Pedro cactus (Cardenas 1989, 283–88). They produce fruits that can be consumed.

The cacti appear in relatively lower ubiquities in the Formative periods but increase in the Tiwanaku period. Camelids have been known to eat cactus

TABLE 5.3. Ubiquity of cacti and aquatic plants through time

	Early Formative (N=192)	Middle Formative (N=384)	Late Formative (N=153)	Tiwanaku (N=57)
Cactaceae	32%	20%	27%	54%
Cyperaceae	72%	60%	97%	86%
Potamogeton sp.	6%	3%	5%	5%
Ruppia sp.	1%	0%	5%	2%

fruits but perhaps not to the extent that they graze on other, less prickly foods. The patterns in these seeds may not be as indicative of their presence on the landscape as sampled by camelids. I will, therefore, examine patterns of cactus as a human food in chapter 7.

AQUATIC PLANTS

The aquatic species of the Cyperaceae family, which includes *totora*, that grow in the lake, along the shore, and in other wet areas such as streams and marshy areas are common in the archaeobotanical record (table 5.3). There are at least three seed types from this family recognizable in the samples, but they are merged as one category here. This is one of the most common families in the plant assemblage with ubiquities of 60–70 percent in the earliest periods, increasing through time up to 90 percent. The high occurrence of these plants reflects the importance of these aquatic species for animal food but also likely their use in the construction of buildings and boats. We also have a few rare finds of the submerged lake species *Potamogeton* sp. and *Ruppia* sp. Their rarity makes it difficult to interpret the significance of their overall presence through time.

These aquatic species could also be indicative of changes in local wetland environments. We might expect that these species would decline in the periods that were relatively drier in the region (chapter 3). Interestingly, however, Cyperaceae ubiquities do not closely track with the paleoenvironmental patterns (Bruno et al. 2021). Instead, there is a general trend of increasing ubiquity of Cyperaceae seeds through time, as there is with other terrestrial species discussed above. These data suggest that people actively gave their herds access to these aquatic plants. Hastorf and I have argued that Taraco herds were not being foddered but likely were grazing across the landscape, which includes several easily accessible wet areas (Bruno and Hastorf 2016).

This could be accomplished by simply moving herds to wet areas along streams, in the *pampa*, or along the lakeshore. In contrast, at Tiwanaku itself, which is even farther from the lake and more of a dry, grassland environment, we find a *higher* ubiquity of Cyperaceae seeds relative to other terrestrial plants. This suggests that the Tiwanaku herds, whose dung supplied the city, had greater access to aquatic plants. This could have been accomplished by keeping herds in places near the lake, such as at the lakeshore provincial center of Lukurmata, or along the Wila Jawira River, at the nearby Choquepacha spring, or possibly near Tiwanaku and provisioned with lake plants. In any of these scenarios, it is clear that these aquatic plant species played an important role in the livelihoods of the people and domesticated animals of the Taraco Peninsula and beyond.

WILD AND WEEDY PLANTSCAPES

In any environment our experiences of it are shaped by the water, topography, and surrounding atmosphere. Plants, however, are often the entities that give a place texture, color, and aroma. They can also shape the access we have to parts of the landscape, either easy walks through low grasses or perhaps tall reeds or dense woods that make it impossible to pass without a tool to cut down the vegetation. They provide us materials with which to make things, they supply food for animals, and they are also intruders in our walkways, patios, and agricultural fields (E. Anderson 1952; Kimmerer 2013). This analysis reveals the great diversity of noncrop plant species that Taraco Peninsula inhabitants interacted with daily.

A review of the wild and weedy plant-actors of Taraco's past provides several avenues for thinking about this landscape: what it would have looked like, how it changed, and what human and more-than-human elements shaped these developments. On the one hand, there are hints of decreasing number of trees through time. Interestingly, the Early and Middle Formative landscapes may have had more pockets of trees, particularly *Polylepis*, that were used to some extent for fuel, but possibly more sustainably than in the Late Formative and Tiwanaku periods. Wood burning seems to increase later in time, possibly having the consequence of reducing the number of local tree populations and necessitating trade in woods from other areas.

Despite an apparent reduction in tree species, there is a notable increase in the diversity of terrestrial, herbaceous species on the landscape. There are several ways ecologists and ethnobotanists describe and quantify "diversity." One basic concept is "richness," which is simply the number of species in

TABLE 5.4. Diversity indices through time

	Early Formative	Middle Formative	Late Formative	Tiwanaku
Richness = Number of Taxa	22	22	25	26
Simpson_1-D	0.77	0.80	0.91	0.88
Shannon_H	2.07	2.37	2.86	2.54
Evenness_e^H/S	0.36	0.48	0.70	0.49

a population sample. If we consider the number of regularly identified wild species in the Taraco samples through time, we do find a slight increase in richness (table 5.4).

The raw number of taxa, however, does not give a sense of how common or rare any given species might be, thus, "evenness," or the distribution of the species, can be calculated. A diversity index can then be calculated to measure the relationship of richness and evenness of a population (Krebs 1989, 329–30). The two most common diversity indices used by ecologists and archaeobotanists are the Shannon-Wiener and the inverse Simpson indices (Popper 1988). In both cases, a higher number indicates both high richness and great evenness. To examine the distribution of evenness of these populations through time, I calculated both the Shannon-Wiener and inverse Simpson diversity indices using the density (seeds per liter) of each taxon per time period (table 5.4). In this case, we do see an increase in diversity across the Formative periods, with a slight decline in evenness in the Tiwanaku period; this could be due, in part, to the smaller sample size for this time.

This study reveals that certain species, particularly grasses, mallows, wild chenopods, and sedges such as *totora*, were fairly constant through time. The views we have today of wide-reaching grassland that terminate at the lakeshore with small sedges and tall *totora* leading to the lake probably looked similar in the past. During periods of relatively lower lake levels, these areas would have been even more expansive, which is perhaps why these species are so prominent in the archaeological record, as the lake was, on average, lower than it is today (chapter 3). While some of the grass species are certainly different and the extent of the lakeshore fluctuated, the most ancient Taraco inhabitants would recognize this combination of predominately herbaceous grassland punctuated with outcrops of trees and bushes in the hillsides and other rocky areas. What appears to have changed most are the other herbaceous species, such as clover, mustards, bedstraw, verbena, amaranth, and sunflowers. These were present across the Early and Middle Formative landscapes but became much more common, and likely noticeably so, to the Late Formative inhabitants. The Late Formative residents even began to encounter new plants that they did not purposefully introduce, including new species of mallow, verbena, and the prickly but possibly useful fuel of the *kayña* bush. These seem to have become commonplace and relatively unchanged into the Tiwanaku period. The biggest change at this juncture may have been a decrease in trees.

The ecological descriptions of the herbaceous species indicate that they were particularly well adapted to disturbed but also nutrient-rich soils. Ethnobotanical accounts both on the peninsula and elsewhere in Bolivia cite them as common volunteer species, or "weeds," in agricultural fields, both those being cultivated and in fallow. They are also widely recognized as being food for animals. Freddy Loza de la Cruz (1998, 83–84) argues that the relative homogeneity of these weedy plant species across different crop and soil types in the Lake Titicaca Basin today is due to the constant rotation of the soil by farmers and by the pasturing of animals in fields throughout the landscape. The archaeobotanical record from the Taraco Peninsula strongly suggests that this process of homogenization began in the Formative period, particularly in the Late Formative.

I have argued (Bruno 2014a) that this dramatic shift in wild plant species is also indicative of agricultural intensification through a variety of practices suited to smallholding, dryland farming as first synthesized by Robert McC. Netting (1993). Many of these activities are described at the start of the chapter: soil modification through tilling to prepare soils for planting, as well as digging to harvest tubers; fertilizing through the addition of dung; weeding to eliminate competition for crops; and diversification of production through the raising of domesticated animals. The plants themselves do not necessarily point to any particular activity but suggest greater overall disturbance of the landscape as well as maintenance of soil nutrients, particularly through the presence of species such as clover and mallows.

Much like we observed for the crops, the patterns of wild plant species in the Tiwanaku period seem to support continuity from the Late Formative period. We find very similar ubiquities of terrestrial and aquatic species with perhaps a decline in the distribution of wild chenopods. Based on other lines of archaeological evidence, particularly ceramics and settlement patterns, we know that many aspects of life on the Taraco Peninsula must have changed during this period, but perhaps the impact on agriculture was insignificant.

With these broad, temporal trends in the botanical landscape established, I will now "zoom in" to more specific spatial and temporal scales as I examine how patterns in plant remains and a suite of other archaeological data at the site of Kala Uyuni can shed light on how these agricultural products were transformed into food. Across the next two chapters, I examine where food-related activities took place, what meals were prepared and served, and the ways in which these practices fed and nourished, both literally and figuratively, social and political relationships among families and communities at the site of Kala Uyuni and in the region.

6

Harvesting and Processing

Transforming Plants into Food (Part 1)

After about a month, the well-tended potato fields were growing tall with green plants and bursting with purple and white flowers. Alejandra told me that once the flowers begin to die, she knows that the tubers are growing in the soil. She let the plants naturally wilt and dry on their own, although some of her neighbors cut down the wilted plants because they said it prevented insects from getting into the tubers. Some years she leaves the tubers in the ground a few more weeks after the plant has died so that they grow larger. This year we were harvesting with a bit of urgency because worms were already beginning to attack the potatoes. Today two neighbors, Julia and her elderly mother, Francisca, were to help Alejandra and me with the harvesting. Alejandra packed up several *chuntillas*, two *totora* reed baskets, two empty *yutis* (plastic sacks), and some bread, cheese, and two bottles of soda pop. We walked out to the field and met up with the two women, who had also helped Alejandra plant this field.

In the field the women instructed me to take hold of the stem of the wilted, dry plant with my left hand, and with my right hand loosen the earth around tuber with the *chuntilla*. Once the earth around the tubers was loose, I could pull the whole plant out of the ground. Next we would shake the tubers to remove the loose dirt, then pick the tubers from the plant and place them in a basket. We would search the soil for any stray tubers and then move on to the next plant. Once our baskets were full, we would dump the potatoes into a growing pile at the side of the field. Two of us worked a row of potatoes and shared a basket. After gathering up a couple of basketfuls of tubers, we would take a short break to look through the harvested pile. The women would inspect each tuber and remove very small or extremely worm-eaten potatoes. Julia complained that this potato harvest was a bit disappointing, bearing only four or five tubers per plant, and many of them quite small and wormy. The reject pile did not go to waste, however, and would be fed to the pigs later. Despite these losses, by the end of harvesting four rows of plants, we were able to fill up one and half sacks of acceptable potatoes. Once finished, I helped hoist the sack onto Alejandra's back, and Julia and Francisca took the smaller one. We each returned home with our harvest. When we returned to the house, Alejandra deposited the sack of potatoes in a cool, dry storage room.

Fortunately, the worms were not affecting the other tuber crops, *oca* and *isañu*, so we could leave those in the ground to continue growing another month or so. Once they were ready, we harvested them in the same manner as the potatoes. The crops whose fruit grow above ground like fava beans, quinoa, maize, barley, and oats could be left in the fields even longer, maturing and then completely drying before being harvested. While worms do not affect these crops, they are at the risk of damage by frost or hail. In 2004 some people lost their fava bean fields to a hailstorm in April. The favas are often the first of the stalk crops to be harvested, as many of them are in the *milli*, but also because people like to eat the beans when they are young. The stalks with the seed heads are pulled up by hand or cut with a sickle at the base. The stalks are placed into piles, either cone-shaped with the head at the top or the stalks on their sides. The plants continue to dry in these piles until they are processed to remove the seeds.

Thus, the harvest in total occurrs over several months, roughly March through May, sometimes even June. Generally, the first crops to be harvested are those in the *milli* (shoreline), as early as December but generally between January and February. With the rains, the lake begins to rise during these months; therefore, the crops must be removed, even if they are not completely ripe. Crops located up the slopes are then harvested as they mature. Once a field is harvested, the animals are tied up in the fields and left to graze on the crop stubble and the many wild plants that have grown alongside the cultigens.

By June, the Quispes and their neighbors had harvested all of their fields. Mounds of tubers were placed in large bags and carried in wheelbarrows or on the back of a donkey to a small storage building between fields near their house. In the cool, dark building the bags of tubers were covered with heavy wool blankets. The crops we harvested on cut stalks such as fava beans, quinoa, and maize were propped up into pyramid-like bundles at the edge of the fields. Across the winter months of June to September, Alejandra or one of the daughters would supervise three to four people, usually women and elderly individuals, to work through these piles of crops to prepare them for their next stage of use: as seed for the next year's planting and as food. The winter months are the best for this work as the days are dry, sunny, and often breezy. There will be an occasional rain or snow flurry, but overall, they are much drier than the summer months. While it can be a comfortable temperature of about 16°C (60°F) in the bright, sunny daytime, winter nighttime temperatures fall below freezing, averaging about −5°C (23°F). As John Murra (1984, 122) aptly observed, however, Andean farmers "use and domesticate the cold," taking advantage of these frigid nights to freeze-dry their tuber crops into forms known as *chuño* and *tunta*, which allow for long-term storage as well as provide culinary diversity (Sammells 2010).

One bright, sunny day in July, I followed Alejandra and Miriam down to the storehouse, and together we pulled out one of the large bags of potatoes and poured them out onto a flat, grassy surface. Alejandra then instructed me on how to separate several "categories" of potatoes: big ones with few worms, medium ones with few worms, small to medium ones with some worms, and "bad" ones rotted or ruined by worms (figure 6.1, *top*). We then spent over an hour sorting through the pile, making new piles, and filling individual sacks with each type of potato. The big ones were carted up to the house and would be the fresh potatoes used in nearly every meal we ate in the house. The medium ones were placed back into the storeroom as they would be the seed for planting come October. Alejandra pointed out that the medium ones with a lot of eyes made especially good seeds. The small ones also went into the storeroom in preparation for being transformed into one of two freeze-dried forms: *chuño* and *tunta*. The "bad" tubers were fed to hungry pigs.

July is usually the coldest month of the year and best for freeze-drying. After watching the skies and consulting the farmer's almanac, Julio and Alejandra determined that the third week of July would provide ideal freeze-drying conditions: sunny and clear days and freezing nights. On Monday after lunch, we headed back down to the storehouse to the same flat, grassy area where we had sorted the tubers a few weeks prior. I helped Alejandra and Miriam lay out about 20 small piles of 30 to 50 small and medium potatoes. They were left there overnight, and as predicted, temperatures dropped, and the exposed piles of tubers froze. Tuesday morning was bright and sunny. When we returned to the piles after lunch, the ice in the potatoes had begun to melt. Alejandra and Miriam then visited each pile of potatoes with bare

FIGURE 6.1. *Processing potatoes.* Top, *sorting out potatoes for different purposes;* bottom, *squeezing out water from a pile of small potatoes that froze overnight in the process of making* chuño.

feet and, in what looked like a well-practiced dance, stepped on the piles in small lateral movements, squeezing out the water and peeling off the skins (figure 6.1, *bottom*). The piles were then left to freeze again on Tuesday night; then water was squeezed out again with the dance on Wednesday. About half of the piles, particularly of the smallest potatoes, continued to undergo this process for four days until all of the water was removed and what looked like black pebbles remained. These are called *chuño*, which are stored in large sacks up at the house until they are needed for a meal. While these stores usually last for a few years, there are accounts that *chuño* can last up to 20 years! *Oca* can also be freeze-dried through this same process, which is called *kalla*. They are not chosen by size, but there is a special variety especially for this purpose called *chuchulla*.

On the second day of freeze-drying, the other half of medium-sized potatoes that were stepped on were gathered into several net bags and tied securely. We loaded these into a wheelbarrow and carted them to a nearby stream that had been modified to create a little pool. Julio helped to lay the net bags into the pool area, and then we used cut grass and hay to cover them so that animals and birds would not disturb them. We left them in the gently flowing water for about two weeks. We removed the nets and brought them back to the processing area. We then spread out the tubers, which had turned completely white, onto the flat, grassy surface to dry. They remained there for a couple of days. Alejandra would visit them to see how they were drying and peeled off any remaining skin so that the final product of snow-white, hardened potato would remain; this is called *tunta*, or *chuño blanco* in some areas of the Andes.

The plants whose seeds need to be retrieved from stalks and outer casings are also processed in the winter in very similar fashion. Alejandra and her neighbors spend most of the winter days threshing and winnowing these crops. Maize is the easiest, as the large heads can be broken off the stalk and the husk peeled away. The entire dried cobs can be stored if time is short, but the seeds will eventually be removed from the cob and either stored or eaten in this fashion. Fava beans and peas are sometimes eaten fresh as they grow, but most are dried on the stalk and then the individual beans are removed from the pods and stored in large bags.

The plants that require the most work are quinoa, wheat, and barley. These plants have small seeds that are encased in layers of flower and leaves, which must be removed before eating or planting. Farmers begin processing them by hitting the seed heads with a wooden stick (figure 6.2, *left*). This releases the fruits from the stalk. What remain are the seeds with abundant casings and small stems. In some cases, it is necessary to perform more threshing with a

FIGURE 6.2. *Processing crops with seeds. Threshing the head of dried barley stalks* (left). *Winnowing barley grains in the wind* (right). *A similar process is used for quinoa.*

smaller stick to loosen these casings. Then, on a slightly breezy day, women will sit in an area where they use perforated metal plates and pans, or simply their hands, to winnow away the lighter debris from the seed (figure 6.2, *right*). From the pile of seeds and casings, they scoop up a moderate amount of material, raise it to about face level, and then slowly let it pour over a clean piece of plastic, emptied flour or sugar bag, or textile. The heavier seeds fall onto the clean surface while the breeze carries the lighter chaff just beyond the seed pile. They will do this several times until what remains is nearly pure seed, which is then stored in bags until needed for either planting or food.

The remnants of this process are not wasted. The thin stalks of barley and wheat are fed to the animals. If still green, thick stalks like those of favas can also be fed to the animals. The larger dry stalks are often burned in piles on fields as a form of fertilizer, and some of them are burned to produce the ashy substance called *lejia*, used in chewing coca to activate the alkaloids. This work of processing provides a variety of foods that can be stored and utilized throughout the year, but especially during the drier seasons and into the start of the summer when fresh beans and tubers are not available. They provide food for daily meals as well as for special occasions. This processing also creates a lot of material that we detect archaeologically.

In chapters 4 and 5, I examined the combined patterns of the major crops and wild/weedy plant species through time at four different sites: Chiripa,

Kala Uyuni, Kumi Kipa, and Sonaji. In this chapter and the next, I take a more detailed view of a single site, Kala Uyuni, which provides insights into transforming crops into food through processing, cooking, and finally eating through a range of archaeological evidence. There are distinct areas of the site where food-related activities took place that represent both daily and specialized food practices. Patterns in carbonized plant density and diversity indicate where people burned and/or disposed of agricultural and food waste, particularly in middens and pits outdoors, while floors and other surfaces, both inside and out, appear to have been kept clean. Differing ratios of crop and weed species, particularly quinoa and *quinoa negra*, provide additional evidence of crop processing and where it was taking place. The activities involved in transforming crops into meals also shaped interactions between individuals in households and their larger communities, thus shedding light on how food-related activities articulated with local and regional sociopolitical dynamics. Before delving into these topics, I provide an overview of the archaeology that provides the evidence for community dynamics through the Formative and Tiwanaku periods at Kala Uyuni.

KALA UYUNI

The site of Kala Uyuni is located on the southern peninsula in the community of Coa Collu (figure 2.1). The southern extent of the site is located on an upper terrace that overlooks a lower plain and the lake. The site extends north up to the top of a prominent hilltop known as Achachi Coa Collu. In his survey of the area, Matthew Bandy recorded two different sites based on surface ceramics, one (T-232) approximately 15 ha on the lower terrace, and another approximately 1.5 ha on the hilltop (T-225), but we've come to understand these two places as one large site that was utilized in different ways beginning around 1500 BCE. TAP excavations focused on four different areas of the site: Ayrampu Qontu (KUAQ), Achachi Coa Collu (KUAC), Kala Uyuni (KUKU), and Siwinka Qontu (SQ)(figure 6.3). Summaries of the TAP excavations here between 2003 and 2009 can be found in Bandy and Hastorf (2007) and Roddick, Bruno, and Hastorf (2014) as well as several reports. Here I describe the primary architectural and occupational features of each of these areas and the insights they provided into the development of community life and food production through time and across space. In general, the Early and Middle Formative activities were concentrated in the KUAQ and KUAC areas, while the activities of the Late Formative and Tiwanaku periods were in the KUKU and KUSQ areas.

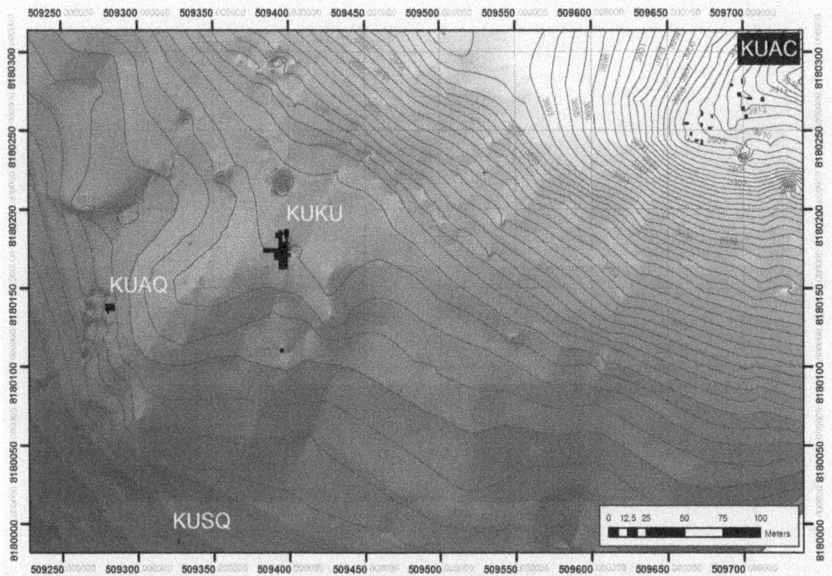

FIGURE 6.3. *Site of Kala Uyuni and the four excavation areas: Ayrampu Qontu (KUAQ), Achachi Coa Collu (KUAC), Kala Uyuni (KUKU), and Siwinka Qontu (SQ). Black rectangles indicate excavation units.*

Ayrampu Qontu (KUAQ)

This area is named after the local toponym, which translates as "hill or mound of Ayrampu," which is a cactus (*Opuntia soehrensii* Britt. and Rose) that grows commonly in rock piles on the peninsula. In this area Bandy identified ceramics from the Early and Middle Formative periods on the surface and suspected it might be an early residential sector. We excavated a 6 × 2 m area here, and while we found some remnants of clay deposits that may have been used for house walls, they were too disturbed by recent plowing to make out any formal structures (Bruno 2007). We did, however, find several horizontal deposits of midden that date between the Early and Middle Formative periods, approximately 900–400 BCE (Bruno 2008; Roddick, Bruno, and Hastorf 2014) (figure 6.4). As will be discussed in greater detail in chapter 7, in addition to relatively high densities of organic materials, these middens primarily contained ceramic wares associated with daily cooking and serving (L. Steadman 2007). Despite the absence of architecture, KUAQ provides a rich record of early daily agricultural and food practices.

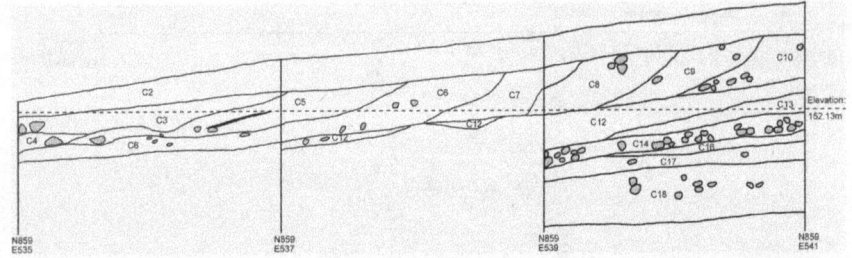

FIGURE 6.4. *Western profile of KUAQ excavations. The southernmost unit shows layers of midden (Events C12–18) that were rich in carbonized plant remains, animal bones, ceramics, and lithics.*

ACHACHI COA COLLU (KUAC)

At approximately 3,900 m a.s.l., the KUAC area provides a prominent view of the terraces and lake below. Bandy (2001) encountered decorated ceramic wares dating to the Early and Middle Formative periods as well as several limestone blocks protruding from the relatively level surface. He hypothesized that ritual architecture typical of these periods was buried below the surface. The excavators strategically placed a series of small (1 × 2 m and 2 × 2 m) units near the protruding stones and then in projected areas surrounding it, verifying that there were, in fact, two sunken courts at the top of the hill (A. B. Cohen and Roddick 2007). Based on the walls encountered in the excavations, we estimate that the "Lower Court" (KU-ASD1)[1] was approximately 18 m × 18 m and the "Upper Court" (KU-ASD3) was approximately 18 m × 15 m (Whitehead and Frye 2003) (figure 6.5). The initial courts were created by digging down into a sterile, red, silty-clay substratum of the hill. This red clay appears to have been used as both an interior and exterior surface for the courts (Goodman Elgar 2004). Although the structures were dug into the ground, the courts were not completely subterranean. It seems that at least portions of the walls would have stood above the surface (A. B. Cohen and Roddick 2007). The walls of the sunken enclosures were constructed of dispersed limestone or sandstone blocks of varying sizes. They filled the gaps between large stones with cobbles and clay-rich fill and mortar. Both courts appear to have undergone at least two phases of reconstruction. At the center of the Upper Court, the archaeologists encountered a nearly 2 m tall sandstone monolith (figure 2.5). The stratigraphy suggests that a pit was dug into an earlier floor to place the monolith. Within the cobble fill surrounding the monolith, the builders also purposefully placed the "Lightning Stone" described in chapter 2.

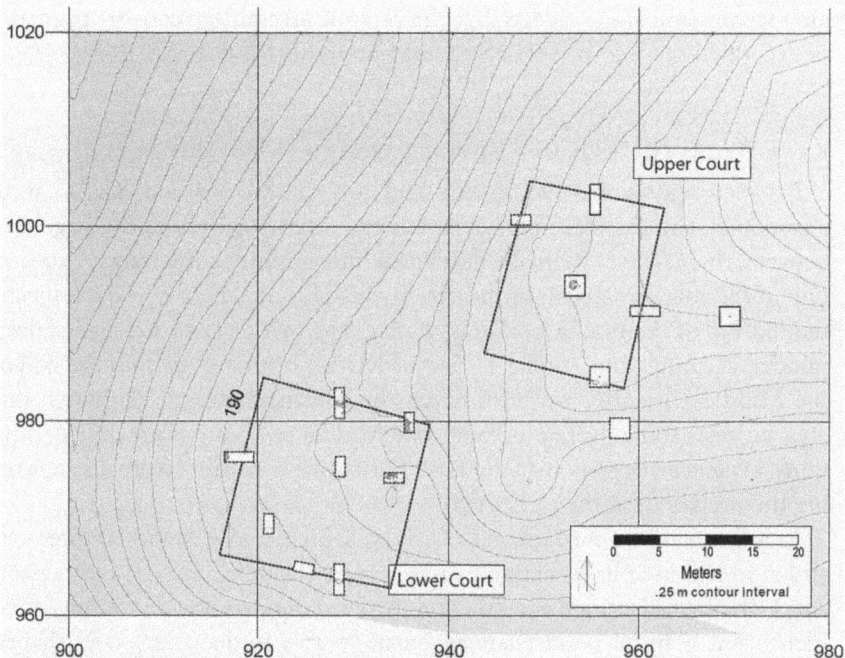

FIGURE 6.5. *Excavation units at KUAC. Dashed lines indicate projection of sunken court walls.*

The Lower Court was also reconstructed at least twice, closing earlier floors, expanding the walls, and placing larger limestone blocks in the walls. In one of the iterations, archaeologists encountered what appeared to be an offering of an adult male with a disarticulated head in the floor matrix. In addition to the structures, the archaeologists found several pits filled with fish bone and botanical remains just outside of the court walls. Several meters east of the buildings, a 2 ×2 m excavation unit revealed an area of midden accumulation, likely associated with the activities at the courts.

The contexts associated with the building and use of the sunken courts primarily date to the Middle Formative period, roughly between 900 and 100 BCE. The earliest deposits, including a midden and small pits filled with organic residues, encountered under the sunken courts date to the Early Formative period, around 1200 BCE (Bruno 2008; Roddick, Bruno, and Hastorf 2014). In contrast to the quotidian nature of the materials encountered in KUAQ, the KUAC area appears to have been an area of ritual importance to the Early and Middle Formative communities. Not only is this reflected in the specialized architecture and stone objects, but the ceramic assemblage consists primarily of decorated serving wares (L. Steadman 2007).

Kala Uyuni (KUKU) and Siwinka Qontu (KUSQ)

Between approximately 100 BCE and 100 CE, KUAQ and KUAC were abandoned, and the focus of occupation and activity shifted to the large area between them, what eventually developed into a prominent terrace. A 2 × 2 m unit at the southern extent of the site, Siwinka Qontu (KUSQ), which means "mound/hill of *siwinka*," a local grass (*Stipa ichu*), revealed another area of deep midden accumulation, similar to that of KUAQ but ranging from the end of the Middle Formative period through the Tiwanaku period. Although this area suggests some overlap between the Middle and Late Formative occupations, evidence suggests that the Late Formative occupants were distinguishing themselves from the earlier era.

At Kala Uyuni we encountered a fairly well-preserved sequence of three construction and use phases dating to 200–500 CE (Roddick, Bruno, and Hastorf 2014). The first identified construction involved digging down into bright red Pleistocene clays to build relatively small (3–4 m in diameter), oval-shaped domestic structures (referred to as KU-ASD9/10) with cobblestone foundations and fine yellow clay floors (Fontenla Alvarez, Sistrunk, and Bruno 2011) (figure 6.6). Although not sunken courts, the practice of digging down into the surface to mark important places may have been carried over from the Middle Formative period. This initial residential area was renovated into a slightly raised platform by placement of nearly a meter of fill that was then capped with a yellow clay (Paz Soria and Fernandez 2007; Roddick 2011). Bright yellow clay was also used to cap surfaces in the process of building the Sonaji platform (Bruno et al. 2006). To the north, excavators found well-preserved foundations of a 3.5 m × 2.8 m oval-shaped structure (KU-ASD2). It had a thick cobblestone foundation (about 1 m wide) and a cobblestone entrance (Paz Soria and Fernandez 2007; Roddick 2011). Two similar structures were exposed to the north (KU-ASD4/6), but they were not well preserved. These buildings all opened to the west, where the yellow platform surface extended. The interiors of these buildings had smooth clay surfaces that appeared to be kept quite clean, but with occupational surfaces that contained both decorated and undecorated ceramic fragments. To the east and "outside" of these structures were relatively dense deposits of middens and burning activities. This architectural complex dates to around 24–337 CE. In the southern extent of the excavations, and possibly contemporaneous with the chambered buildings,

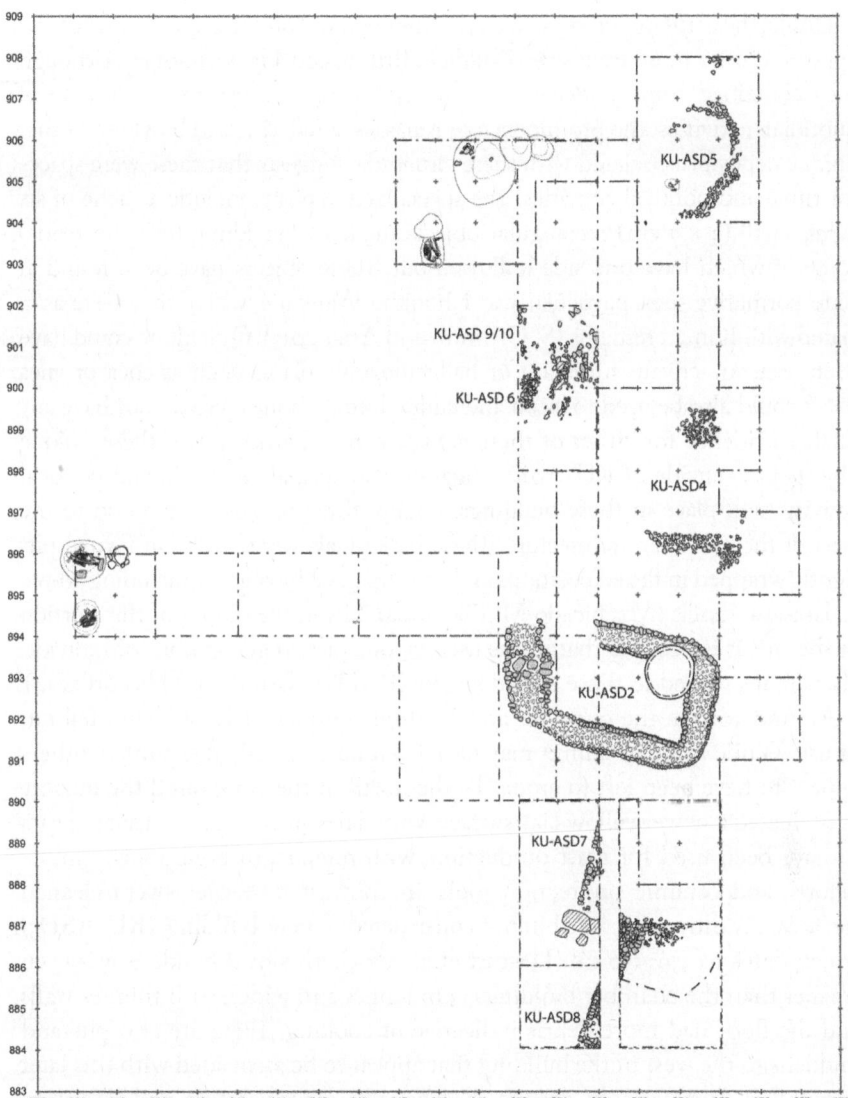

FIGURE 6.6. *Plan view of excavations at KUKU indicating the architectural subdivisions (ASD) encountered.*

we encountered portions of linear cobble walls and surfaces (KU-ASD7/8) that may have been "bounded compound space" or a patio for activities, similar to what would be a common architectural arrangement later at Tiwanaku (Capriles Flores and Machicado Murillo 2011).

Unlike the earlier, open sunken courts, the chamber buildings were smaller and appeared to be more exclusive (Roddick, Bruno, and Hastorf 2014). Although they contained some undecorated utilitarian ceramics, possibly indicative of quotidian activities, the prominence of Kalasasaya red-rimmed bowls and other unique deposits associated with these structures suggests that these were spaces for ritual and political activities. The specialized deposits include a cache of six *cubos*, small (3 × 7 cm) rectangular objects made of quicklime (calcium oxide), some of which have one side hollowed out. These objects have been found at Late Formative sites, particularly at Khonkho Wankané, where they were associated with human remains (S. C. Smith and Arias 2015). Quicklime could have been used to activate stimulant or hallucinogenic plants such as coca or vilca, but it could also be used to clean and curate human bones. We do not have any further evidence for either of these activities, but the deposit of these unique objects just outside of KU-ASD2 suggests that specialized ritual and political activity took place in these buildings. Finally, three burials were found to the west of the chamber architecture. These individuals were buried in formal pits, tightly wrapped in flexed positions and accompanied by objects, including whole Kalasasaya vessels (Machicado Murillo 2008). Given the dating of this portion of the site, it is possible that it was used by one or two generations of individuals, perhaps related to those buried nearby (Roddick, Bruno, and Hastorf 2014).

Around 300 CE the chamber architectural complex at Kala Uyuni fell out of use. While some buildings may have been purposefully dismantled, others appear to have been left to erode. To the north of the compound the inhabitants created a newer yellow clay surface, with dates of 256–422 CE, that appears to have been used for craft production, with remains of bone tools, spindle whorls, and ceramic production tools, in contrast to earlier swept/cleaned surfaces. Additionally, inhabitants constructed a new building (KU-ASD5), which dates to 356–550 CE (Hastorf et al. 2005). This oval building was even smaller than the chamber buildings (3 m long × 2 m wide), with thinner walls, and the floor had more debris indicative of cooking. There are also pits and middens to the west of the building that appear to be associated with this later occupation. Interestingly, despite the changes in architecture and the more quotidian nature of the activities, the ceramic assemblage is quite similar to the previous phase of use with the continued presence of Kalasasaya red-rimmed and zonally incised vessels (Roddick 2009). The persistence of Kalasasaya red-rimmed wares as well as other common undecorated forms and paste types into the Late Formative II period reveals that using the Qeya style of decorated vessels to demarcate the size and nature of the population here could be misleading. Bandy suggested a population decline based on surface ceramics, but that interpretation was based on the expectation that there was a distinctive change in pottery at this time. Our excavations, however, reveal a continued occupation of the area that may appear less focused on hosting ritual and political events and more focused on residential activities. This could reflect shifting political dynamics between the other Taraco Peninsula political centers, Sonaji and Kumi Kipa. Even if the political prominence of its residents may have declined through time, families continued to reside there, even when the center of political and cultural influence coalesced at Tiwanaku.

We identified two major Tiwanaku occupation zones overlying the Late Formative period phases at KUKU. Two rather substantial (10–40 cm deep) horizontal strata indicate long-term occupation reflecting a wide range of activities (Paz Soria and Fernandez 2007; Roddick, Bruno, and Hastorf 2014). Although we did not find any intact architecture, we did encounter several Tiwanaku period burials (Machicado Murillo 2008; M. J. Miller et al. 2022) and pits. The pit features ranged from 25 cm to 5 m in diameter and from 50 cm to 2 m deep (Roddick, Bruno, and Hastorf 2014), and their contents varied from rock fills to midden fills. Kala Uyuni may not have been a major administrative or ritual outpost for the Tiwanaku, as developed at Lukurmata and Chiripa, but there are indications that residents adopted a Tiwanaku "way of life" in terms of material culture and belief system. The area then appears to be largely abandoned into the Late Intermediate and Inka periods, or there was simply a shift to agricultural fields, which continue to be cultivated into the present by local Coa Collu landowners.

With this general overview of the Kala Uyuni archaeological record spanning the entirety of the Formative and Tiwanaku periods, we can now turn to patterns in the archaeobotanical record. I start with general trends in the density and diversity of botanical materials across the major types of contexts that we encountered at Kala Uyuni. This sheds light on a range of activities and their depositional characteristics. From these general patterns I begin to tease apart what specific assemblages might indicate about a range of agricultural and food practices at Kala Uyuni. I focus specifically on identifying some of the crop-processing activities described in the opening vignette.

PLANT REMAINS AND FOODWAYS AT KALA UYUNI
Contexts and Plant Remains

In order to make comparisons of general plant use across different areas of Kala Uyuni, I categorized all of the analyzed samples into eight different types of contexts: architecture, burial, fill, in situ burning, midden, occupation zone, pit, and surface (table 6.1). While there is variation within these groupings, comparison of the density (average count of items per liter of soil) and richness (number of identifiable taxa) of carbonized plant remains provides an overview of important patterns in plant preservation, use of fire, and specific activities (table 6.2; figure 6.7).

Contexts associated with architecture, prepared surfaces, and occupational zones tend to be relatively sparse in plant remains. Despite the low number of items encountered in these contexts, there is a relatively wide range of species, from as few as 12 in architectural deposits to as many as 26 in occupation zones. These low densities suggest that, much like today, past Taraco residents did a good deal of activity outdoors and aimed to keep formal surfaces inside buildings and even outdoor patio areas relatively clean. They probably tried not to spill, and if they did, it was swept up. Moreover, the things that may have been spilled or left on surfaces were usually not burned and thus would not have preserved. The relatively high diversity of species represented in these lower-density deposits, however, suggests that these plant remains could represent a range of different activities that were taking place in and around the buildings. There will be a more careful examination of species' distributions in the following chapter.

Contexts such as middens, fills, pits, and, unsurprisingly, purposefully (in situ) burned contexts have the highest density of carbonized plant remains. They also have a slightly higher number of taxa, ranging from 24 to 30 species, which is to be expected given the higher density of remains (Lepofsky and Lertzman 2005). This also reflects a wider range of activities associated with plants that were eventually deposited and preserved in these contexts. Middens also contain high quantities of pottery and animal bone that lend additional insights into the activities that produced these assemblages.

Finally, the specialized contexts of burials have very low densities and richness of plant remains. Much like surfaces, they were quite "clean" and did not have what might have been perceived as garbage inside of them. Plants were likely used in these contexts as material for wrapping the body and as food. Individuals were commonly interred with whole serving vessels such bowls and drinking cups and even cooking vessels, which stand the test of time (Machicado Murillo 2008). Unfortunately, organic items that accompanied buried community members were likely fresh and degraded.

Past Crop Processing

In addition to shedding light on waste disposal practices at Kala Uyuni, this overview gives us some insight into where work associated with food

TABLE 6.1. Description of context categories in alphabetical order and number of samples of each type

Context Type	Description	Number of Samples
Architecture	Formal walls made of adobe or stone, wall fall/slump, wall trench	4
Burial	Human internment, most commonly in a pit	10
Fill	A purposeful deposit associated with leveling off or filling in an area to make level or for a new construction	19
In situ burning	Clearly defined area of burning	6
Midden	Horizontal deposit with moderate to high density of organic remains (plant and bone) as well as pottery and lithics	33
Occupation zone	Area with accumulation of human activity but not formally a building or midden	31
Pit	Feature dug into a surface with a distinctive fill	26
Surface	Formal surface (interior or exterior) made of clay or modified substrate	51

TABLE 6.2. Patterns in density and richness of carbonized plant remains in different types of contexts at Kala Uyuni, in order of least to most dense

Context Type	Average Density (count/L)	Number of Taxa
Architecture	0.47	12
Surface	1.04	23
Burial	1.35	23
Occupation zone	1.83	26
Midden	3.10	27
In situ burning	3.60	24
Pit	3.94	30
Fill	4.31	25

production, such as crop processing and storage, would have taken place. As we see with these activities today, cleaning crops down to parts that can be stored, eaten, and planted as seeds the next year takes place outside. Of the crops we find in the archaeological record, quinoa takes the most processing from harvest to seed. It also requires the assistance of a breeze to winnow away the smallest pieces of the plant. Doing this outside, near a residence or a field where it was drying, would be more common than inside. The remnants of the winnowing process include both the cleaned seed as well as the leftover chaff.

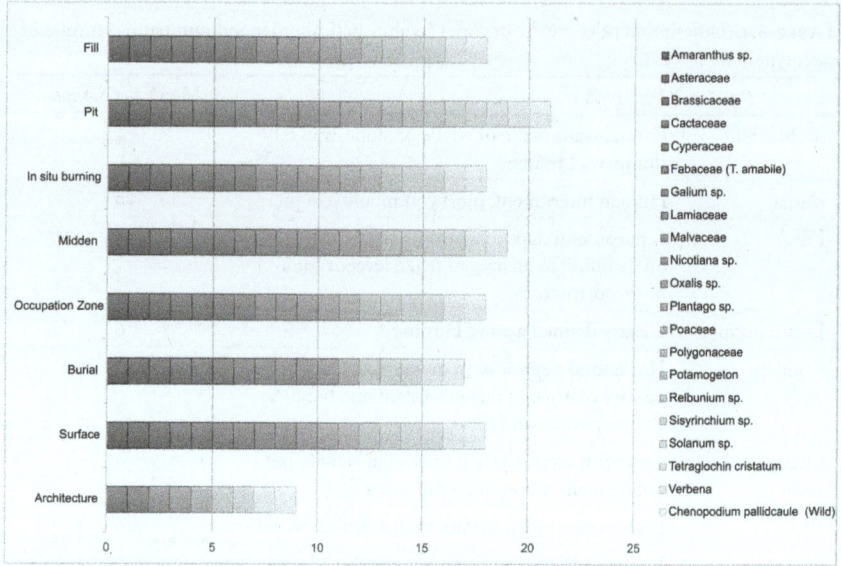

FIGURE 6.7. *Number of wild taxa present across each type of context at KUKU.*

I observed that the chaff was often collected and fed to animals, or I was told that it is sometimes burned to ash to be chewed with coca. Feeding it to animals and subsequent use of camelid dung for fuel would result in this material being incorporated into the waste remains that we find on the site.

The archaeobotanical record does offer some additional evidence for processing quinoa to be stored and eaten. Indications of purposeful cleaning can be seen in the proportions in which we find the seeds of cultivated quinoa relative to those of the weed *quinoa negra*. Higher percentages of crop quinoa versus *quinoa negra* most likely represent a food or storage context rather than processing or introduction through dung. The most impressive discovery of such a context is from the specialized buildings or "Houses" of the Chiripa Montículo. In a sample from a bin of Upper House 5, Whitehead (2007, 98–99) encountered over 2,000 *Chenopodium* seeds and less than 1 percent were the weedy *quinoa negra* seeds (Bruno and Whitehead 2003, 350). Bennett and Bird (1949, 142) also found a cache of *Chenopodium* seeds in Bennett's excavations, but we have not had the opportunity to examine these. It's quite likely that they were a similar composition to the TAP context.

Although we did not find specialized storage architecture at Kala Uyuni, we may have a precedent for what would eventually emerge at Chiripa of the association of cleaned quinoa seeds, and possibly storage, at KUAC. The highest densities of cleaned quinoa seeds across all of Kala Uyuni are from Early and Middle Formative contexts on the hilltop. A pit (Event KU-A121) found under the first floor of the Upper Court (KU-ASD3) contained 268 quinoa seeds, and only 6 *quinoa negra* seeds. Later an ashy lens above the floor in the same building (Event KU-A158) contained 488 quinoa seeds, and only 41 *quinoa negra* seeds. I will discuss the activities at these sunken courts in more detail in the following chapter, but these two contexts show that people in the earliest Formative periods were obtaining mostly clean quinoa grains, burning, and burying them in this important location.

We do not find such discrete deposits of quinoa in the Late Formative or Tiwanaku contexts, but as discussed in chapter 4, quinoa continues to appear in high ubiquities across these phases, suggesting that it remained an important crop that would have required processing. Interestingly, the Late Formative period has several contexts with relatively high quantities of *quinoa negra* seeds. At Kala Uyuni a pit (KU-B48) contained 165 *quinoa negra* seeds and only 91 quinoa seeds. At the site of Sonaji we also found two in situ burning contexts that contained very high amounts of *quinoa negra*: Event SN-A67 contained 177 *quinoa negra* seeds and 134 quinoa seeds, and Event SN-A68 contained 282 *quinoa negra* seeds and only 43 quinoa seeds. As discussed in chapter 5, weedy species increased across the landscape through time; however, the careful collection and deposition of *quinoa negra* suggest that it may have had another use, possibly as food in times of scarcity (see chapter 7).

Given the evidence of potatoes and *oca* in the archaeobotanical record, we might also envision that processing of these tubers into their freeze-dried versions, *chuño*, *tunta*, and *kalla*, would have taken place outside homes and near fields. As described earlier, the process requires exposure of the tubers to freezing temperatures at night during the dry, winter months and then squeezing out the water under the bright daylight sun by stepping on them. This task is difficult to detect archaeologically; however, recent work on the study of potato starch grains suggests that the processes of creating both *chuño* and *tunta* modified the grains in a diagnostic manner (Melton, Biwer, and Panjarjian 2020). We unfortunately do not have such evidence available yet for Kala Uyuni, but future analyses may provide such insights.

With these initial steps of transforming the harvested crops into storable and edible forms, we can now turn to the evidence in plant remains and other artifacts that sheds light on the foods that were prepared, consumed, and disposed of at Kala Uyuni through time. We can also begin to examine how particular meals, and the etiquette around them, may have connected this local community to larger peninsular and southern Titicaca Basin political landscapes.

7

Eating

Transforming Plants into Food (Part 2)

The products of yearlong agricultural work ultimately provide most ingredients in daily and special-occasion meals on the peninsula. While a portion of a yearly harvest will be given to family members living in the city or possibly to a local or city market, most of it gets stored and consumed in an array of meals throughout the year. These items are supplemented with purchased ingredients such as rice, bread, onions, sugar, salt, and chili peppers. In general, however, the farming families of the Taraco Peninsula still subsist on what they grow each year.

With the Quispes and other families with whom I ate, the daily meal schedule was very regular and only deviated on days with special occasions. The morning started with a piece of fresh bread (brought in from La Paz and purchased at the corner store), a piece of cheese (homemade or purchased from a neighbor), and a hot, sugary beverage, usually tea or coffee.[1] Each would then proceed with their morning tasks and return home around 11:00 a.m. to have the main meal of the day, a large lunch. The lunch usually consisted of at least two, if not three, starches—rice or noodles, potatoes, and possibly *chuño*, *tunta*, *oca*, or another tuber—a small piece of meat (chicken or beef) or fried cheese, and a sauce, usually a combination of onions, garlic, chili peppers, and tomatoes. After a short rest, everyone would return to work until *tecito* or "teatime," usually around 5:00 p.m., which included another piece of bread and a warm beverage. A few more tasks could usually be completed before nightfall, and then everyone would gather in the warmest room, usually the kitchen or parents' bedroom. Either a small pot of soup was prepared, or some leftover lunch would be consumed as a light supper. Many elements of this schedule are clearly introductions from European colonists: bread, tea, coffee, sugar, and several of the ingredients of the main meals, particularly rice and noodles. The timing of meals, particularly breakfast and tea, is also likely a European introduction. Julio *often* commented to me that this was not the way his parents ate.[2] He said that they would not have bread and tea in the morning but a big bowl of quinoa porridge to start the day. Quinoa had been replaced by rice and noodles in this Taraco household as well as in many others according to my interviews. Mary Weismantel (1998) documented how products like bread and rice were replacing traditional Andean grains in the Ecuadorian highlands. As products like bread and rice became more accessible, it was often children who pleaded with their parents to have those items instead of quinoa or barley. Despite these ongoing changes in local pantries and dishes, many meals still had very strong, local elements. One, in particular, that was always greeted with excitement in the Quispe household was *wallaque*, a fish stew.

As described in chapter 1, it was a common task for male members of the household to gather up the fish from nets in the morning. During my time on the peninsula, most of the fish were packed up into wooden boxes and sent into La Paz on a bus to be sold.[3] On days when Alejandra would prepare *wallaque*, about 20 of the biggest fish were kept at home. Although most cooking is now done on a gas stove with an aluminum pot, I often heard comments that the most flavorful food is prepared in clay pots over a dung- and wood-burning stove. In the Quispe household the kitchen was one of the smaller rooms of the house complex. Inside there was a gas stove and a table where ingredients were stored, but it was not used for chopping, as is common in North American or European households. Women squatted or sat on low stools to prepare foods by peeling and cutting over plastic or metal basins and pots, which caught the residues or were filled with ingredients. Just outside of the enclosed kitchen was a corner of the patio where they built a stove of clay and stone and where meals could be prepared in clay pots with fire (figure 7.1).

Today Alejandra decided to cook in the clay pot and started by boiling water with some chopped onions that she purchased at the market and an herb called *khoa* (*Clinopodium bolivianum*), which grows in the Taraco hills. The herb is in the mint family and has a pungent aroma that is an essential ingredient in *wallaque* (Hastorf and Bruno 2020). Miriam and Alejandra began to prepare the fish that would be added to the water once it boiled and could be

FIGURE 7.1. *An outdoor kitchen with clay oven and clay and metal pots. A drying stack of quinoa awaits processing in the background.*

reduced to a simmer. The most common native fish of Lake Titicaca is the *karachi* (*Orestias* spp.). There are several species that occupy different depths of the lake, and unfortunately the largest (*Orestias cuvieri*) has gone extinct by overfishing. The most common size brought home was about 8 cm in length. They are relatively fat but very scaly and bony. Thus, before the whole fish is placed into the pot, most of the outside scales are scraped off with a knife. Another native fish that is caught in shallower waters is the *suchi*, or catfish (*Trichomycterus rivulatus*), which has no scales and can be placed directly in the pot. Finally, a recently introduced species, *pejerry* (*Odontesthes bonariensis*), earns more money in the markets and so was usually sent off to be sold. This, however, was the preferred fish for frying in a pan to eat over rice and potatoes.

Next, fresh potatoes were peeled and placed in cold water. They would be added to the boiling broth with enough time to cook before serving. Alejandra then prepared a paste of garlic cloves and rehydrated yellow chili, called *aji amarillo*, by grinding them with the family's stone mortar and pestle. This

FIGURE 7.2. Bowls of wallaque *waiting to be eaten.*

paste was then added to the simmering broth, resulting an aromatic, spicy, fishy broth. In addition to the potatoes, Miriam prepared *chuños* that would be served alongside the soup. The dried potatoes had soaked in water overnight. Miriam drained the soaking water and steamed them with a small amount of water in a separate clay pot.

With the meal prepared, Alejandra called everyone to the interior patio to eat lunch outside. We set up benches and blankets in a circle, each awaiting to be served. Alejandra removed the pot of soup from the stovetop and served each person one by one. As the houseguest, I was always served first, then Julio, and then the kids. The cooks were always last. Alejandra ladled the steamy broth with chunks of cooked potatoes in the bowls. She then placed three or four tender fish on the top (figure 7.2). The steamed bowl of *chuño* was placed in the middle of the floor, and each person helped themselves. We sipped the hot, flavorful broth with a spoon or simply from the side of the bowl. I could easily gobble down the tubers, but the fish presented a real challenge to an inexperienced eater! The white flesh must be picked out from inside the skin and around the numerous tiny bones. The uneaten bones, innards, and skins were tossed onto a piece of plastic in the middle of the floor. I fumbled around each delicate part of the fish and slowly managed to eat most of the fish I was served. The parents and teenaged kids, however, quickly and deftly picked through the bones, handing the youngest children bone-free chunks of fish. The other family members had finished at least three fish by the time I'd eaten one! By the end of the meal a pile of fish bones accumulated in the middle of the floor. The cat received a few nibbles, but the remainder got cleaned up and tossed into the garbage pit out near one of the agricultural fields. Once everyone had digested, Julio sent Nicolas to the store to buy a bottle of soda pop. We sat around, and each person was served a plastic cup of soda until we emptied the bottle.

Although *wallaque* is a unique dish, the basic components of this meal were present in all of the meals I ate while living with the Quispes and as a guest in several other households. As several scholars have noted, an Andean meal really is not a proper meal without a potato in some form, either fresh or freeze-dried, ideally both. In fact, Sammells (2010) argues that Bolivian highland meals must include at least two starches. While fresh potato or *chuño/tunta* usually serves as a primary starch, other tubers (*oca, isañu, papa lisa*), maize, and fava beans may accompany the potato, but commonly today these are served over mounds of rice or noodles. Nearly all meals have a protein—fish, meat, or eggs—although it is usually a smaller portion than the starch. A nonfish soup will always be prepared with a bone or small chunks of meat with small pieces of meat doled out to each person. Some families have enough money to buy fresh meat and bone at the weekly market. Many families also have stores of dried animal meat called *charqui*.[4] When a family animal is slaughtered, most often a sheep but occasionally a cow or llama, thin strips of meat are hung out on a line to dry through the cold evenings and hot sunny days. In *wallaque*, the spicy paste is added to the broth, but it is more common for a spicy relish called *llajwa* to be served in a small bowl that eaters can add to their dish based on their individual preference. It is also made in the mortar and pestle, ground together with a tomato, the fresh chili pepper *locoto*, and an herb, usually the asterid *quillquiña* (*Porophyllum ruderale*). Home meals are always served on a single dish or bowl and normally eaten with a spoon, but it is also common to eat with the hands. It is rare to eat the skin of a potato. When served whole, potatoes are quickly peeled by hand before eating. Remnants of skin on a *chuño* are scraped off.

Special Meals

Daily meals are usually with members of the family, but sometimes individuals who have helped with a task are invited to join. Serving food is also an important element of any group or community gathering. Elements of these meals are also prepared in individual households, but the amount of food is increased by help from neighbors or each household contributing to the larger meal. Although there might be occasion for a special meal anytime of the year, the largest number of celebrations on the Taraco Peninsula occur in the winter months, particularly July and August, when there are several national holidays (Bolivia's independence and the founding of La Paz), local holidays celebrating the founding of the towns of Taraco and Santa Rosa, and celebrations marking the winter solstice.

In the year that I lived with the Quispes, the eldest son and his wife, who now resided in El Alto, had been named the sponsors (*padrinos*, literally "godparents") of the Santa Rosa town festival. This involved the preparation of a huge amount of food and required resources from the entire family and their friends. Not only did they have to prepare meals for the family staying in town for the party, but they were required to feed at least one big meal for three days to everyone participating in the dance troupe. Despite the larger scale of these meals, they still consisted of the same elements as the daily meals: at least two primary starches, a protein, and a spicy sauce or relish. A dish common for such special events is *fricase*. It is a pork stew in a chili- and garlic-based broth served with boiled maize and *chuño*. Just as they do at a home meal, people arrive to the location, often a rented room at the school or the large patio inside a building, take a seat on the ground or a bench, and wait to be served. The cooks, all women, set up their kitchen with several large gas stoves in a smaller room off to the side. Then bowls of steaming broth, maize, and a large portion of pork are served with heaping piles of *chuño* on the side. Any bones or pieces of food not consumed are piled up on the floor or are scooped into the empty bowl.

As archaeologists working in the winter months, we participated in many smaller community celebrations associated with a national or local holiday. Since the early 2000s, winter solstice celebrations have become increasingly popular, as they have successfully attracted large groups of tourists to the major archaeological site of Tiwanaku (Sammells 2012). In hopes of also attracting tourists to their local sites, the communities of Chiripa and Coa Collu have begun to host their own celebrations. In 2012, I participated in the inaugural *solsticio* event in the town of Coa Collu atop the Achachi Coa Collu peak and archaeological site. At dawn on top of the hill an offering (*waxta* or *misa*)

FIGURE 7.3. Local authorities in the community of Coa Collu lay out boiled potatoes, oca, and chuño on textiles with bowls of llawja as a relish.

was burned to Pachamama with singing and dancing. Later in the morning the participants gathered outside the museum that the Taraco Archaeological Project had just completed, which housed the artifacts from our excavations. The authorities, called *mallkus*, and their wives were responsible for providing the food. Around noon the wives arrived in their finest hats, *polleras*, and shawls with bulging *bultos* (a blanket filled with goods) flung around their necks. After a few speeches, libations, and some dancing, colorful blankets were laid out in a long row on a flat area of the grassy hillside (figure 7.3). The women carefully unpacked their *bultos* and poured out mountains of tubers, fava beans, and maize onto the blankets. They then unwrapped small ceramic bowls of *llajwa* and placed them between the food mounds. Finally, some women brought blocks of homemade cheese and broke pieces into the *llawja* or left chunks out among the potatoes. Other than the cheese, no other proteins were served. With a nod from the hosts to the visitors and low murmuring of *licenciamapi* (Aymara) and *permiso* (Spanish), translated as "excuse me" or "permit me," the guests reached into the mounds of food, taking a handful tubers, dipping one or two into the hot sauce, grabbing a chunk of cheese, and then sitting back around the blanket to enjoy the special presentation of foods that are eaten almost every day at home. Nearly every morsel of food was consumed. What remained was wrapped back up in the blankets in which they had arrived, and the remnants, such as potato peels and fava bean casings, were disposed of at people's homes, either in a garbage pit or, more likely, fed to the pigs.

If not used as seed, the final destination of a cultivated crop is in a meal, transformed through cooking, combined with other elements to be served, and ingested in a home or at a village gathering. While eating fulfills energy needs for humans to survive, it is an activity that occurs multiple times a day and is structured not just by particular ingredients, which are grown, but by ideas about how to prepare, combine, serve, and consume them. As Hastorf (2017, 2) emphasizes, "Food is a social fact," and it plays an "active role . . . in creating, enacting, and sustaining cultural and social processes." The social and political arrangements of food intersect with the broader agricultural landscape and can shed light on community dynamics at different periods of time.

I now turn to patterns in the plant remains and other associated evidence that illuminate how the processed crops were transformed into meals for household and community consumption. The Taraco Archaeological Project has employed a wide range of analyses aimed at discerning foodways. Through the input of our many specialists, multiple lines of evidence are providing an increasingly clear picture of meals consumed both daily and on special occasions. Below I examine how chenopods, tubers, camelids, fish, and other wild plant and animal species became ingredients, taking on different roles in each meal. I then consider evidence for how they were prepared through boiling, roasting, and fermentation. Ceramic vessels are particularly important for revealing the key role of soups and porridges. They also reveal changes in how such meals were served during ritual and political occasions. Plant remains and human isotope signatures shed light on the introduction of maize to the peninsula as a fermented beverage served on special occasions to important people. Understanding how these meals were prepared and shared connects the products of the Formative and Tiwanaku period agricultural landscapes to local and regional social and political dynamics.

ANCIENT TARACO MEALS

Ingredients

Meals are created from ingredients prepared in particular combinations and presentations (Douglas 2018; Hastorf 2016). Cross-cultural studies of foodways reveal that meals are often composed of common categories of ingredients: (1) a starchy base provided by plant foods, (2) a protein that is often derived from animal meat or milk but can also be from protein-rich plants, and (3) a "relish" or something that adds flavor, texture, and nutrients. The relish can be plant or animal derived. Using these categories along with the combinations employed on the peninsula today, TAP archaeologists have been able to think about our lists of plant and animal species as particular ingredients that contributed to meals (Hastorf 2012; 2016; Roddick and Hastorf 2010) (table 7.1).

From chapter 4 we are already familiar with the crops that contributed the plant, starchy basis of ancient Taraco meals: tubers, such as potatoes and *oca* (and likely others we have not yet identified), and quinoa as well as possibly *kañawa*. Although maize begins to make an appearance in the Late Formative period, its rarity suggests that it may not have been consumed as a starch but rather a beverage, a point that I will elaborate below. Tubers still feature prominently as primary starches in Taraco meals today. Although quinoa is less common, grains such as rice and even noodles are always the basis of any meal. Given the prominence of both tubers and quinoa through time on the peninsula, it is likely that combinations of these formed the basis of all past Taraco meals. As tubers became more common into the Late Formative period, their contribution to meals likely increased relative to quinoa.

The Taraco Peninsula would have been particularly rich in protein sources derived from wild and domesticated animals that thrive in this abundant environment. The zooarchaeological record, analyzed primarily by Katherine Moore and José Capriles, is dominated by camelid bones (K. M. Moore, Steadman, and deFrance 1999; K. M. Moore et al. 2010; K. M. Moore 2011b). Analysis of size distributions of the bones suggests there were domesticated llamas (*Lama glama*), alpaca (*Lama pacos*), and also possibly wild guanaco (*Lama guanicoe*) and vicuña (*Vicugna vicugna*). Although there are some fluctuations through time, much like tubers and quinoa, camelids are highly ubiquitous, suggesting that they were the primary source of protein in Taraco meals across the Formative and Tiwanaku periods (Bruno et al. 2021; K. M. Moore 2011a; K. M. Moore et al. 2010) (figure 7.4).

Fish bones are also quite common in the Taraco faunal assemblage, and we systematically recover them through flotation (Capriles 2006; Capriles et al. 2014; K. M. Moore, Steadman, and deFrance 1999). Both density and ubiquity of fish remains fluctuate through time, but they are ever present. Furthermore, they do not appear to correlate with high or low lake levels (Bruno et al. 2021; Capriles et al. 2014), suggesting that even when the lake was low, people went

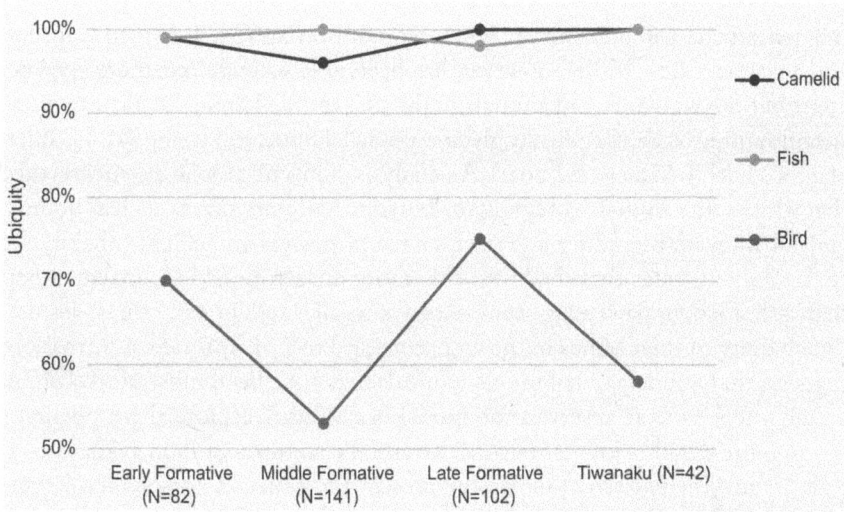

FIGURE 7.4. *Ubiquity of animal food sources through time at all Taraco sites (based on Bruno et al. 2021).*

out of their way to acquire them. The abundance of fish bones suggests that the lake provided a critical source of protein for Taraco residents.

There also are bones from other wild animals such as birds (both lake and terrestrial) and deer, indicating that hunting was part of the food procurement repertoire (K. M. Moore 2011a; K. M. Moore et al. 2010; K. M. Moore, Steadman, and deFrance 1999). Rodent bones are also present, such as guinea pig (*Cavia* sp.), but present in rather low quantities and ubiquities, suggesting that this Andean domesticate was not particularly important to the residents of the Taraco Peninsula. Taken together, these other protein sources make up a much smaller portion of the record compared with both camelid and fish.

While we have primarily depended on patterns in plant and animal remains to understand the various ingredients in Taraco meals through time, innovative analysis of isotope ratios from human remains and pottery residues by Melanie Miller has unveiled patterns in consumption that have been surprising. As discussed in chapter 4, traditional analyses of bulk carbon and nitrogen ratios have demonstrated the significant contribution of C_3 plants such as quinoa and tubers to Taraco diets across time (M. J. Miller 2005; M. J. Miller et al. 2022; M. J. Miller et al. 2021). In the Late Formative and Tiwanaku periods, however, there were several individuals with $\delta^{13}C$ ratios (-16 to -15‰) from dental collagen that could suggest an increase in the consumption of C_4 plants, in this case maize, but it was unclear if fish were potentially contributing to this pattern, as fish and maize signatures can overlap (M. J. Miller, Capriles, and Hastorf 2010). Miller, however, has been able to tease out more specific contributions of plants and animals to the diet through analysis of compound-specific amino acids, specifically glycine, phenylalanine, and lysine (M. J. Miller et al. 2022; M. J. Miller et al. 2021). An analysis of juvenile molar enamel reveals that while some animal proteins contributed to the diets, plants such as quinoa and tubers were providing a greater source of protein to ancient inhabitants. It also demonstrates that the lower $\delta^{13}C$ ratios are attributable to maize rather than fish. Fish, in particular, seem to play a smaller role in daily diets, despite the ubiquity of their bones in the archaeological record. This new information suggests that animal contributions to meals may have been more of a relish in a daily meal or were reserved for special occasions. I explore these possibilities in more detail below as we consider specific contexts of food at the site of Kala Uyuni. The pattern of increasing presence of maize in Taraco diets beginning in the Late Formative period corresponds well with the botanical record, where remains are quite sparse in the early periods but increase through time (chapter 4). The contexts and ways in which maize would have contributed to these meals will also be explored in more detail below.

Although a bit more elusive, we do have some evidence for plant species that could have contributed to meals as spices (Hastorf and Bruno 2020). There are several local, wild species that are collected to add flavoring to a range of dishes, particularly special-occasion meals. One already mentioned is the aromatic shrub *khoa*, which is a critical ingredient in the fish stew *wallaque*. According to the ethnobotanical interviews, another mint species, locally called *salvia* (*Lepechinia meyenii*), is also used as flavoring or spice in cooking (Bruno 2008). While we have not identified these specific species in the archaeobotanical record, seeds of the same mint family (Lamiaceae) increase in ubiquity through time, first in 1–3 percent in the Early and Middle Formative periods, then up to 10–12 percent in the Late Formative and Tiwanaku periods. Another family that contains important flavors for dishes is the sunflower family (Asteraceae). In the ethnobotanical interviews the herb known as *chhijchhipa* (*Tagetes multiflora*) is used in a dish often prepared for Easter called *queso humacha*. This is also the family of the herb *quillquiña* (*Podophyllum ruderal*), which does not grow locally but is purchased or grown in small home gardens and incorporated into the most common relish, *llajwa*. This sauce was occasionally prepared in the Quispe household for dishes that had boiled potatoes and cheese; it is always prepared for the communal, outdoor meals, or *fiambres*, such as the one I described for the solstice celebration. As with the mints, while we have not been able to identify particular species of the asterids, they are quite common in the archaeological record and through time (table 5.2). While we cannot say for certain that these seeds represent the use of these plants as flavoring, particularly in the earliest periods where they are quite sparse, we should not ignore their potential contributions to past recipes (Hastorf and Bruno 2020).

An important spice used frequently in cooking today, which is absent from our samples, is the chili pepper (*Capsicum* spp.). The archaeological record of chili peppers goes back nearly 8,000 years on the coast of Peru and around 3,000 years in the highlands of Peru (Chiou et al. 2017; Perry et al. 2007). Unfortunately, we have yet to find any evidence for them on the Taraco Peninsula. While it is possible they were used in such small quantities that they have not preserved, it is also possible that this condiment was introduced to the region later in time.

Finally, the contributions of other wild plant foods as relishes such as seeds, greens, and fruits should also be considered. While most of the wild species discussed in chapter 5 are known fodder for camelids and may have arrived indirectly through burning of camelid dung (Browman 1989; Bruno and Hastorf 2016; Hastorf and Wright 1998), it is worth considering how they may have occasionally been human foods. Browman (1989) argues strongly for the use of lake plants as food, for they contain high quantities of protein and vitamins. The corm (root) of the *totora* (Cyperaceae) reed can be eaten fresh, and for the Quispe family it was a common snack enjoyed while carrying out tasks on the lake such as fishing or collecting reeds to feed to animals (table 5.3). Two other categories of wild plants that are likely candidates for common foods are amaranth, chenopods, and cactus. The wild amaranths and chenopods found archaeologically have edible leafy greens (Brack Egg 1999, 27) (table 5.2). I was not witness to any used in this way, but it could have been more common in the past. Their seeds could also be used as a primary starch or sprinkled in to add texture to a dish.

The role of wild *kañawa* or *illama* as an early wild plant food or garnish is particularly compelling at the courts of KUAC (Bruno 2008). While densities were relatively high in the midden area, they were also present in the small pits near the courts. The Early Formative pit (Event KU-A121) with abundant quinoa seeds also had 259 *illama* seeds (see chapter 6). An ash- and fish-bone-rich deposit (Event KU-A33) that covered the final clay floor of the Lower Sunken Court had 620 *illama* seeds (over 80 seed/L of soil). There were very few other plant species in these contexts, suggesting that *illama* was specifically selected and burned in this place. Its association with domesticated quinoa seeds and other foods such as fish suggests that it could have been collected for the special meals consumed here. Interestingly, it does not seem to be important enough to cultivate until much later in time. The first domesticated *kañawa* seeds appear in the Late Formative period and become more common in the Tiwanaku period (Bruno 2023).

The other wild chenopod, *quinoa negra*, seems to have a distinctive trajectory compared with *illama*. It is not until the Late Formative period that we find high concentrations of *quinoa negra*, suggesting that it might have been purposely collected and possibly stored (chapter 6). The purposeful separation of quinoa and *quinoaambered negra* reflects processing, but many Taraco residents have commented to us that it is used as a food during periods of low productivity, particularly during droughts (Bruno 2008; Hastorf and Bruno 2020). The strategy of saving this seed for dry periods appears to have become more prevalent later in time.

Finally, cactus fruits are today a special treat that people eat as they pasture animals on the hillsides and children walk around and play (chapter 5). They tend to grow in undisturbed, rocky outcrops, and the seeds that are not digested are left where the fruit was consumed. Thus, cactus as field snack is very unlikely to show up in the archaeological record. Cactus seeds are present in the samples but in relatively low densities, usually just a few seeds per samples. Their occurrence in middens, then, could indicate their purposeful collection and use for meals in the past, likely as a relish. It should be noted that camelids do eat them, so they could also arrive through dung burning, but perhaps not in the quantities we encounter. Across the samples, cactus seeds are more ubiquitous in the Early Formative period (32%), decline slightly in the Middle and Late Formative periods (20%–26%), and increase significantly in the Tiwanaku period (54%) (table 5.3). The decline in the Late Formative period, when other wild species that enter the record through dung increase, suggests that their patterns in the archaeological record could be more indicative of availability on the landscape and/or food preferences. I have argued that increased disturbance due to agricultural clearing may have caused a decline in cactus on the peninsula during the Late Formative period (Bruno 2014a). The marked increase in the Tiwanaku period could perhaps indicate that cactus became a preferred food at that time. Interesting patterns in cactus diversity and distribution at Kala Uyuni will be explored in more detail in chapter 7.

Preparations

With a list of ingredients, we can now consider how these elements were transformed into edible forms through the application of heat as well as fermentation. We can look to some archaeological features such as pits and

TABLE 7.1. Ingredients of past Taraco meals and their potential categories of use

	Primary Starch	Primary Protein	Relish	Spices
Early Formative	quinoa tubers	quinoa camelid fish	bird *cuy* (guinea pig) cactus *illama*	mint asterids
Middle Formative	quinoa tubers	quinoa camelid fish	bird *cuy* (guinea pig) cactus *illama* maize	mint asterids
Late Formative	quinoa tubers	quinoa camelid fish	bird *cuy* (guinea pig) *quinoa negra* *kañawa* maize	mint asterids
Tiwanaku	quinoa tubers *kañawa* maize	quinoa camelid fish	bird *cuy* (guinea pig) cactus *quinoa negra*	mint asterids

burned areas, possibly hearths, to consider the cooking technologies employed. Some patterns in the plant remains themselves shed light on how they were cooked, although this is somewhat limited given that the macrobotanical remains are all carbonized. For example, there are some indications of the processes by which cooks removed the bitter saponins from quinoa. María Laura López and colleagues (López, Capparelli, and Nielsen 2011) documented the patterns present in quinoa seeds after various stages of toasting, soaking, and finally cooking in the Lípez region of southern Bolivia. They found that a combination of soaking and grinding removed not only the outermost layer known as the pericarp, which contains most of the saponins, but often also the seed coat (testa). They also found that this could result in separation of the embryo from around the central perisperm. In my analyses of the different types of chenopods in the Taraco samples (Bruno 2006), I identified a very common form with a large, truncate perisperm (typical of domesticated chenopods) but lacking the embryo and entire seed coat. Based on the findings of López and colleagues, this could be indicative of the soaking and toasting process prior to boiling. Patterns of burning on animal bones can also indicate the type of cooking employed to convert animal products into food (K. M. Moore et al. 2010), particularly differences between boiling and roasting. Perhaps the most direct indication of cooking technologies, however, is in the ceramic remains. Below I review various lines of evidence for different food preparations found across the Taraco sites, particularly at Kala Uyuni.

Boiling

The vignette of cooking the fish stew *wallaque* highlights one of the most common techniques that we have evidence for in the past: boiling. Fragments of cooking pots, *ollas*, are among the most common vessel forms encountered in Taraco archaeological sites with their shapes and sizes varying through time (L. Steadman 1999; 2007; Roddick 2009; Roddick, Fontenla Alvarez, and Reilly 2017). Often, we find these fragments with encrusted burned remains inside and burned on the outside from the fire. The burned exteriors showing the hottest areas of the vessels were at the base, with less intense sooting in the upper portions of the vessels. This indicates that pots were placed directly on the fire. While most kitchens today use metal pots and gas stoves, some people still use adobe stoves with a combination of wood, grass, and dung as fuel (figure 7.1). Clay pots are propped up above the fire below. We do not have any archaeological evidence of such ovens, but we might imagine some similar technology used to keep the boiling pots in a safe location while the food simmered. The materials from which these pots were made changed through time, starting with fiber tempers and stuccoed bases in the Early Formative phase, with pastes and walls eventually becoming a bit finer and tempered with mica. Both technologies would help to maintain temperatures long enough to cook the contents without burning them.

Boiling with a relatively large amount of water could cook fresh tubers or quinoa. Today boiling is the most common way to prepare maize kernels. Often the kernels are removed from the cob, then placed to boil over several hours, and then eaten with tubers and cheese. A lower ratio of water to quinoa or tuber could make more of a soup or a thicker porridge. Quinoa or even *chuño* flours could also be added to thicken a watery dish. A small amount of water could be used to steam and rehydrate freeze-dried potatoes or meats. As is common today, animal proteins could be added to these liquids as part of the main dish or simply to flavor and add fat to the dish. Fragrant plants could then be added to increase the dish's flavor.

Roasting

Across the Andes and on the Taraco Peninsula, specifically, the most common traditional form of roasting is in an earth oven, called a *w'atia* in Aymara.

FIGURE 7.5. *A small* w'atia *to roast potatoes prepared in a harvested field.*

This involves digging a pit in the ground, adding fuel such as wood and dung, and heating the pit until hot (figure 7.5). Ingredients such as tubers and meats are placed directly into the hot embers, covering it all with more earth until the ingredients are cooked. Today this preparation is used only occasionally. Tubers are commonly prepared in a small *w'atia* after a day of work harvesting them. Larger roasts that include a wider range and number of tubers and meats (often pork) are prepared for special occasions, such as the closing celebrations of our archaeological projects.

Unfortunately, there are not many clear archaeological indicators of this type of cooking. They do not require ceramic vessels, and according to the zooarchaeologists, the moist heat that would cook animal bones leave a similar signature on bone as boiling (K. M. Moore et al. 2010). We have often speculated as to whether some of the many pits we encounter at the Taraco sites served as roasting pits, and I will examine a few such contexts below. Most, however, appear to be accumulations of garbage, which could, of course, have first been used as a roasting pit and/or include the remnants of such meals.

Finally, roasting in open air, or grilling, is another cooking technology that is not used frequently on the peninsula today. Moore, however, sees some indications on bird and guinea pig remains that this preparation may have been used in the past.

Fermenting

In the Andes fermentation is employed to produce beer, known widely across the Americas as *chicha*. *Chicha* is no longer a common drink in the Lake Titicaca Basin but is still very common in lowland valleys such as Cochabamba (Cutler and Cárdenas 1947; La Barre 1938). Maize beer is the most common form found throughout the Andes today, but residents of the peninsula indicate that *chicha de quinua* used to be brewed. On the peninsula today people purchase bottled wheat/barley beer or grain alcohol for special events. Maize *chicha* is never consumed, and maize is consumed only as a boiled food.

As discussed in chapter 4 and earlier in this chapter, archaeological evidence for maize is relatively sparse, suggesting that it was a rare, specialized ingredient (M. J. Miller et al. 2021). We do not find maize cupules, fragments of the cob, until the Tiwanaku period, suggesting that whole cobs were rare if not absent in the Formative periods. The few kernels found as well as maize phytoliths and starch grains on ground stone from Kala Uyuni suggest that it may have been brought in small amounts and ground locally, likely in preparation for *chicha* (Logan, Hastorf, and Pearsall 2012). We do not find large fermentation jars, such as those that became quite common at Tiwanaku, but this may not have been necessary for the scale at which it is was consumed here. It is also possible that the people consuming higher quantities of maize beer were not doing so on the peninsula but while visiting places where it was served. This may have been particularly prevalent during the Tiwanaku period, when maize beer consumption became a central part of its statecraft (Goldstein 2003; Janusek 2002, 2004b). The abundance and quality of *kerus* (specialized drinking mugs) and large fermentations jars at the site of Tiwanaku itself suggest that those leaders hosted large ceremonies and feasts featuring *chicha* for visitors to the city. Such practices were even replicated in distant regions where the Tiwanaku state also had influence, particularly in the lower valleys of Moquequga, Peru, and Cochabamba, Bolivia. In fact, Tiwanaku likely colonized and influenced local populations in these areas because they were places where maize grew well (Goldstein 2003). Evidence for maize fermentation and consumption at Kala Uyuni will be examined in more detail below.

Finally, it is worth mentioning that the freeze-drying processes for both tubers (*chuño* and *tunta*) and meat (*charqui*) does include fermentation. The microbes involved in transforming these products into dry, storable goods also produce distinctive, stronger flavors than those of their fresh versions. Thus, the freeze-drying process should be thought of as not just a storage mechanism but one that also added different layers of flavor to the Taraco cuisines. We currently do not have direct evidence for *chuño, tunta,* or *charqui,* but we should include these elements of flavor and texture when envisioning Taraco meals.

Serving

The combinations of boiling and roasting present several possibilities for how these dishes were served and consumed. In addition to the presence of *ollas,* the likelihood that soups, stews, and porridges were common preparations is also supported by the abundance of bowls found in the Taraco archaeological record, particularly at Kala Uyuni (Roddick 2009; Roddick, Fontenla Alvarez, and Reilly 2017; L. Steadman 1999, 2007). In domestic middens we find undecorated bowls made of coarser pastes. The most common bowls, however, are found in ceremonial or special-occasion contexts and are made of finer pastes and forms. There are some very interesting changes in size and shape of bowls through time, which will be discussed in more detail below.

Many of the foods that people eat today can also simply be placed on a textile or pulled from a pot and eaten by hand. While people use spoons today, many of the meals we shared on the peninsula were consumed without utensils, plates, or bowls, both in a family kitchen and in larger communal meals. Today a meal consisting primarily of boiled or steamed tubers, fava beans, and/or maize laid out on a textile is called a *fiambre* (or *merienda*). It is often accompanied by a relish such as cheese, chili sauce (*llajwa*), or meat such as fish or *charqui*. People serve themselves the starches by hand, and another person, usually a woman, hands out the relish (Sammells 2010). Sammells (2010) notes how the dense *chuño* can be split apart and used to scoop up sauces, acting as both utensil and food. Although textiles and mats do not preserve in the *altiplano* archaeological record, their use and importance are recorded in dry, coastal regions to the west. The remains of bone weaving tools (K. M. Moore 2011b; K. M. Moore, Steadman, and deFrance 1999) and ceramic spindle whorls (Roddick 2009; L. Steadman 2007) are evidence that woven fabrics were an important element of Taraco living and likely provided eating surfaces in the home and in larger public gatherings.

The bowls encountered could have also been drinking vessels. Bowls or wood gourds, for which we have no archaeobotanical evidence, could have been used when *chicha* first appeared on the peninsula. The first versions of the specialized drinking cup, *keru*, began to appear at the terminal end of the Late Formative period on the peninsula and elsewhere. Such "proto-*kerus*" have been found in the earliest occupation levels at Lukurmata, and we recovered one at Kala Uyuni (Marsh et al. 2019). During the Tiwanaku period the *keru* became formalized and elaborated and was incredibly widespread across all sectors of society and to the various regions it influenced. It became emblematic of *chicha* drinking and the Tiwanaku state (Goldstein 2003; Janusek 2002). At Kala Uyuni, *keru* fragments were found in middens, and complete vessels were encountered in burials as well as pits. Although the evidence for large-scale *chicha* production and consumption is limited at Kala Uyuni, the beverage clearly was present.

FEEDING FAMILIES AND COMMUNITIES AT KALA UYUNI

With the range of ingredients, preparations, and serving elements reviewed, we can take a closer look at their distribution and combinations to gain insights into specific meals across a range of contexts and time periods. As discussed in chapter 6, most food remains at Kala Uyuni come from middens, pits, and burned contexts that are likely accumulations of past activities and types of meals. By examining specific deposits and the composition of plant remains and other artifact categories, we can tease out some interesting patterns indicating more specific recipes and meals as well as the settings in which they were prepared, consumed, and discarded. Below I examine the patterns in these food contexts through time, noting continuities and changes and how these practices in the community of Kala Uyuni articulated with broader social and political dynamics unfolding across the peninsula.

Early Formative Period

While there are only a small number of Early Formative deposits at Kala Uyuni, they provide important insights into the beginnings of social and political life of this long-lived community. The oldest dates for the site, approximately 1200 BCE, come from discrete deposits on the KUAC hilltop. As mentioned in chapter 6, we find early evidence of quinoa cultivation and processing here. For example, a pit (Event KU-A121) contained high densities of cleaned quinoa seeds (29.78 seeds/L) and parenchyma/tuber fragments (13 fragments/L). There were also cactus and *illama* seeds. The high density of plant food remains and the scant evidence of post-depositional disturbance indicate there was a fire in this pit and it was buried very quickly (K. M. Moore et al. 2010). It appears that the earliest settlers on the peninsula visited this prominent location to carry out special ceremonies, possibly offerings of food on top of the hill. While *illama* could have been a wild food used as a relish in this meal, it is also possible the plant was burned for its aroma or other significance. Today there are reports in Bolivia that *illama* is burned as an offering for a good harvest (Serrano Quezada 2012).

Later in the Early Formative period a hamlet was established below the hill at KUAQ, where a midden began to accumulate. Events KU-C18 and KU-C17 represent the earliest deposits at the site (see figure 6.4), and they contain small quantities of quinoa and parenchyma but not cactus. This suggests that the offerings at the hilltop were rooted in the foods consumed in the home, quinoa and tubers, but that cactus might have been a special-occasion food. The KUAQ deposits are distinct from those of KUAC, as the food species occur in slightly lower densities (1–3 seeds or fragments/L), and there are more of the wild/weedy species present, particularly grasses and *quinoa negra*. This indicates that the KUAQ deposits accumulated gradually and contain the residues of a wider range of activities from daily cooking, agricultural work, and craft production.

The Early Formative ceramic assemblages in both areas are undecorated and are primarily *ollas* for cooking and storage. Lee Steadman (2007) describes the ceramics in both areas as overwhelmingly "domestic," especially in comparison to the assemblages at Chiripa, which have relatively more Early Formative decorated vessels, larger *ollas*, and bowls. Steadman (2007, 69) did identify one decorated bowl fragment from KUAC, suggesting that perhaps some special food serving took place there, but overall, the ceramic assemblages are quite similar at this time.

Despite the paucity of bowls from these contexts, the prominence of cooking pots and quinoa (which must be contained in a vessel to cook) suggest that soups or stews were being prepared by these early inhabitants. It is also possible that quinoa was prepared as a thicker porridge that could have been eaten by hand or with the help of tubers. Boiled and steamed tubers as well as camelid and fish were components of the earliest meals here as well and could be eaten from a pot or served on a mat or textile. These ingredients and preparations set the stage for meals for generations to come.

Middle Formative Period

As the population grew at Kala Uyuni, the two areas—KUAQ, a more residential area, and KUAC, the special-use, ceremonial area of the sunken courts—became even more distinct, providing us greater insights into differences between the "domestic" and "ritual" spheres of the community (Bruno 2007; A. B. Cohen and Roddick 2007). This distinction is relevant because at Chiripa, the best-studied site for the Middle Formative period, these two spheres overlapped a good deal, suggesting that those two arenas of life were greatly intertwined there (Dean and Kojan 2001). The distinctions at Kala Uyuni came in the form of specialized, ritual architecture at the two sunken courts at KUAC, while general midden accumulation occurred down the hill at KUAQ. Additionally, the residents created and used very distinctive pottery assemblages in the two areas (L. Steadman 2007). The KUAQ ceramic assemblage continued to consist of primarily undecorated pots, jars, and just a few bowls. The KUAC assemblage, however, contained some undecorated cooking and serving vessels, but also a high number of decorated bowls and serving jars made of fine pastes (as described in chapter 2). The decorated wares were found in association with the two courts and the nearby midden. Among the assemblage of fine-ware bowls, Steadman recorded an extra-large bowl (> 30 cm in diameter) with a red slip and cream-colored paint. This bowl is like those found in the Chiripa Montículo and are interpreted as being part of ritualized, public eating and drinking during this period. While there were a few decorated fragments reminiscent of the northern-lake-basin Qaluyu style at KUAC, most of the pottery appears to have been produced locally. The "special-use" ceramic assemblage also includes fragments of instruments, or *trompos*, and bowls with evidence of burning inside, believed to be incense burners (L. Steadman 2007). While there are some cooking vessels, they are made of finer pastes than those from KUAQ and represent a relatively lower percentage of the assemblage.

Patterns in plant remains and pottery between KUAQ and KUAC suggest that much of the food was prepared at home and then brought up to the hilltop. The overall density of plant remains in the KUAC midden area (average 0.89 items/L soil) is lower than the KUAQ middens (average 1.66 items/L soil), suggesting that less burning activity, including cooking, took place on the hilltop. As mentioned in the previous chapter, the floors of the buildings tended to be kept clean of debris. Additionally, the "utilitarian" KUAC ceramic assemblage consists primarily of storage and serving vessels, with few cooking pots. This contrasts with ritual areas of Chiripa where archaeologists frequently encountered large cooking pots (L. Steadman 2007, 75–76), indicating the preparation of large meals at these specialized locations. Interestingly, the remains of large cooking pots were found in the KUAQ midden. These patterns suggest that participants brought already

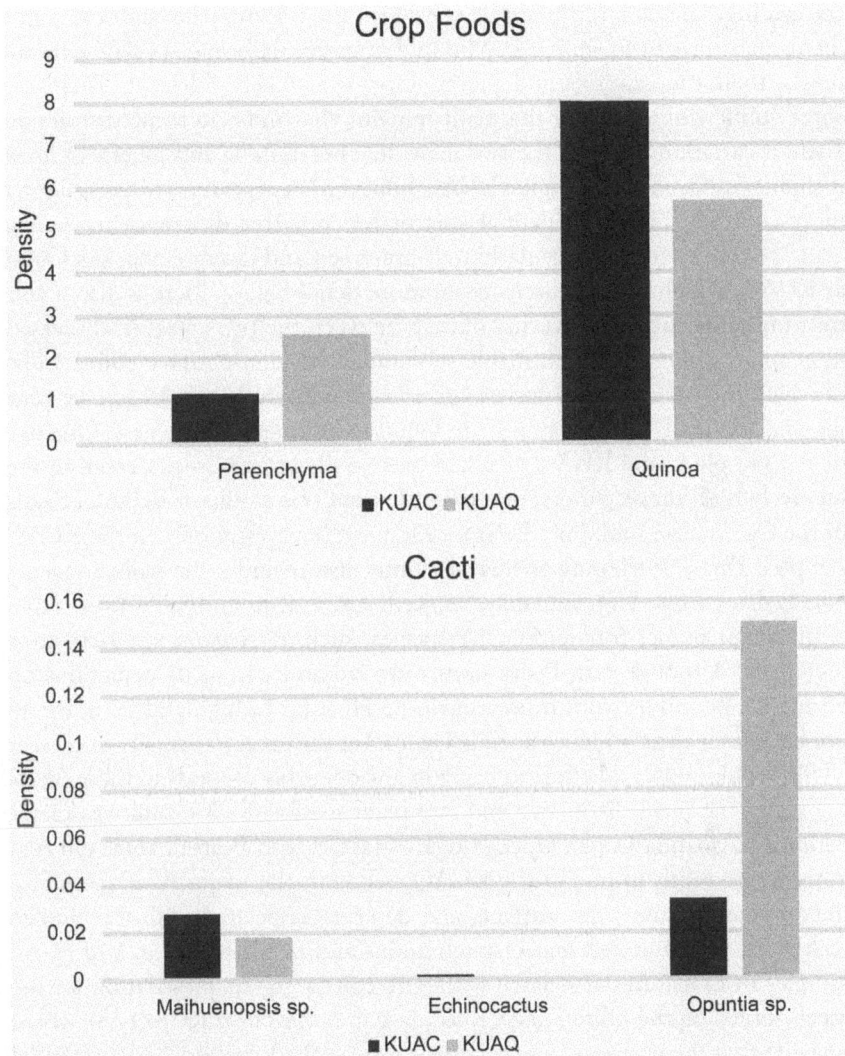

FIGURE 7.6. *Comparison of crop foods and cacti at KUAC and KUAQ based on average density of plant remains per liter of soil.*

cooked items up the hill in ceramic vessels, or as is common today, wrapped in textiles.

While pottery assemblages are distinctive, the plant remains at KUAQ and KUAC are quite similar (figure 7.6). Quinoa, tubers, and cacti are now common in both areas, again indicating the connection between homegrown and cooked ingredients and the meals served on the hilltop. Although the ingredients may have been similar in Middle Formative daily and special-occasion meals, their preparations and presentation were likely different. There are some subtle differences in the plant remains that indicate some distinction. There is variation between the two main starches, quinoa and tubers. Quinoa is slightly more common on the KUAC hilltop whereas parenchyma is slightly more common in the residential area of KUAQ. This difference in quinoa could be due to some particularly well-preserved and discrete deposits found at KUAC, which will be discussed in more detail below. There is also a contrast in the density and diversity of cacti between the two areas. As discussed in chapter 4, the three identifiable subfamilies of cacti produce edible fruits, of which the Opuntoidea species, *Opuntia* sp. and *Maihueniopsis* sp., are common on the landscape today and are found in both areas of the site. One particular sample in the KUAQ area had over 50 *Opuntia* sp. seeds, creating the relatively high density there; otherwise, it would be similar to KUAC. Seeds of the Cactoideae subfamily *Echinocactus*, however, appear only in the KUAC samples. This is intriguing as this subfamily also includes the hallucinogenic San Pedro cactus. Unfortunately, its seeds are indistinguishable from other nonhallucinogenic, fruit-producing species, such as *Rebutia* sp., that grow regionally. Although San Pedro cactus use is known from its depictions on Formative period artwork from Chavín de Huantar in highland Peru, we do not have such clear evidence at Kala Uyuni. Yet the greater diversity of cacti at KUAC could reflect an effort to bring in a wider array of foods to these meals.

Finally, the most distinctive and rare plant food at Kala Uyuni was maize. Although Amanda Logan (2006; Logan, Hastorf, and Pearsall 2012) did find a maize phytolith in one of the KUAQ middens, the majority of the maize microremains came from artifacts and deposits associated with the sunken courts. She encountered maize starch grains and/or phytoliths in 8 of 13 soil samples from features associated with both courts. Again, preparation for the meals served on the hilltop likely took place in homes near KUAQ. We might imagine that the imported maize kernels were soaked, ground, and fermented in a home kitchen. It would have then been brought to the hilltop to be consumed, likely from the large painted bowls. Also intriguing is the fact that a maize phytolith was identified on the teeth of the individual buried in the floor of the Lower Court, suggesting that this person had consumed maize, likely *chicha*, prior to his or her death.

The presence of bowls in both areas of the site suggests that liquid meals were prepared and consumed daily and on special occasions. The presence of pots and jars as well as large, decorated bowls at KUAC indicates that these soups, stews, and/or drinks were served in a communal manner (Roddick and Hastorf 2010). Whole tubers or pieces of meat or fish could have also been passed around in these large bowls and/or presented on specially woven textiles. Perhaps there were different phases of the special meal, and the bowls were filled with different items as the festivities progressed.

We find several unique deposits at KUAC that shed light on the meals associated with use of the courts. On the exterior surfaces of the Lower Court, excavators encountered two pits filled with ash and very high densities of fish bone (figure 7.7). Moore and colleagues (2010) found that the fish bones had indications of being burned post-deposit rather than during cooking. These pits had very little pottery. According to Steadman (2007), both pits contained utilitarian wares, but they are distinct from each other. Event KU-A26 had more cooking vessels whereas Event KU-A29 had more serving/storage vessels. Perhaps some of the serving vessels still contained part of meals or were recipients for the residue, such as fish bone. Although KU-A26 did have plant food remains, including parenchyma (3.30 fragments/L as well as a tuber fragment), quinoa (2.75 seeds/L), and cactus (*Echinocactus* and *Maihueniopsis*), KU-A29 had even higher densities of chenopods (12.57 seeds/L) as well as parenchyma (3.8 fragments/L) and cacti (*Opuntia* sp. and *Maihueniopsis*). The combination of remains in these features suggests that these were the burned remnants of meals that took place at the courts.

These features also highlight another ingredient that may have been particularly important for the meals taking place in this ritual space, fish. The surprising amino acid isotope data highlighted the fact that fish were likely not a common, daily food item, as it seems to be today. The zooarchaeological record does indicate that camelid bone is ubiquitous in this period, and there has been no indication that there was a difference in its use between the two areas of the site. The abundance of fish in these pits associated with the courts suggests that they could have been particularly important during these events. They could have been the primary protein served in a warm soup or stew, like today's *wallaque*, or possibly roasted or steamed and passed around in the large bowls or presented on a textile.

Although we do not have such discrete deposits in the KUAQ midden, the range of plant and animal species found in the Middle Formative deposits suggests that daily meals consisted primarily of quinoa, tubers, and camelid meat. Soups, stews, *fiambres*, and porridges with occasional cactus fruits and a range of condiments from local herbs continued to sustain the families living in the area. As we see in important community gatherings today, such as the solstice festival, these individual households likely contributed portions of

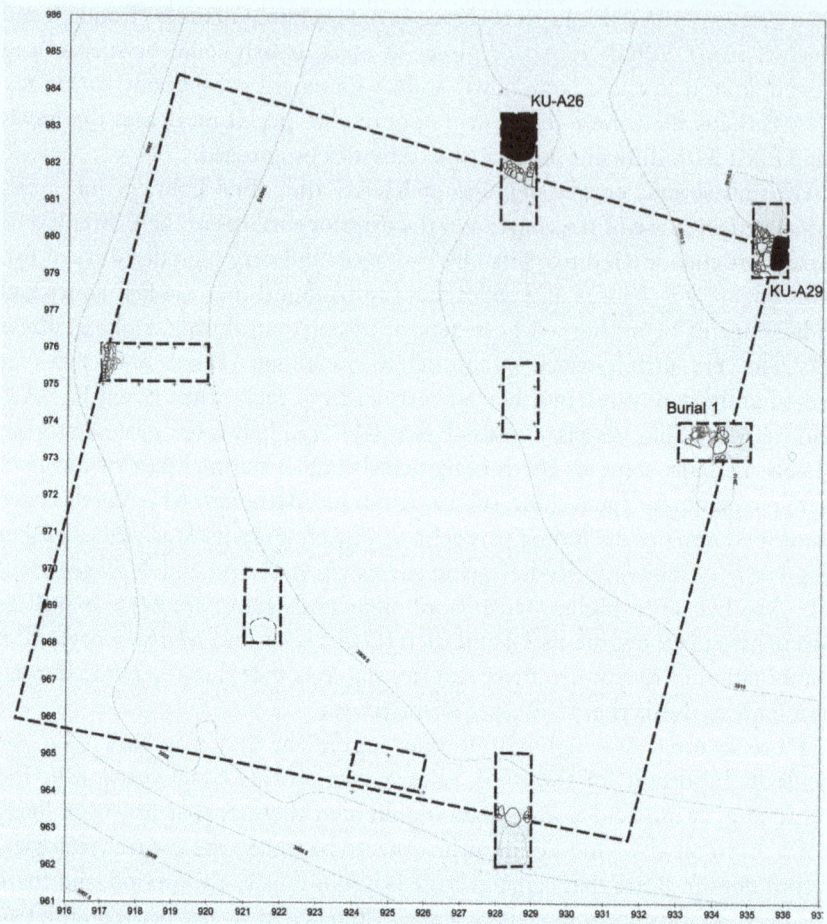

FIGURE 7.7. *KUAC Lower Court (KU-ASD1) indicating the location of the "fish pits" and burial under floor.*

these staple foodstuffs to the special gatherings that took place across the year on the KUAC hilltop.

Late Formative Period

Many changes transpired between the Middle and Late Formative periods (chapter 2). The community at Kala Uyuni underwent several transformations, including a shift to a new settlement in the central area of what would become a prominent terrace. Both the KUAQ and KUAC areas were abandoned, and new traditions in architecture and pottery emerged, indicating new dynamics of local social and political life (chapter 6).

Rather than the spatial differences in ritual and domestic spheres that we were able to explore for the Middle Formative period, the KUKU sector history is temporal with a vertical sequence of occupations that shifted in use and activity through time. Through this sequence we can track patterns in food remains and associated artifacts that indicate some important continuities from the Early and Middle Formative practices as well as some changes.

Initial Late Formative Village

The first discernible phase of occupation of the KUKU sector includes portions of two small, oval structures, KU-ASD9/10, whose size and associated artifacts suggest a residential function. The ceramics found on the surfaces inside and outside of the KU-ASD9 structure include fragments of Late Formative decorated red-rimmed bowls as well as incised decoration, but also a ceramic polishing tool signaling local pottery manufacture (Harkey and Steadman 2011). As with other structures, the floors associated with this building had relatively low densities of plant remains, and the food remains are quite familiar: remains of quinoa (1.29 seeds/L) and tubers (0.55 fragments of parenchyma/L) (figure 7.8). There were, however, no cactus seeds. The animal bones recovered from inside of the structure showed a high degree of burning, but it appears to be from post-deposition firing, not from cooking. The highest density of animal bones, however, was outside of the structure (K. M. Moore 2011b). The animal species are like previous periods with mostly large mammals (camelids), some fish, and a little bird.

Another area of early Late Formative domestic refuse is in the area of KUSQ, where we recovered a small sample of a domestic midden (see figure 6.3). There we found higher densities of quinoa (5.6 seeds/L) and parenchyma (4.8 fragments/L), as well as one seed of the *Maihueniopsis* sp. cactus. Thus, despite the growth and reorganization of the community, which could include local population change as well as newcomers from other areas of the peninsula or further afield, the basic ingredients of daily meals persisted from previous generations.

Expanding Political Center

The next phase of occupation at KUKU is characterized by expansion and is the period when this community served as the political center of the Taraco Peninsula Polity. The initial residential buildings were covered, and a period of construction involved at least three oval structures (the chambers),

KU-ASD2/4/6, in the central area of the site, and the linear-walled structures KU-ASD7/8 to the south. To the west of these structures were yellow clay surfaces that appear to constitute a patio or plaza, as well as several pit deposits and burials. To the east, "outside" of the chamber compounds, are the dense middens and pits discussed in the previous chapter (figure 7.8). The ceramics associated with this area are similar to those of the earlier era, consisting of cooking and storage *ollas* and bowls, although their manufacturing techniques changed significantly (see chapter 2; Roddick 2008). The most common form associated with the structures and many of the pits/middens is the bowl, the majority of which were decorated in the Late Formative "Kalasasaya" style with a painted red rim as well as some with incised, painted decoration. These fine serving vessels have been found across the basin but appear to have been particularly popular at Kala Uyuni. The high percentage of decorated bowls as well as unique features, such as the cache of *cubos*, found in association with these unique buildings, have led us to interpret this architectural complex as a central place of social and political activity on Taraco's Late Formative landscape. Several lines of evidence suggest that food and drink consumption was an important part of the activities taking place here.

In the previous period, it appeared that food preparation was primarily carried out in homes and food was brought to the KUAC ritual center, consumed, and disposed there. In contrast, the distribution of midden, pit, and in situ burning features as well as the composition of the plant remains suggest that cooking took place near the KUKU complex. Figure 7.8 illustrates that the highest density of carbonized plant remains are outside of the chambered buildings and in pits to the west.

Unlike the middens and discrete burning deposits found in association with the sunken courts at KUAC, the botanical remains from these features, while containing some food plants, particularly quinoa and parenchyma, contain much higher densities of wild/weedy species (Bruno 2008). The botanical remains here suggest the burning of high quantities of camelid dung and grasses for fuels (K. M. Moore et al. 2010). Given their proximity to the architectural complex and the prominence of cooking and serving wares associated with these features, these residues are likely associated with food preparation and disposal. For example, Event KU-B77, an exterior surface of KU-ASD2, contained mostly cooking vessels and many sooted sherds (L. Steadman 2007). As described in the previous chapter, we may have evidence for the processing of quinoa, with the relatively high occurrence of *quinoa negra* seeds found in these nearby features. We also begin to find larger pit features compared with

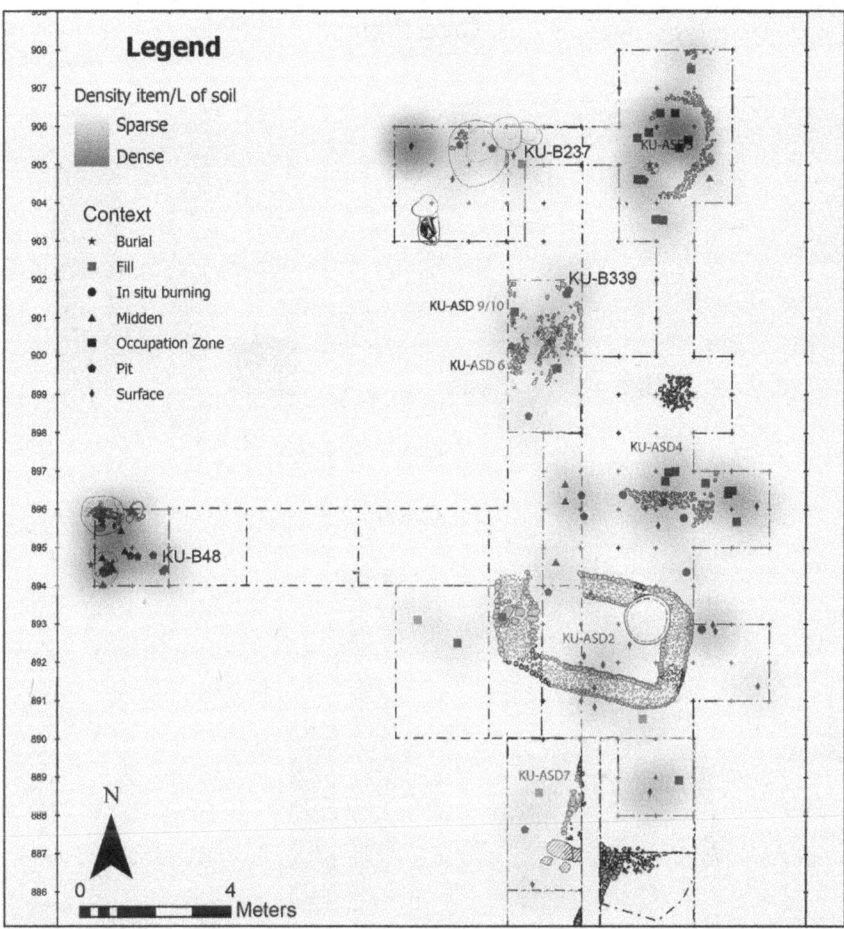

FIGURE 7.8. *Density of carbonized plant materials and contexts across the site of KUKU. All Late Formative period samples are represented. Location of several features mentioned in text are indicated.*

the Middle Formative period. While there were discrete pits filled with food remains at KUAC, indicating the residues of specific meals, the KUKU pits are larger and filled with more wild/weedy species. It is possible that these pits were first dug as earth ovens, where tubers and meat would be placed with fuel, including wood and dung, for roasting. The food items would be removed and served, with the residues of the fuel, burnt seeds, left behind. The same pit could then be used to dispose of the waste from the meal.

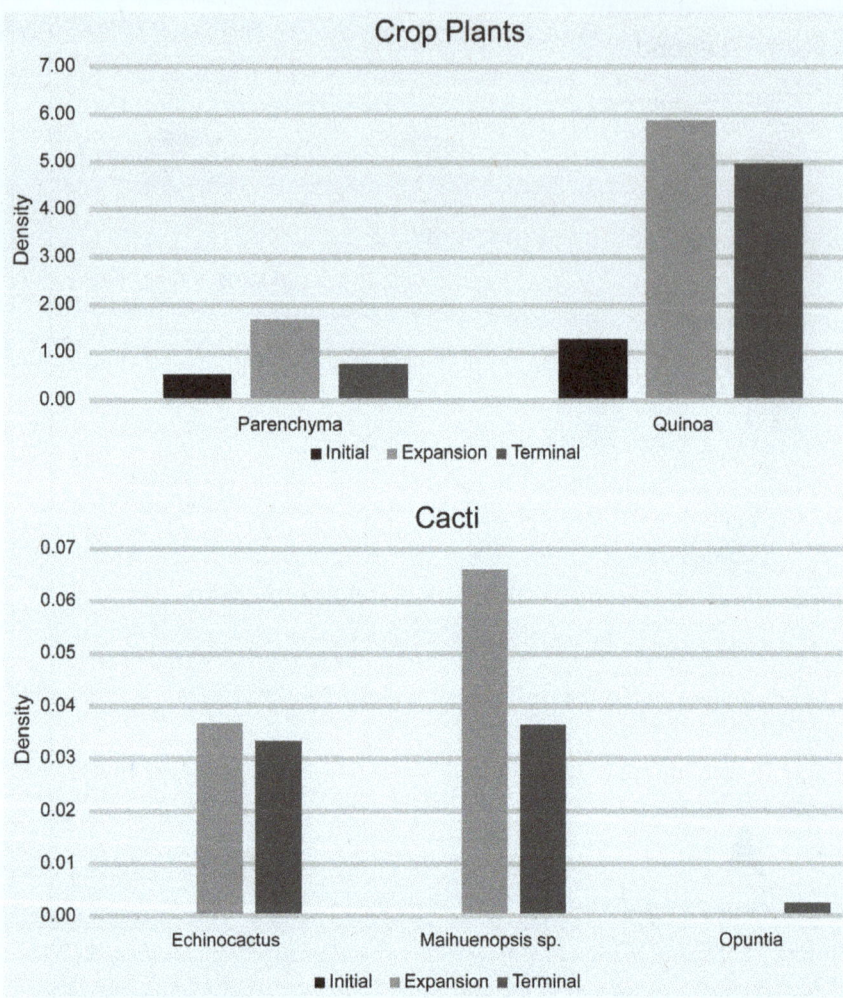

FIGURE 7.9. *Comparison of crop plants and cacti across the Initial, Expansion, and Terminal occupations of KUKU based on average density of plant remains per liter of soil.*

We find a similar range of food species as we did for the earlier time periods (figure 7.9). Quinoa and tubers continue to be the primary starches of Taraco meals, although there does appear to be an overall increase in the presence of tubers in this phase. This could coincide with the evidence for pit roasting, as this technique produces distinctive flavors and textures of tubers compared with boiling or steaming.

Cacti are less prominent at KUKU (fewer than 0.6 seeds/L) than they had been at KUAC (as high as 0.14 seeds/L). The seeds are encountered with less frequency than in previous periods (chapter 4). The decline in cactus could reflect a shift in taste whereby this ingredient was no longer as important as it had been in the Middle Formative period. It is also possible that cactus fruits were not as readily available given that more area of land was being disturbed for farming. It may have shifted to more of an occasional snack that people consumed when they were out on the hillsides, no longer associated with the special activities in the center.

Maize remains are present but relatively sparse in this phase of the Late Formative occupation. Much like the KUAC pattern, none of the events associated with the structures or middens contained macrobotanical remains of maize. Logan (2006), however, found maize phytoliths and starch grains in five different soil samples from the interior floor and a silt lens associated with the KU-ASD2 structure and from a midden deposit (KU-B91) to the west. Thus, there appears to be continued use of maize, likely in the form of *chicha*, in special events. Miller analyzed the isotopes from the collagen of five individual teeth that correspond to this phase, and all of them have signatures for diets containing C_3 plants (M. J. Miller et al. 2022; M. J. Miller et al. 2021). This suggests that maize consumption was low and not significant enough to influence the bone chemistry of the individuals buried during this period at KUKU.

Camelids continue to be an important food source at KUKU and appear to be slightly more prominent than in the earlier Formative periods (K. M. Moore 2011b). Although portions of meat may have been cooked and served, some of the discrete features at the site contain relatively high densities of fragmented bone, suggesting that large mammal bones may have been crushed to release the marrow in soups (K. M. Moore et al. 2010). Fish, however, decline in comparison to their use in the Middle Formative period (24% of the animal assemblage). While scales and bones are present in nearly all of the samples, they do not occur in such high densities as they did in the previous period. This could be due to the absence of the "fish pits" like those at the KUAC sunken courts, which contained extraordinarily high densities of fish bone. This could also be because the lake was, on average, lower across the Late Formative period than it had been during the Middle Formative period (Bruno et al. 2021; Capriles et al. 2014). Yet, as Capriles and colleagues (2014) point out, this did not mean fishing ceased. Fish were still captured for meals at Late Formative KUKU and in some ways may have been even more relished, as they would have required more effort to obtain.

Finally, there is a notable increase in the presence of bird bone in this phase. Birds appeared in less than 1 percent of all weighed bone in the Middle Formative period at Kala Uyuni and increased to 6 percent in this expansive period. Eggshell was also recovered in small quantities from events associated with these buildings. An in situ burning context associated with KU-ASD6 (KU-B339) had a particularly high density of bird bone (figure 7.9). Plants did not preserve very well in this context, possibly because of the high temperature of the fire, but the bird may have been the residue of a particularly unique meal served here.

Thus, in terms of plants, the ingredient list of this phase of Late Formative special occasion meals appears much the same as that of the earlier generation, with a slight decrease in cactus. The animal contributions may have changed with greater importance on camelid meat, less fish, and possibly more bird. There is also strong evidence that the forms of serving and eating etiquette changed, which could also mean that different recipes were served. Bowls continue to be the principle serving vessel, but they change in form and size compared with those present in the Middle Formative period. They are much smaller in diameter, approximately 16 cm, in contrast to the large (> 30 cm) bowls of the previous era (Roddick 2009; Roddick and Hastorf 2010; L. Steadman 2007). The smaller, finer serving bowls first suggest more individualized serving portions. Rather than a large bowl of food being shared among a group, it seems each person had his or her own vessel. The smaller, almost cuplike bowl, which could fit into the palms of a person's hands, might also reflect the preparation of more brothy soup or smaller portions of a porridge. There might only be space for one large potato or piece of meat. Instead, it is possible that those larger items could have been presented on textiles and eaten by hand. The increase in tubers, which may have been roasted in the earth ovens, much like the large *w'atia* feasts today, may have been served in this communal manner and simply eaten without a ceramic vessel. These bowls may have also been important personal items as indicated by a burial in the western sector of the excavations where an adult individual (sex indeterminate) was interred with a red-rimmed bowl (Bruno and Leighton 2007). The tomb was also lined and capped with a large grinding stone or *batán*, adding another layer of food-related meaning to this individual's afterlife. If bowls were personal items, then they may have been brought to these events or possibly were given as gifts by the host and used for years after the event.

Thus, we can detect some important changes as well as some continuities in the character of foodways at the height of the KUKU political center. The change to smaller bowls indicates a shift from communal dishes to individual servings, and there were changes in recipes utilizing quite similar ingredients from the earlier era. The overall increase in tubers and pits with evidence of burning might suggest the use of earth ovens for roasting tubers and possibly meat for these events. If these roasted items were presented on textiles, this aspect of the meal may have been more communal; yet individuals could select their own portions. Soups or *chicha* could then be served to individuals in their own bowls from a larger pot. Although we did not encounter a discrete residential area, as we did in the Middle Formative period, it does appear that more food preparation was taking place near the location of the special events in the chambered buildings.

Terminal Late Formative Village

The final phase of Late Formative occupation at KUKU involved the closure of the chamber architecture and the creation of a new occupation surface, the construction of an oval-shaped building (KU-ASD5), and the continued accumulation of middens and pits with residues of a variety of activities. The materials associated with these new spaces appear to be more domestic in nature, perhaps coinciding with the decline in political influence of Kala Uyuni. The new clay occupational surface (KU-B237) had the highest occurrence of ceramic tools associated with textile (spindle whorls) and ceramic production (polishing tools), and, for the first time, we find evidence for food preparation inside of a building.

The terminal Late Formative building (KU-ASD5) was much simpler, with smaller foundations and thinner walls. It had a prepared floor but not as thick, yellow, or clean as that of the previous structures. Unlike the floors of the chamber architecture, the occupational surface of this building (Event KU-B249) had a much higher density of remains on the surface (figure 7.9). Unlike KU-ASD4, which showed evidence for a good deal of disturbance and may explain a higher density of material compared with KU-ASD2, this building was well preserved, as the northern sector had collapsed, covering the materials that had been left there, including a broken cooking vessel. Here we found a very high density of quinoa seeds (79% of chenopod seeds) and in relatively high proportion compared with *quinoa negra* (21% of chenopod seeds), suggesting a space where it was being cooked or consumed rather than processed (Bruno 2008). Unlike the discrete burned, cache-like deposits of chenopods encountered at KUAC, these seeds were dispersed across the structure floor, more indicative of spills that come with cooking rather than purposeful deposition. In contrast, few parenchyma fragments were encountered, but there were some cactus seeds. Unfortunately, this surface was not sampled for microbotanical remains, so we do not know if maize would have been prepared or consumed here.

This building contained the highest density of sooted and charred sherds from any event at the site (Roddick 2009; L. Steadman 2007). Most of the forms were cooking pots, and many of the sherds were fire-clouded, a pattern that appears when a pot is placed over a fire. There were also some storage and serving vessels. Despite the quotidian nature of the undecorated ceramics, fragments of the decorated Kalasasaya red-rim and incised vessels, including cups, were still quite common here (Roddick 2009). The question remains as to whether this building was for daily, household meals or the preparation of special-occasion meals that were being served elsewhere. It could have fit one or two people and is reminiscent of the cozy kitchen spaces, commonly associated with households today, where both cooking and eating take place. Plant remains and ceramics found outside of the building suggest that although KUKU may have been a less important political or ceremonial center in this later phase, special food preparation and consumption were still taking place to some extent.

In the thick clay surface (KU-B237) west of KU-ASD5, excavators encountered a "proto-*keru*," with thick red and black vertical designs (Roddick 2009) (figure 7.10). Examples of these early drinking cups have been found at only a few other sites in the entire basin (see chapter 2), suggesting that the people here still had some special prestige or political affiliations. We also find the first macrobotanical evidence of maize, fragments of two charred maize kernels, in a pit (Event KU-B48) in the western sector of the site (figure 7.9). This pit also contained some rare fragments of Late Formative II ceramics. This pit contained one of the highest densities of plant remains at the entire site (615.40 items/L), including high densities of wild/weedy plant species, which could indicate the presence of fuel, possibly associated with cooking (Bruno 2008; K. M. Moore et al. 2010). This pit also contained a very high percentage of bird bone (nearly 16% of the total assemblage by weight) (K. M. Moore 2011b). Although we finally encounter some macrobotanical evidence of maize, its overall signature is still low, suggesting it continued to be a unique and prestigious ingredient.

In spite of the changes during the terminal Late Formative occupation of KUKU, many patterns persisted in the meals served there. Tubers, quinoa, and camelid meat continued to be the principal ingredients, complemented by cactus and fish. There are no indications for shifts in preparations or serving, although the scale of special meals was likely smaller. Although KUKU may have lost its role as the primary location for peninsula-wide political

FIGURE 7.10. *Proto*-keru *and Tiwanaku* keru *from Kala Uyuni.*

gatherings and meals, the remains of specialized ingredients, particularly maize and bird, as well as the presence of fine-ware bowls and proto-*kerus* suggest that the people here still had prestige and access to goods and food practices that marked a higher social and political status, at least at a local scale.

TIWANAKU PERIOD

The entire southern Lake Titicaca Basin experienced a major social and political shift with the rise of the first state and urban center at Tiwanaku, just 20 km away from the peninsula and Kala Uyuni. Two substantial strata (Events B-8 and B-25) containing numerous features, including pits, burials, and disturbed remnants of architecture, indicate that the descendants of the Late Formative period KUKU community and political center continued to inhabit this area during this time. We unfortunately do not have any undisturbed architectural features dating to the Tiwanaku period at Kala Uyuni. While we found a few alignments of cobblestones and adobe that may have once been the foundation of a house or other building, we could not delimit any walls or floors (Bruno and Leighton 2007; Bruno and Roddick 2011; Capriles and Machicado Murillo 2011). Because these occupations are closest to the modern-day surface and active agricultural fields, many of them are quite disturbed, not just from plowing but the activities of plant roots, insects, and animals that turn over these deposits. However, insights into the foodways of the Tiwanaku period KUKU inhabitants as well as the potential influence of the nearby state center can still be accessed through the less-disturbed deposits, particularly the ubiquitous pits. Although pit digging dates to the Formative period, this practice was taken to a new level during the Tiwanaku period, both in Kala Uyuni and at Tiwanaku itself (Janusek 2013). At KUKU we recorded at least 25 pits, some so large—more than 2 m in diameter—that we thought they were horizontal strata when first encountered in smaller excavation units (Fontenla Alvarez, Sistrunk, and Bruno 2011, 30–31)! For this analysis, I focus on patterns seen across three types of contexts with food remains: pits (6 samples), occupation zones/middens (3 samples), and one in situ burning context.

Once again, across all types of contexts, we find a similar suite of plant foods, quinoa and parenchyma, as well as cactus. The diversity of cacti, however, diminished compared with earlier periods, with only *Maihueniopsis* sp. seeds being encountered (figure 7.11). As expected, the in situ burning context (KU-B202) had the highest density of plant remains, among the densest at the site (436 items/L). Although it contained a relatively high density of quinoa (> 18 seeds/L), it was particularly dense in wild/weedy species, especially the wild legume *Trifolium* sp. (185 seeds/L) and grasses (41 seeds/L). The discrete nature of the burned deposits certainly suggests that plants and possibly dung were used for fuel, but they could also be the remnants of crop processing, as it appears to have been in an outdoor surface/occupation zone. The midden/occupation zones contained similar plants at slightly lower densities (figure 7.11). The pits, in contrast, contained relatively low densities of plant food remains with primarily wild and weedy species, suggesting the remains of garbage but also possibly cooking activities.

The analysis of ceramics from some of these pits does indicate that cooking occurred in the area. Pits KU-B322 and KU-B-320 contained high densities of ceramics, including large cooking pots and fragments with burning on the exterior and interior of the sherds (Roddick, Fontenla Alvarez, and Reilly 2017). Bowls continued to be common in the Tiwanaku period, some of which appear to be a continuation of forms used in the Late Formative period. The size of the bowls, however, increased in diameter slightly (8–22 cm). Interestingly, there were some ceramic pieces with Kalasasaya decoration in these Tiwanaku contexts. While this could represent mixing of earlier contexts, it could also indicate continued use and possibly even production of this style later in time (Roddick, Fontenla Alvarez, and Reilly 2017, 24).

While the plant food patterns appear quite similar to the previous periods, several lines of evidence point to increased maize consumption. We

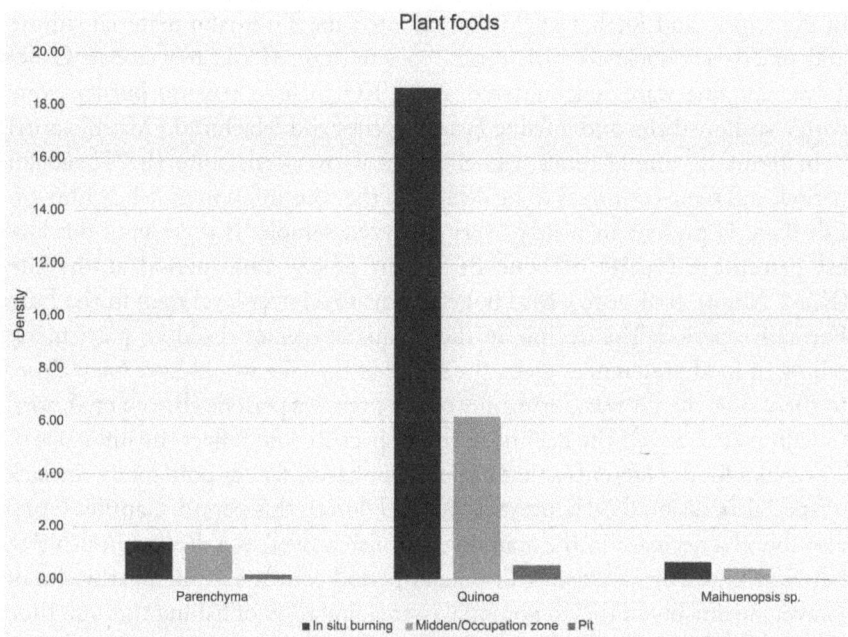

FIGURE 7.11. *Comparison of food taxa across different Tiwanaku period contexts at KUKU based on average density of plant remains per liter of soil.*

encountered both macrobotanical and microbotanical remains of maize for the first time during this period. We identified carbonized remains of the cob (cupule) from the latest Tiwanaku occupational layer (Event KU-B8) as well as maize starch grains embedded in the teeth of an adult male buried with a black, burnished *keru* and an incense burner (Logan 2006; Machicado Murillo 2008). This man also had an isotope signature indicative of maize in his diet (M. J. Miller et al. 2022). Another individual, a child (3–7 years old) who was also buried with a complete ceramic jar (Machicado Murillo 2008), also had $\delta^{13}C$ values indicative of maize in the diet. This certainly raises an interesting question as to whether children were fed maize or if this particular child was nursing a mother who had consumed maize. The presence of maize at the site, as well as at Sonaji, suggests that it was being prepared locally and that people were not just consuming more of it at Tiwanaku itself, although that could certainly be contributing to the higher isotopic signatures. Finally, Tiwanaku-style *keru* fragments as well as whole vessels are common in these deposits (Harkey and Steadman 2011; Roddick, Fontenla Alvarez, and Reilly 2017; L. Steadman 2007). This pattern is like that of other communities in the region and further afield that adopted the Tiwanaku material culture and practices associated with maize consumption (Goldstein 2003). Other Tiwanaku fine-wares encountered at KUKU include incense burners, one with a scalloped rim and a feline face (Capriles and Machicado Murillo 2011).

In terms of animal foods, camelid appears to persist into the Tiwanaku period, and there continues to be decline in the consumption of fish. Although fish bone is present in nearly every analyzed sample, it represents the lowest percentage (13.2%) of bone by weight of any time period at the site (K. M. Moore et al. 2010). Bird bone returns to a lower level than in the Late Formative period. The decline in these aquatic species could be particularly telling of food preferences given the fact that the lake would have been closer to these sites than it was during any of the previous periods (Bruno et al. 2021; Guédron et al. 2023). The decline in these species could reflect the influence of Tiwanaku food preferences that did not emphasize fish or potentially the lack of special-occasion food contexts at KUKU during this period. Capriles (2013) also found a decrease in the abundance of fish as well as a decline in fish size between Late Formative and Tiwanaku period contexts at the nearby site of Iwawi. He attributed this to potential overexploitation of fishing through time, which provides another intriguing explanation.

Overall, there appears to be much continuity in food practices from the Late Formative into the Tiwanaku period at KUKU, with some influence coming from the new urban and ritual center. While some important residents may have had greater access to maize, other individuals from this period continued to be eating primarily quinoa, tubers, and camelid (M. J. Miller et al. 2021). This pattern is, in fact, not much different from what is found in many of the neighborhoods at Tiwanaku itself. Analysis of plant remains from across the site indicates high ubiquity (over 80%) of chenopod and tuber remains, with maize found in up about 20 percent of samples analyzed (Wright, Hastorf, and Lennstrom 2003). So, while maize consumption may have been higher at Tiwanaku itself, it seems quinoa and tubers still provided the primary staples for meals.

The continued presence of *ollas* and bowls at KUKU during this period suggests that soups and stews remained important dishes. Greater variation in bowl size and shape does suggest that there was less focus on a standardized presentation of these meals. This could reflect the fact that these bowls are the remains of more mundane daily meals, or that the people living at Kala Uyuni were now on the receiving end of special meals rather than the hosts. The greatest influence of the Tiwanaku state on Kala Uyuni foodways, however, is the subtle but not irrelevant increase in the presence of maize and *kerus*. Drinking maize beer was not new to Kala Uyuni, but perhaps increased access to maize through Tiwanaku networks made it more accessible, at least for some people living here. While they were consuming it more at Tiwanaku itself, the increased presence of maize macroremains and *keru* fragments at KUKU suggests that they were brewing it themselves. It is also possible that Taraco farmers began to experiment with growing it locally as the peninsula presented favorable conditions.

This detailed analysis of how the products of farming were incorporated into daily and special-occasion meals at Kala Uyuni through time provides insights into the smaller, more intimate scales of Taraco agricultural landscapes. It sheds light on how preferences for particular ingredients in specific meals might have shaped the practices and desired outcomes of the activities involved in producing them. Although changes are apparent in meal preparation and serving etiquette across time at Kala Uyuni, the continuity of locally grown ingredients, particularly quinoa, tubers, and camelids, unveils the fundamental structures of these meals. Both daily and special-occasion meals were built around plant-based starches, sometimes accompanied by meat as a protein or relish, all of which were flavored and given different textures by a range of wild plant and animal species.

Such consistent patterns in these food remains suggest that while many aspects of political and social life changed through time, systems of food production and consumption were more conservative. In the concluding chapter, I return to a broader temporal and spatial scale of analysis to consider how each of the landscape elements discussed thus far intersected as part of seasonal agricultural taskscapes. I explore the development of these taskscapes using a temporal framework that foregrounds patterns in multispecies entanglements. This not only provides a new perspective on the trajectory of human history on the Taraco Peninsula but highlights the ways in which these Indigenous communities provide a model for sustainable agriculture and living.

8

Agricultural Taskscapes

Resurgent Communities of the Taraco Peninsula

One clear day in March, after the morning chores, Alejandra packed up an *aguayo* of bread, fruit, and two bottles of soda pop as well as two picks. Julio harnessed one of the family bulls and loaded up some additional tools onto its back. I accompanied them as well as their daughter Marta to a field on the *laderas* owned by another family, the Blancos. We were assisting this elderly couple and their adult daughter in planting their potato field. We arrived, and Julio hooked up his and the Blanco family bulls to the *yunta*. As we did in the Quispe family fields, the men directed the *yunta* across the field and the women followed behind, placing the potato seeds. The *yunta* would return and cover the seeds. After about an hour of work, we took a break. Alejandra laid out the *aguayo* on a grassy spot near the field and spread out the food. Señora Blanco added cookies and fruits to the blanket. Another small blanket of coca leaves was also set out. The soda pops were opened, and as each person helped themselves to fruit and bread, Alejandra served everyone the soda pop from a single glass. Before drinking the glass, each person would pour out a small amount of the beverage onto the ground as an offering to the earth, *Pachamama*, before drinking the remainder themselves. This was repeated until all the soda pop was consumed and most of the food eaten. Refreshed by the snack, work resumed for another hour and a half. We then all headed to the Blanco house where the daughter had already returned to start cooking lunch. Gathered in the small sitting room, everyone was served a hot bowl of soup made of potatoes and mutton. Comments were made about the successful work and hopes of an abundant harvest. On our way home, I asked about this arrangement. Why had we gone to plant this field? Alejandra told me that because many of the Blanco children were now living in the city of El Alto, the two older parents and one adult could not do all the work alone. The two families were close friends, and they offered to help with the planting. In return, the Quispes were served a nice lunch and will get some of the harvest; this was a task most neighbors seemed happy to do, in part, because they knew assistance would be returned at some point in the future.

Many of the agricultural tasks that I witnessed in my year on the peninsula included several people from outside of the family. In addition to going to other homes and fields, individuals were invited to help with tasks on the Quispes' property. People who assist at any stage of the cycle normally receive part of the final harvest. Thus, people who have little land or live alone, such as elderly folks or single mothers, are often invited to help because they may need extra food assistance. I was told that this is type of aid is called *yanaptaña*, which simply means "to help." Another common arrangement is when one family provides land, and the invited individuals provide some seed. They all work to plant the crop and then share the harvest. In Aymara this is called *waki* (Carter and Mamani 1982, 136).[1] In general, the sharing of agricultural labor on the peninsula seemed to be a fluid and somewhat informal process that took place on an individual level. Families or friends would make agreements to help provide a bull or a worker, and the exchange of goods in return was automatic.

Larger work projects, however, were organized on the community level. The plaza in Santa Rosa was undergoing reconstruction while I was there, and the local leaders, known as *mallkus*, had a list of every member of the community based on land ownership. Each member was expected to contribute both time and money to the completion of the plaza. I was not present for any large agricultural works projects, but they likely would have been organized in a similar fashion. Christine Hastorf told me that when TAP and the community of Chiripa built the first small museum there in 1998, each family contributed a certain number of homemade adobe bricks to the construction. With funds provided by grants and the labor and materials from the community, the building was constructed together.

Many studies of Andean lifeways emphasize the organizational role of the *ayllu*, which has been defined as "a number of unrelated extended families living together in a restricted area and following certain common rules of crop rotation under more or less informal leaders" (Rowe 1963, 253). According to many colonial documents and ethnographies, Andean peoples were organized in this manner (Abercrombie 1998; Klein 1993; Murra 1984). Although the *ayllu* is often presented as an unchanging social institution of the Andes, many scholars have pointed out the wide range of social groups that this word encompasses (Fabricant 2010; W. Isbell 1997; Klein 1993). Chiripa was the only community I worked with that utilized the term *ayllu*. In this case, it defined two sides of the community that were divided by a natural ravine. West of the ravine is the *ayllu* Ocorani and east of the ravine Chiripa (Soriano 2017). Every year the primary political positions shift between the two *ayllus*. Within each group, like the other communities, the positions rotated among landholding families. The other communities did not have this division, and the rotation of leadership and participation in events and projects simply rotated through a single list.

Although the rules surrounding land ownership and work relationships today are strongly shaped by colonial impositions and more recent political developments, particularly the agricultural reforms of the 1950s, this discussion leads us to think about how agricultural work articulated with broader social and political processes on the Taraco Peninsula in the past. Agricultural work requires collaboration and communication. It also takes place across a finite area of land, and as populations grow and/or lands contract (such as when the lake rises), coordination and negotiation is needed to determine who can plant where and when. In this concluding chapter, I bring together the various lines of evidence that have been examined across each chapter to consider how agricultural activities articulated with the construction of Taraco Peninsula societies through time. By considering the material, historical, grown, and lived elements of Taraco agricultural landscapes, we can envision what they might have looked like during certain time periods and how they contributed to shifting sociopolitical landscapes. Building on Roddick's (2013) call for an "archaeology of inhabitation" in the Lake Titicaca Basin, I examine agricultural taskscapes, particularly the stages of work that marked the agricultural year. I consider how agricultural tasks might have changed or persisted as broader structures shifted such as population size and political entities as well as environmental elements that impacted the lands upon which agricultural production took place, particularly rainfall, lake level, soil types, wild plant ecologies, and other activities such as pastoralism and fishing. In thinking through the agricultural taskscapes of Taraco Peninsula history, I hope to illustrate how people dwelled in this landscape through time, bringing the material and historical conditions to life (*sensu* Barrett 1994).

This landscape approach reveals a different story from the traditional archaeological culture histories, which have been based largely on changes in ceramic production and architecture that were believed to reflect cultural evolutionary shifts (Graeber and Wengrow 2021; Swenson and Roddick 2018). In the traditional southern Lake Titicaca Basin cultural chronology, the biggest "rupture" or transition among the four time periods was between the Late Formative and Tiwanaku periods—thus the nomenclature indicating two different cultural phenomena. When focusing on the patterns of agricultural landscapes, particularly the plants, the most significant "rupture" or change in local livelihoods is between the Middle and Late Formative periods. For this final discussion, I move away from these traditional temporal labels and organize it around the characteristics of the multispecies communities that emerged. This reorientation of Taraco Peninsula history changes our view of these communities, bringing into focus the elements of "resurgence" that allowed for long-term success in this dynamic place.

ESTABLISHING AND EXPANDING MULTISPECIES COMMUNITIES, 1500 BCE–250 CE

Around 1500 BCE, as rainfall became more abundant and regular and the lake began to fill, the first people settled into permanent homes on the peninsula. These small groups of people lived in dispersed houses with plentiful space for fields and herds. The lake would have been a few kilometers away but close enough to occasionally fish and collect other lacustrine resources like *totora* reeds and birds. This early phase of farming was likely one of experimentation. People were learning how crops grew in different soils, where animals could be tended, how to manage the variables of changing weather patterns, and the reactions of the wild plant and animal species living in the area.

The work of preparing fields in this early period was light. With ample planting areas to choose from, the first fields were likely located in the areas easy to manipulate. Men and women with simple stone tools made of wood and local quartzite could select loose soils along the rising, yet fluctuating, lakeshore, near springs, or along streams where the *laqa* soils could easily be turned over. Men punched holes for tubers or scraped the surface for quinoa while women followed behind planting the seeds. This work could be done by an immediate family of grandparents, parents, and children, but neighbors and distant kin may have joined to learn about this land as it became newly farmed.

These first farmers grew quinoa and tubers, likely potatoes and *oca*, and possibly *isañu* or *papa lisa*. Quinoa was an easy crop to cultivate; it required little tillage and could be sown by broadcasting. The archaeological record suggests quinoa was more common than tubers. The tubers would have required digging more deeply into the earth and then covering them. This would be easiest in the looser soils. Multiple varieties and species could be planted in the same plots. The crop rotation used today is meant to maximize soil nutrients for the different needs of each crop. The newly planted Taraco soils would still be rich in nitrogen and phosphates, so a rotation was not yet necessary. Additionally, the plentiful space would have also allowed for longer fallow periods, 10 or more years, helping to maintain the nutrients of the soils each year.

Camelid herds would have had ample grazing areas, but as crops began to grow and bloom, they would be moved to areas where these cultivated plants would not be disturbed. The low-lying *pampa* areas that have dense soils, difficult to turn over for crops but able to support expanses of grasses and sedges, would have been excellent for feeding camelid herds. Aspects of life during this time may have been quite mobile. Longer walking distances to plant, herd, and fish may have been a part of everyday life that was carried over from previous generations of more mobile hunting and gathering. This would allow families to adjust to drier years, with a more distant lake, for herding areas and fields.

These early Taraco inhabitants also interacted with many wild plant species growing across the landscape. The most prominent species were grasses, malvas (mallows), and wild chenopods, but also pockets of clovers, amaranths, and verbenas. It may have been necessary to remove these species from cultivated fields to aid in crop success, but the macrobotanical record suggests these plants were not particularly dense or diverse. Thus, the work of tending fields and weeding may have been minimal or possibly nonexistent. People were also learning about the usefulness of these plants for medicines, spices, dyes, and relishes. People would have encountered wild *Chenopodium* species, *quinoa negra*, and *illama*, in their fields. These may have been allowed to grow until they had seeds but then removed from around growing quinoa or potatoes. The seeds could be saved to serve at special meals or for times when harvests were low; they may have even been fed to camelids. *Illama* was saved and burned, along with quinoa, in the first sacred activities conducted on the hilltop of Achachi Coa Collu.

As the rainy season ended and the crops matured, families would return to the fields to pull out the quinoa stalks and dig up the tubers. The dry months would have been spent processing the harvest, whacking the dried stalks with wooden sticks, and winnowing the dried fruits with baskets and textiles to release the small seeds. Once the freezing nights began to arrive, piles of potatoes could be laid out to freeze-dry to make *chuño*.

While fields and herds thrived, the lake provided additional resources such as *totora* reeds and sedges for roofs, boats, and basketry. The birds in the lake and land were harvested occasionally for food and sources of feathers for adornments. Fathers, sons, and cousins made trips out into the lake to harvest fish, possibly for occasional special home meals, but particularly in preparation for the festivities that would take place in the sunken courts that were being built in communities across the peninsula.

The first generations of settlers on the Taraco Peninsula were successful and populations grew. Families would become more wedded to particular *pampas*, hillsides, valleys, and hills. The hamlets in places like Chiripa and the area of Ayrampu Qontu at Kala Uyuni became villages where residents elaborated their ritual spaces with new architecture and ceremonies. At Achachi Coa Collu they constructed two sunken courts and remodeled them over a span of several hundred years, adding new floors and providing space for offerings of humans and sacred stones. The creation of these places and the events taking place there were extensions of the communal work that was involved in agriculture. They were places intimately connected to the success of the communities' fields and herds. Unfortunately, there are no plant or animal species that indicate when these rituals would have taken place, but it is quite likely they were seasonal. Today celebrations associated with the Catholic calendar, particularly Carnaval and Easter, occur in the rainy season when crops are growing. Offerings are made to ensure successful harvests, and we might imagine that early farmers would have performed rituals at this initial stage of the agricultural year as well. As sunken courts became important places to celebrate, however, the dry season may have been a more appropriate time to gather. Crops would have been harvested and would have contributed to the special meals. Additionally, there would not be the threat of a rainstorm that might leave water in the courts. Although processing work needed to be done, the dry season is not as busy without pressures to plant or harvest at the appropriate time. Today many community celebrations take place in this season, including the celebration of the winter solstice.

Although by 800 BCE Taraco inhabitants developed new methods and styles of pottery and architecture, the archaeobotanical record indicates continuity in agricultural activities. Quinoa continued to be the primary crop, with tubers still playing a lesser role. Certainly new varieties were developed and propagated of both, though we cannot yet detect them in the remains. These farmers would have been very familiar with the wild plant species that had been thriving there for generations. Continuity in the diversity and density of wild plant assemblages suggests that soil disturbance, either through agriculture or herding, was not greatly impacting the local plant ecology. There may have been increasing efforts to remove those growing alongside crops, however. The stored caches of cleaned quinoa found in the bins at the Chiripa Montículo attest the efforts to keep weedy plants, particularly *quinoa negra*, separate from crops as well as to process the clean seed. Yet these wild plants may still have been collected for greens or seed as relishes for meals. Another wild plant that appears to become an important food as court ceremonies were elaborated, at least at Kala Uyuni, is cactus. An increase in these seeds suggests that they were used for more than just a snack while herding camelids but were brought up to Achachi Coa Collu as part of the meals served there. *Illama* continues to be present in very high densities in the court activities, including the discrete pits that contained other food remains. The presence of cactus fruit could indicate that these ceremonies were taking place toward the end of the rainy season and the start of the dry season, when fields were ripening and the harvest was being processed.

While more fields may have been planted, there was still enough space to allow them to fallow for relatively long periods of time and for the local flora to reestablish itself. The residents were now more familiar with the peninsula, and while still exploiting the easiest soils to cultivate, they would be learning when and how to utilize the more difficult soils, such as the clay-rich, *k'inku* areas in the *pampa* and even some of the *q'ala*, rocky soils on the hilltops. They would now be experts in how particular crops responded to different soils and when to begin planting based on the yearly rainfall. Fields closer to the lake, springs, and streams may have been utilized in times when rainfall decreased, and those higher up the *ladera* and hilltop may have become useful in wetter periods. As more space began to be used for planting, more coordination would have been required to move herds out of the way. Some areas may have become designated specifically for grazing.

With expansion of agricultural land and the need to feed more people, the work of preparing soils for planting would have increased. An increase in the density of stone tools, still made of mostly local stone, in the Middle Formative period indicates more digging was taking place at this time (Bandy 2001; Bruno 2014a). This additional work would have required greater coordination with relatives or neighbors outside of the household. There may have even been community efforts to prepare some of the more difficult-to-till soils. Again, the elaboration of ceremonial architecture, such as the Montículo at Chiripa and the sunken courts at Achachi Coa Collu, certainly attests to an ethic of communal work within these growing villages that could have initially been based in agricultural work or expanded to it.

The pattern of food remains in the domestic midden of Ayrampu Qontu and the sunken court deposits at Achachi Coa Collu sheds light on the dynamic of food production, preparation, and consumption at these villages. The similarity in plant species in both places strongly suggests that the foods served during the special events held at the sunken courts were grown, processed, and prepared with local ingredients in local homes. While there is some food refuse on the Achachi Coa Collu hilltop, we do not find the density of materials that are present in the Ayrampu Qontu midden. This indicates that the processing of crops after harvest was done at home, while the remnants of the special meals served at the sunken courts were disposed of in small pits and a larger midden on the hilltop. While the ingredients of the Achachi Coa Collu meals may have been the same as those at home, their preparations were likely different and their presentation and consumption, in large, painted bowls and colorful textiles, would have set them apart. Finally, a special drink, *chicha*, made of a nonlocal crop, maize, would have added another element of distinction to these meals. The fizzy, fermented drink was shared in the large serving bowls. It is possible that not all participants drank this beverage, but knowledge of this mildly intoxicating and foamy drink made from an exotic plant would have been remembered and valued within these communities, perhaps sparking the first attempts to grow it on the peninsula.

INTENSIFYING AND DIVERSIFYING MULTISPECIES COMMUNITIES, 250–1150 CE

There is a clear change in the elements that constitute the agricultural landscapes on the Taraco Peninsula after 200 BCE. There are also some prominent changes in other aspects of the archaeological record between about 200 BCE and 250 CE across the southern Lake Titicaca Basin. Across much of the region, the location of communities and their activities changed. For example, at Kala Uyuni, Achachi Coa Collu and Ayrampu Qontu were abandoned, and the central area known as Kala Uyuni grew (Bandy 2007; Roddick, Bruno, and Hastorf 2014). At Chiripa, while there are a few remains of Late Formative activities, there is a clear decline in ritual activity (Hastorf 2003). By 250 CE, many aspects of life changed on the Taraco Peninsula and beyond: new ceramic and stone sculpture styles emerged, villages grew larger and more centralized, and new monumental architectural spaces were constructed. It is also at this moment when we find the most significant changes in the archaeobotanical record, particularly in the wild plant assemblages but also in crop preferences. Interestingly, many of these patterns in the plant remains persist into the subsequent period of major political change, around 500 CE, when the Tiwanaku state comes to prominence.

Population growth does seem to be an important factor in the new developments seen in the Late Formative period (Bandy 2006; Bruno 2008; Stanish 2003). Whether it be from local growth or movement of people into the area, the sites on the Taraco Peninsula and elsewhere in the southern basin are larger and more concentrated than in the Middle Formative period. This meant less space for the more extensive agricultural practices common in the prior era and would have required changes in how the landmass was utilized to raise crops and animals (Boserup 1965). Elements of water and soil also continued to change, with the lake level gradually increasing through time, punctuated with periods of drier conditions. Managing this dynamic environment would have continued to play a central role in sustaining these communities as they grew. The Taraco archaeological record indicates that the agriculturalists of this later period employed a variety of practices that are typical of smallholder, dryland farmers around the world when experiencing pressure to intensify production; that is, produce the same amount or more from the same area of land (Bruno 2014a; Netting 1993). These strategies can be explored through changes in seasonal taskscapes.

Preparing the earth for planting became more involved. Several lines of evidence suggest that local farmers increased soil manipulation on the peninsula. The first is an increase in the presence of stone hoes. While some were still made from local quartzite, there is an increase in more durable, imported andesite (Bandy 2001; Hastorf et al. 2022). By now, the Taraco farmers would have been very knowledgeable about the various soils present on the peninsula—where they were located, when they should be planted, and how to plant them. Expanding into more variable soil types likely began in the Middle Formative period, but the necessity to continuously plant across all of these areas undoubtedly grew in the Late Formative period. Thus, this period may have seen the beginnings of sectoral fallowing, a rotation of planting across different soils interspersed with fallowed fields. Another way to increase the production of crops in a smaller area of land is to reduce fallow. The most indicative change that fallow periods shortened and more continuous field preparation was required is the dramatic shift in wild plant ecology. While many of the same species common on the landscape in the previous era persisted and, in some cases, increased, several species that had been sparse became very prominent. Species that thrive in disturbed environments—sunflowers, clovers, mustards, and verbenas—would have now filled the landscape both in fallowed and growing fields. These would have certainly been excellent fodder for sustaining camelid herds, but they made more work for weeding.

The increased pressure on land use may have made areas exposed by lower lake levels during dry periods even more desirable. As has been described for historical periods, farmers may have clamored to reclaim the land recently exposed by falling lakeshores. These lands would have even been easier to till and been more fertile, although possibly a bit saline. Those newly exposed areas may have relieved land pressure for periods of time. When the lake rose again, however, the loss of these lands would become more problematic as the population size and food needs would remain the same. It would have been in these instances where the soil manipulation and water management practice of raised field agriculture became an integral practice of farming on the peninsula and elsewhere. While there may have been some experimental use of this practice in the Middle Formative period, it would have become a necessity during periods of higher lake levels during the Late Formative and then into the Tiwanaku period. The labor required to maintain these different areas of production could have come from individual households, but community efforts would have made raised field construction and maintenance more feasible.

The zooarchaeological record indicates that camelids continued to be an important part of Taraco landscapes and foodways into the Late Formative and Tiwanaku periods. In fact, data suggest that herd size may have increased. Recent strontium analysis on camelid teeth from the peninsula suggests that they lived most of their lives there and were not taken to other places to be herded (Hastorf et al. 2022). Although some Andean scholars have viewed agriculture and pastoralism as opposing, with one giving way to the other, in fact, the diversification of production through the raising of domesticated animals is another intensification strategy used by agriculturalists worldwide (Netting 1993). The space and timing of herding would have been coordinated with growing crops, and perhaps the lower, grassy *pampas* were used exclusively for camelid herding until fields were harvested. The weeds and processing waste derived from agriculture, however, could have been fed to animals. The animals could be set to graze in harvested and fallowed fields, a practice common on the peninsula today. Their grazing helped to prepare fields for planting. Camelid dung is an important fertilizer. Camelids tend to defecate in the same location, creating discrete piles of dung across the landscape. Farmers would need to disperse it across the fields, but this extra work would be a critical input as soil fertility, particularly nitrogen, would have diminished with decreasing fallow periods. We still have not been able to demonstrate purposeful fertilizing with camelid dung, as has been shown in other parts of the Andes (Santana-Sagredo et al. 2021; Szpak and Chiou 2020), but we continue to look for traces of it. Finally, another indication that grazing was a contributing factor to the increased soil disturbance on the peninsula during the Late Formative period is the appearance of the spiny bush *Tetraglochin cristatum*.

At this turning point, we also see a shift in the composition of domesticated plant species. Quinoa continues to be a core crop and food, but two lines of botanical evidence suggest that tubers became increasingly important: an increase in the ubiquity of parenchyma fragments and an increase in the ubiquity of *Solanum* sp. and *Oxalis* sp. seeds. While people do not eat these seeds, some of which could be from wild counterparts, their increased presence in the archaeological record suggests that potatoes and *oca* were more abundant on the landscape. The increase in tuber species also converges with the evidence for greater soil disturbance as excavation is required to both plant and harvest the tubers.

The work to tend quinoa and tuber fields also increased significantly during this period. The abundance of wild species suggests that weeding would now have become a more important agricultural task during the growing season. Today this is done primarily by women, and it is possible that this division of labor may have developed at this time. Women would have continued to observe the various species growing in the fields and feeding some of them to their camelid herds, while others would have been kept for spices, medicines, and relishes. *Illama* continues as a common weedy species but is joined by a greater number of other weedy species compared to the earlier periods. *Illama*'s resilience to cold temperatures, however, may have been noted by women tending to fields and left to grow, collected, and eventually purposefully planted in the next year, initiating the process of domestication of *kañawa*.

The work of harvesting and processing these crops would have been like that of previous generations. With the increased production of tubers, other forms of preservation through freeze-drying may have developed, including the practice of first submerging potatoes in water and then leaving them out to freeze-dry, producing the form known as *tunta*. Although there may have been an increase in the contributions of tubers to peninsula foodways, the suite of ingredients for meals—quinoa, tubers, camelid meat, and some fish—remained consistent. Changes in ceramic serving vessels, particularly fine-wares, does indicate a shift in the ways these foods were consumed, at least in more formal contexts. Bowls are still prevalent for serving soups and porridges, but they are smaller, individual-sized servings. Although we cannot see textiles, we might also image that a spread of boiled, steamed, and roasted tubers could also be laid out on the clean, clay surfaces of the chamber buildings, as is common at community feasts today. Given the high density of midden remains just outside of the Kala Uyuni chambered rooms, it is likely that the foods for these occasions were prepared there and the remains disposed of afterward. While the ingredients continue to be primarily local during this period, the organization of who prepared food and how it was prepared for special occasions appears to have shifted. Rather than community members all contributing a prepared portion of their harvests to the meals, they provided ingredients that were prepared and served by particular individuals at the event.

There is a very slight increase in the presence of maize, both in the botanical remains and isotope signatures, but it is still very rare. The preparation and consumption of *chicha* would have continued to be a very specialized and exclusive aspect of peninsular celebrations and ritual life. Maize was likely not grown locally yet, and it may have taken several generations of experimentation and breeding to arrive at the variety that grows in the basin today. The experimentation may have begun with these generations as the demand for the plant increased.

The intensification of agriculture and herding across the Taraco landscape during the Late Formative period would have required increased coordination and negotiation around where fields could be planted and herds could be grazed; thus territoriality may have increased at the time. Most models of how leaders emerged on the Taraco Peninsula have focused on either access to exotic products and trade control or ritual prowess (chapter 2). The need to help organize and coordinate increasing agricultural labor and lands has not been recognized by archaeologists until the Tiwanaku period for state control of raised fields, but the basis for this likely emerged in the Late Formative period. The ability to help ease disputes that would have arisen around land access and even designation of communal lands for both farming and herding could have been an arena in which emerging leaders at Late Formative village centers may have found success and influence. The ability to help resolve disputes, carry out rituals that would ensure successful harvests, and help to organize labor related to farming and other village activities would have been increasingly important. These events seem to have shifted from large, communal rituals to more intimate occasions where food was served in small vessels with smaller-scale rituals. This would facilitate negations in the chambers and small patios managed by local leaders.

The emergence of the region's first state at nearby Tiwanaku around 500 CE was a major social and political transformation that changed many aspects of material culture, ritual and religious practice, and subsistence and economic practices in the southern Lake Titicaca Basin and beyond. Upon beginning this study, I expected there to be a significant "rupture" in farming and food on the Taraco Peninsula with the rise of the Tiwanaku state. I speculated that the importance of raised field agriculture just to the east at Pampa Koani might have shifted people's attention there, resulting in some disintensification at sites like Kala Uyuni. Roddick (2013, 303) suggests that Tiwanaku could have redefined the timing of agricultural practices, bringing people to work on the large fields during specific times of the year, which would have "staggered" the agricultural season, presenting a "new form of temporal reasoning." He asked, "whether staggering generated disjointed temporalities, or whether it permitted local agricultural cycles to work in harmony with state projects."

The data examined here suggest that there was little disruption to Taraco Peninsula agricultural taskscapes and that any new demands of the Tiwanaku state "worked in harmony" with previous practices. People in the area certainly adopted the new decorated ceramic styles and even garbage disposal practices of creating large pits. Yet the archaeobotanical record looks remarkably like that of the Late Formative period. A similar suite of wild plant species continued to dominate the landscape. The women of the region would by now be very familiar with these species and accustomed to removing them from growing fields and utilizing them for a range of purposes, including fodder for herds. The crops also remain similar, with tubers continuing to be more prominent than in the earliest Formative periods and quinoa remaining a reliable and valued food. At this time domesticated *kañawa* was integrated into the rotation system or intercropped with quinoa. We do see the first increase in the ubiquity of maize macrobotanical remains as well as more individuals with isotope signatures indicative of maize. These patterns are not quite as elevated as they are in the center of Tiwanaku, but it appears that Taraco residents now had greater access to this food, very likely through their relationships with the state. Farmers in the basin may have been closer to developing the lake variety, but it is unlikely that they could produce enough for the demands at the city and ceremonial center. Thus, it is unlikely that maize had yet become a regular member of the annual Taraco crop rotation, as it is today.

The more intensive agricultural practices established in the Late Formative period, consisting of greater efforts to till a range of soils in preparation for planting a rotation of crops across the landscape, persisted into the Tiwanaku period. The population structure of the Taraco Peninsula remained largely the same in the Tiwanaku period with some slight shifts (Bandy 2001, 226–27). As long as productivity remained consistent and no greater demands were placed on production, the soil management practices established in the previous period could continue. One factor that may have changed during this period is that the lake level became relatively higher compared with that of the previous periods, with one drier episode around 1000 CE. While this would reduce planting area, rainfall would be more abundant, perhaps resulting in larger harvests on smaller amounts of land. The topography of the western peninsula, near Kala Uyuni, does not have a lakeshore floodplain where raised fields could be expanded, but raised field systems were built and maintained near springs and streams in Chiripa. Unmodified, these areas would be poor for crops like potatoes because water accumulates, but the elevated beds would allow for drainage of soils as well as the other thermic and nutrient benefits of raised field farming. These smaller clusters of fields in Chiripa could have been managed by extended families but may have even been communal fields for the village.

Although the Taraco political centers and leaders at places like Kala Uyuni lost their broader influence, the local populations appear to have remained in their communities and adopted aspects of Tiwanaku material and political culture. This was not the case in other locations, such as in the Tiwanaku Valley itself and at the eastern end of the peninsula in the Katari Basin. The population structures there shifted to the city of Tiwanaku and the burgeoning "second city" Lukurmata. The reasons for this could be many but very likely related to two significant shifts in economic production in these two regions: (1) the lure of economic specializations in the heartland such as potting, stoneworking, and possibly even textile production at the city center and (2) the importance of larger-scale raised field farming in the Pampa Koani near Lukurmata. While residents of Kala Uyuni and other Taraco villages may have traveled to Tiwanaku to participate in its festivities and even perhaps contributed food to those events, such as potatoes, quinoa, camelids, and even fish, they could easily return to their homes and continue about their daily lives, albeit in the shadow of the city to the west.

While we find *keru* fragments and maize remains at sites across the peninsula, there are no major changes or modifications to local ceremonial architecture, with the possible exception of the Montículo at Chiripa (Browman 1978a). At least at Kala Uyuni the Tiwanaku occupation appears to be primarily residential. The people residing in the area could have been the descendants of important leaders who adopted aspects of Tiwanaku culture. Burials, which are similar in form and orientation to the Late Formative period (Machicado Murillo 2008), often included Tiwanaku fine-wares, and several of the interred individuals, including a child, had isotopic signatures for maize.

Overall, the material remains suggest that Taraco inhabitants integrated several aspects of Tiwanaku culture into their daily practices but continued to farm and herd much in the same way that they had done for generations. Thus, the tasks and tempos of daily life related to the agricultural calendar remained much the same. Political and ritual events at Tiwanaku may have required leaving for short periods of time, but they do not appear to have caused much disruption to the local agricultural practices and landscapes.

Taking this long view of Taraco Indigenous history from the perspective of the elements that contributed to agricultural landscapes reveals striking continuities, particularly in relationships with domesticated plants and animals. Human communities began cultivating a suite of plants, quinoa and tubers, alongside the rearing of camelids about 3,000 years ago, and they continued to do so through the end of the study period around 1,000 years ago. There are more invisible changes in the development and use of different varieties and species of quinoa, tubers, and camelids; yet the suite of species is consistent across the Early and Middle Formative periods with a slight shift in relative importance during the Late Formative period and Tiwanaku periods. This persistence in plant and animal management does not align well with the many notable changes that humans made in ceramic production, architecture, stone sculpture, religion, and politics. This suggests that agricultural practices were among the most conservative of human activities, learned and passed down over generations to allow for success in the face of a very dynamic Titicaca Basin environment. There were certainly moments of food scarcity and political strife, but the routines associated with seasonal agricultural taskscapes, which could shift under a variety of conditions, brought people through hard times. These difficult moments may have also resulted in the development of new varieties of crops such as *kañawa* and maize as well as new techniques such as raised fields, all of which provided tools for challenges that would face subsequent generations. In other words, the practices and multispecies interactions underwriting the creation of agricultural landscapes on the Taraco Peninsula between 1500 BCE and 1000 CE are an example of both sustainable agriculture and sustainable lifeways.

RESURGENT COMMUNITIES: PAST, PRESENT, AND FUTURE

Over the course of this book, I have explored how Indigenous Taraco communities have interacted with land, water, animals, and plants to create sustainable agricultural practices. This has involved examining the material, historical, lived and grown, and social and political aspects of landscapes.

Examination of these long-term patterns also reveals meaningful elements of these places. This includes the values that these communities placed on the nonhuman elements of their world and the beliefs about what was required to succeed and thrive in their place over many generations. The labor invested to ensure that plants and animals flourished not only kept family members from going hungry but reflects an ethic of living in balance with a diversity of plant and animal species. It also involved intimate knowledge and understanding of the behaviors of soils, rainfall, and lake, spring, and stream waters, which were beyond their immediate control. Overall, their actions minimized harm to other entities and, in fact, encouraged them to thrive. Fish and birds that lived in the lake were harvested but do not appear to be overexploited. Although there are some indications that tree species, and possibly cacti, declined as agriculture expanded, herbaceous and bushy wild species prospered and multiplied. While these species presented competition to growing crops, they also provided flavors, textures, sustenance, and medicine to humans and other animals; therefore, they were also valued and respected. This epitomizes what Anna Tsing (2017, 51) describes as "multispecies resurgence," a viable way of living through interactions with many nonhuman actors—a sustainable way of living.

Future studies on the peninsula should examine the elements of agricultural landscapes through the Late Intermediate, Inca, and Spanish colonial periods. This would illuminate how the practices highlighted here endured or changed during these particularly tumultuous and violent periods of Lake Titicaca Basin history. The ethnographic and historic data gathered for this study shed light on some of the very significant changes that transpired over this time, particularly with Spanish colonization: the introduction of new crops and animals, tools and technologies, as well as fundamental reorganization of landholdings. On the Taraco Peninsula, quinoa as well as *illama* lost their primary places as the principal domesticated species, and native wild species like *illama* have all but disappeared, giving way to Eurasian mustards and grasses. Yet a diversity of tubers, potatoes, *oca*, *isañu*, and *papa lisa*, continue to be cared for across these communities, indicating elements of persistence and resistance rooted in ancient agricultural practices. The practices developed to care for Andean domesticated plants and animals have been applied to introduced species such as fava beans and sheep, all of which have been integrated into seasonal taskscapes and meals. Regular harvest of the Titicaca Basin maize variety also reflects the success of previous generations in growing this crop locally; although it is no longer used for *chicha*, the kernels contribute to daily and community meals. The tools of farming have also greatly changed. Metal plows, both animal and engine-powered, now till the earth, but the ethnohistorical records suggest that the gendered pattern of men tilling and women planting persists. Knowledge of rainfall patterns and soil characteristics remain fundamental to successful harvests on the peninsula and likely would have been constant over subsequent changes in land ownership. While the distribution of soils and who has access to them has changed, it is certain that the generational knowledge of Indigenous farmers of how best to cultivate these soils enabled the continued productivity of this landscape, including when the lands were unjustly usurped by outside hacienda owners. It was not only Indigenous labor that was exploited at these times but their expert knowledge of this landscape. A large part of what has made these communities resurgent over millennia, even in the face of harsh mistreatment by colonizers, has been their ability to adapt, resist, and rebound by maintaining their relationships with the more-than-human entities of their environment through continued agricultural production. This model of sustainability is not static but very dynamic.

It is important to note that the Taraco existence is not perfect, and the desire to stay on the peninsula and continue to farm is less appealing to younger generations. A tension that exists in Taraco and other rural communities is that this way of living appears antithetical to modernity and development in the twenty-first century. Gaining an education and opportunities to work in the city provide the younger generations entry into global economies and lifeways. Farming is hard work, and many rural areas of Bolivia, including the Taraco Peninsula, still lack many of the basic modern amenities such as plumbing, stable electricity, and, increasingly important, internet connectivity, all of which make living in the countryside less desirable to many. I would argue, however, that they and *we* need these places to continue to thrive if we truly value all aspects of sustainability, not just the health of the planet but also cultural diversity.

I now return to the question I posed in the introduction: what if we *all* placed greater value on other lifeways, learned from them, and worked toward maintaining the beneficial aspects of them? What might those of us living in urban, nonproducer, non-Indigenous contexts learn from this example of resurgent communities based in agriculture? While we cannot replicate the particular multispecies relationships or taskscapes of the Taraco Peninsula, we can actively engage more closely with those more-than-human actors in our respective worlds through establishing community gardens, volunteering at local farms and environmental projects, supporting local, organic farmers and food justice initiatives. We can also engage with local, Indigenous initiatives based in environmental justice and food sovereignty. It is also critical to engage in international movements and support policies that bolster Indigenous sovereignty, foodways, access to land, and the management practices that they have developed over centuries. Such actions ultimately demonstrate that we value these diverse ways of life and acknowledge their critical contributions to our overall well-being and survival. It is my hope that through sharing this history of Indigenous sustainability on the Taraco Peninsula, readers will be inspired to reciprocate by creating and supporting their own resurgent communities.

CHAPTER 1: INDIGENOUS AGRICULTURE AND RESURGENT COMMUNITIES

1. All of the names used here are pseudonyms as the vignettes are composites of the ethnographic experiences that took place between 2003 and 2022.

2. This included participant observation of agricultural practices and semi-structured interviews about the agricultural cycle. I also conducted ethnobotanical collections of wild and domesticated plants as well as mapping of fields accompanied by interviews to record their planting and fallow histories. Further methodological detail of this work can be found in Bruno (2008).

3. An "Aymara-ization" of the Spanish word for mustard, *mostaza*.

CHAPTER 2: TARACO PENINSULA COMMUNITIES

1. A hectare is 10,000 square meters or 2.47 acres. This is the most common unit of measurement for land used in the region.

2. In 2015 the old *sede social* where we lived was converted into a room for the school, and the community constructed a new two-story, multiroom *sede* just to the west (figure 2.2). Additionally, the Taraco Municipality renovated the hacienda house, and it is now a functioning hotel for tourists and archaeologists.

3. According to historical research done by Jewell Soriano (2017), Ocorani is likely the original name of the location

of the Montículo and hacienda house. The whole community was named Chiripa by the Iturralde family, who became the sole landholders in 1910; prior to this the whole area had been divided and sold to 11 different landowners in the late 1800s.

4. In the Andean literature the Archaic periods are defined in terms of uncalibrated years BP while the rest of the archaeological chronology is defined in calendar years (BCE/CE).

5. Carlos Ponce Sangines assigned this moniker to these red-rimmed vessels based on his excavations at the Kalasasaya sector of Tiwanaku.

6. This style was defined by Dwight Wallace from a large collection of complete vessels at the site of Qeya Qollu Chico on the Island of the Sun.

7. Remains of bone and ceramic wool processing and weaving tools are present throughout the Formative period, but sadly we have very little evidence of actual textiles and designs. Because Tiwanaku's influence extended to the dry Pacific Coast, examples of colorful and intricate Tiwanaku textile craft provide us greater insight into what this medium might have contributed to the material culture.

CHAPTER 3: FIELD PREPARATION

1. Other studies found similar soils terms among Aymara groups in Bolivia and Peru (Onofre Mamani 1997; Tschopik 1963).

2. This statement was confirmed through the crop rotation interviews I conducted.

3. Tschopik (1963, 513) recorded similar topographic descriptions in other areas of the lake basin.

CHAPTER 4: PLANTING

1. For a description of how planting is now done following a tractor in place of a *yunta*, see Sammells (2010).

CHAPTER 5: TENDING

1. In many flora *Relbunium ciliatum* is called *Galium corymbosum* (Ruiz and Pav.). Pestalozzi and Nina (1998, 181) also collected both of the species mentioned above but classify them as *Galium corymbosum* R. and P. and *Galium* cf. *richardianum*.

CHAPTER 6: HARVESTING AND PROCESSING

1. TAP labels discrete architectural features as "architectural subdivision," or ASD. The label includes an abbreviation for the site—in this example, Kala Uyuni (KU) and a sequential number based on order of discovery.

CHAPTER 7: EATING

1. During my dissertation fieldwork, I kept a detailed food log using a FileMaker database created by my colleague Clare Sammells, who was also conducting doctoral fieldwork on food and tourism in Tiwanaku, Bolivia.

2. Also see Sammells (2010) for a similar discourse among the Aymara family she lived with in Tiwanaku.

3. In the nearly 20 years that have passed, very few families, including my host family, still fish for income. Those who have stopped commented to me that it was because there are fewer fish in the lake and that the earnings are not worth the effort. Those families that do still fish for income now use plastic buckets to transport their morning catch.

4. The Quechua term for dried meat from which the English term *jerky* derives.

CHAPTER 8: AGRICULTURAL TASKSCAPES

1. In many regions of the Andes these types of social work relations have particular names, such as *ayni* or *m'inka* in the Quechua language (Mayer 2002). *Ayni* refers to reciprocal work; if someone helps a family, then that family is expected to help that person without any type of pay (Carter and Mamani 1982, 132). There is also paid labor called *m'inka*. The person works for a certain amount of time and is paid with cash or sometimes with part of the harvest (Carter and Mamani 1982, 133).

References

Abbott, Mark B., Michael Binford, Mark Brenner, and Kerry Kelts. 1997. "A 3500 14C Yr High-Resolution Record of Water-Level Changes in Lake Titicaca, Bolivia-Peru." *Quaternary Research* 47: 169–80.

Abercrombie, Thomas A. 1998. *Pathways of Memory and Power: Ethnography and History among an Andean People*. Madison: University of Wisconsin Press.

Adelaar, Willem F. H. 2004. *The Languages of the Andes*. Cambridge Language Surveys. Cambridge: Cambridge University Press.

Aellen, Paul, and Theodor Just. 1943. "Key and Synopsis of the American Species of the Genus *Chenopodium* L." *American Midland Naturalist* 30 (1): 47–76.

Albarracin-Jordan, Juan. 1996. *Tiwanaku: Arqueología Regional y Dinámica Segmentaria*. La Paz: Editores Plural.

Albó, Xavier. 1979. "Khitipxtansa? Quienes Somos? Identidad Localista, Etnica y Clasista en los Aymaras de Hoy." *Américan Indígena* 39 (3): 477–528.

Albó, Xavier. 2000. "Aymaras entre Bolivia, Perú y Chile." *Estudios Atacameños (En línea)*, no. 19: 43–74. https://doi.org/10.22199/S07181043.2000.0019.00003.

Albó, Xavier, and Josep María Barnadas. 1985. *La Cara Campesina de Nuestra Historia*. La Paz: UNITAS.

Alconini Mujica, Sonia. 1995. *Ríto, Símbolo e Historia en la Pirámide de Akapana, Tiwanaku*. La Paz: Editorial Acción.

Aldenderfer, Mark S. 1989. "Archaic Period in the South Central Andes." *Journal of World Prehistory* 3 (2): 117–58.

Aldenderfer, Mark S. 1999. "The Late Preceramic–Early Formative Transition on the South-Central Andean Littoral." In *Pacific Latin America in Prehistory: The Evolution of Archaic and Formative Cultures*, edited by Michael Blake, 213–22. Pullman: Washington State University Press.

Aldenderfer, Mark S., and Luis Flores Blanco. 2011. "Reflexiones para Avanzar en los Estudios del Período Arcaico en los Andes Centro-Sur." *Chungará, Revista Antropología Chilena* 43: 531–50.

Allen, Catherine. 1988. *The Hold Life Has: Coca and Cultural Identity in an Andean Community*. Washington, DC: Smithsonian Institution Press.

Allmendinger, Richard W., Teresa E. Jordan, Suzanne M. Kay, and Bryan L. Isacks. 1997. "The Evolution of the Altiplano-Puna Plateau of the Central Andes." *Annual Review of Earth and Planetary Sciences* 25: 139–74.

Altaweel, Mark. 2008. "Investigating Agricultural Sustainability and Strategies in Northern Mesopotamia: Results Produced Using a Socio-Ecological Modeling Approach." *Journal of Archaeological Science* 35: 821–35.

Altieri, Miguel A. 2004. "Linking Ecologists and Traditional Farmers in the Search for Sustainable Agriculture." *Frontiers in Ecology and the Environment* 2 (1): 35–42.

Altieri, Miguel A., and Parviz Koohafkan. 2004. "Globally Important Ingenious Agricultural Heritage Systems (GIAHS): Extent, Significance, and Implications for Development." In *Proceedings of the Second International Workshop and Steering Committee Meeting for the Globally Important Agricultural Heritage Systems (GIAHS) Project*, 7–9. Rome: FAO.

Altieri, Miguel A., and Victor Manuel Toledo. 2011. "The Agroecological Revolution in Latin America: Rescuing Nature, Ensuring Food Sovereignty, and Empowering Peasants." *Journal of Peasant Studies* 38 (3): 587–612.

Anderson, Edgar. 1952. *Plants, Man, and Life*. Boston: Little Brown.

Anderson, Karen. 2013. "Tiwanaku Influence on the Central Valley of Cochabamba." In *Visions of Tiwanaku*, edited by Alexei Vranich and Charles Stanish, 87–112. Monograph 78. Los Angeles: Cotsen Institute of Archaeology, University of California, Los Angeles.

Anderson, Patricia, ed. 1999. *The Prehistory of Agriculture: New Experimental and Ethnographic Approach*. Monograph 40. Los Angeles: University of California, Los Angeles.

Anshuetz, Kurt F., Richard H. Wilshusen, and Cherie L. Scheick. 2001. "An Archaeology of Landscapes: Perspectives and Directions." *Journal of Archaeological Research* 9 (2): 157–211.

Ansión, Juan. 1986. *El Árbol y el Bosque en la Sociedad Andina*. Lima: Proyecto FAO/Holanda/INFOR.

Appadurai, Arjun. 1981. "Gastro-Politics in Hindu South Asia." *American Ethnologist* 8 (3): 494–511.

Argollo, Jaime, Leocaido Ticcla, Alan. L. Kolata, and Oswaldo Rivera. 1996. "Geology, Geomorphology, and Soils of the Tiwanakau and Catari River Basin." In *Tiwanaku and Its Hinterland, Archaeology, and Paleoecology of an Andean Civilization*, vol. 1, *Agroecology*, edited by Alan L. Kolata, 57–88. Washington, DC: Smithsonian Institution Press.

Arkush, Elizabeth. 2006. "Collapse, Conflict, Conquest: The Transformation of Warfare in the Late Prehispanic Andean Highlands." In *The Archaeology of Warfare: Prehistories of Raiding and Conquest*, edited by Elizabeth Arkush and Mark Allen, 286–335. Gainesville: University Press of Florida.

Arnold, Denise, Domingo Jiménez Aruquipa, and Juan Dios de Yapita. 1992. *Hacia un Orden Andino de las Cosas*. La Paz: Talleres Graficos Hisbol.

Arnold, Denise Y., and Christine A. Hastorf. 2008. *Heads of State: Icons, Power, and Politics in the Ancient and Modern Andes*. Walnut Creek, CA: Left Coast Press.

Arnold, Denise, and Juan Dios de Yapita. 1996. *Madre Melliza y Sus Crias—Ispall Mama Wawampi: Antología de la Papa*. La Paz: Hisbol.

Arnold, T. Elliott, Aubrey L. Hillman, Mark B. Abbott, Josef P. Werne, Steven J. McGrath, and Elizabeth N. Arkush. 2021. "Drought and the Collapse of the Tiwanaku Civilization: New Evidence from Lake Orurillo, Peru." *Quaternary Science Reviews* 251 (January): 106693. https://doi.org/10.1016/j.quascirev.2020.106693.

Baitzel, Sarah I. 2018. "Cultural Encounter in the Mortuary Landscape of a Tiwanaku Colony, Moquegua, Peru (AD 650 1100)." *Latin American Antiquity* 29 (3): 421–38.

Baker, Paul A., Sherilyn C. Fritz, J. Garland, and E. Ekdahl. 2005. "Holocene Hydrologic Variation at Lake Titicaca, Bolivia/Peru, and Its Relationship to North Atlantic Climate Variation." *Journal of Quaternary Science* 20 (7–8): 655–62.

Baker, Paul A., Geoffrey O. Seltzer, Sherilyn C. Fritz, Robert B. Dunbar, Matthew J. Grove, Pedro M. Tapia, Scott L. Cross, Harold D. Rowe, and James P. Broda. 2001. "The History of South American Tropical Precipitation for the Past 25,000 Years." *Science* 291: 640–43.

Baleé, William. 1994. *Footprints of the Forest: Ka'apor Ethnobotany—The Historical Ecology of Plant Utilization by an Amazonian People*. New York: Columbia University Press.

Balée, William. 1998. "Historical Ecology: Premises and Postulates." In *Advances in Historical Ecology*, 13–29. New York: Columbia University Press.

Bandy, Matthew S. 1999. "The Montículo Excavations." In *Early Settlement at Chiripa, Bolivia: Research of the Taraco Archaeological Project*, edited by Christine A. Hastorf,

43–50. Contributions of the University of California Archaeological Research Facility 57. Berkeley: University of California, Berkeley.

Bandy, Matthew S. 2001. "Population and History in the Ancient Titicaca Basin." PhD diss., University of California, Berkeley.

Bandy, Matthew S. 2004. "Fissioning, Scalar Stress, and Social Evolution in Early Village Societies." *American Anthropologist* 106 (2): 322–33.

Bandy, Matthew S. 2005. "Energetic Efficiency and Political Expediency in Titicaca Basin Raised Field Agriculture." *Journal of Anthropological Archaeology* 24: 271–96.

Bandy, Matthew S. 2006. "Early Village Society in the Formative Period in the Southern Lake Titicaca Basin." In *Andean Archaeology III: North and South*, edited by William H. Isbell and Helaine Silverman, 210–36. New York: Springer.

Bandy, Matthew S. 2007. "Kala Uyuni and the Titicaca Basin Formative." In *Kala Uyuni: An Early Political Center in the Southern Lake Titicaca Basin, 2003 Excavations of the Taraco Archaeological Project*, edited by Matthew S. Bandy and Christine A. Hastorf, 135–43. Contributions of the Archaeological Research Facility 64. Berkeley: University of California, Berkeley.

Bandy, Matthew S. 2013. "Tiwanaku Origins and Early Development: The Political and Moral Economy of a Hospitality State." In *Visions of Tiwanaku*, edited by Alexei Vranich and Charles Stanish, 135–50. Monograph 78. Los Angeles: Cotsen Institute of Archaeology, University of California, Los Angeles.

Bandy, Matthew S., and Christine A. Hastorf, eds. 2007. *Kala Uyuni: An Early Political Center in the Southern Lake Titicaca Basin, 2003 Excavations of the Taraco Archaeological Project*. Contributions of the Archaeological Research Facility 64. Berkeley: University of California, Berkeley.

Bandy, Matthew S., and John W. Janusek. 2005. "Settlement Patterns, Administrative Boundaries, and Internal Migration in the Early Colonial Period." In *Advances in Titicaca Basin Archaeology—1*, edited by Charles Stanish, Amanda B. Cohen, and Mark S. Aldenderfer, 267–88. Los Angeles: Cotsen Institute of Archaeology, University of California, Los Angeles.

Barbieri, Chiara, Paul Heggarty, Loredana Castrì, Donata Luiselli, and Davide Pettener. 2011. "Mitochondrial DNA Variability in the Titicaca Basin: Matches and Mismatches with Linguistics and Ethnohistory." *American Journal of Human Biology* 23 (1): 89–99. https://doi.org/10.1002/ajhb.21107.

Barrett, John C. 1994. *Fragments from Antiquity: An Archaeology of Social Life in Britain, 2900–1200 BC*. Oxford: Blackwell.

Basso, Keith H. 1996. *Wisdom Sits in Places: Landscape and Language among the Western Apache*. Albuquerque: University of New Mexico Press.

Bastien, Joseph W. 1985. *Mountain of the Condor: Metaphor and Ritual in an Andean Ayllu.* Long Grove, IL: Waveland Press.

Batai, Ken, and Sloan R. Williams. 2014. "Mitochondrial Variation among the Aymara and the Signatures of Population Expansion in the Central Andes." *American Journal of Human Biology* 26 (3): 321–30. https://doi.org/10.1002/ajhb.22507.

Bateson, Gregory. 1972. *Steps to an Ecology of Mind: Collected Essays in Anthropology, Psychiatry, Evolution, and Epistemology.* San Francisco: Chandler Publishing.

Bauer, Andrew M., and Peter G. Johansen. 2011. *The Archaeology of Politics the Materiality of Political Practice and Action in the Past.* Newcastle upon Tyne: Cambridge Scholars Publishing.

Bauer, Andrew M., and Steve Kosiba. 2016. "How Things Act: An Archaeology of Materials in Political Life." *Journal of Social Archaeology* 16 (2): 115–41. https://doi.org/10.1177/1469605316641244.

Bauer, Brian, and Charles Stanish. 2001. *Ritual and Pilgrimage in the Ancient Andes: The Islands of the Sun and the Moon.* Austin: University of Texas Press.

Bazile, Didier, Sven-Erik Jacobsen, and Alexis Verniau. 2016. "The Global Expansion of Quinoa: Trends and Limits." *Frontiers in Plant Science* 7:622.

Beck, Robin. 2004. "Architecture and Polity in the Formative Lake Titicaca Basin, Bolivia." *Latin American Antiquity* 15 (3): 323–43.

Bellentani, Federico. 2016. "Landscape as Text." *Tartu Semiotics Library*, no. 16: 76–88.

Bennett, Wendell C. 1934. *Excavations at Tiahuanaco.* Anthropological Papers of the American Museum of Natural History 34, pt. 3. New York: American Museum of Natural History.

Bennett, Wendell C. 1936. "Excavations in Bolivia." *Anthropological Papers of the American Museum of Natural History* 35 (4): 329–507.

Bennett, Wendell C., and Junius B. Bird. 1949. *Andean Culture History.* Handbook Series, no. 15. New York: American Museum of Natural History.

Bentley, Jefferey W., Morag Webb, Silvio Nina, and Salomón Pérez. 2005. "Even Useful Weeds Are Pests: Ethnobotany in the Bolivian Andes." *International Journal of Pest Management* 51 (3): 189–207.

Benton, Jane. 1999. *Agrarian Reform in Theory and Practice: A Study of the Lake Titicaca Region of Bolivia.* Brookfield, VT: Ashgate.

Berenguer Rodriguez, José Angel. 1998. "La Iconografía del Poder en Tiwanaku y su Rol en la Integración de Zonas de Frontera." *Boletín del Museo Chileno de Arte Precolombino* 7: 19–37.

Beresford-Jones, David. 2011. *The Lost Woodlands of Ancient Nasca.* New York: Oxford University Press.

Bermann, Marc. 1994. *Lukurmata: Household Archaeology in Prehispanic Bolivia.* Princeton, NJ: Princeton University Press.

Berryman, Carrie Anne. 2010. "Food, Feasts, and the Construction of Identity and Power in Ancient Tiwanaku: A Bioarchaeological Perspective." PhD diss., Vanderbilt University.

Binford, Michael W., Alan L. Kolata, Mark Brenner, John W. Janusek, Matthew T. Seddon, Mark Abbott, and John H. Curtis. 1997. "Climate Variation and the Rise and Fall of an Andean Civilization." *Quaternary Research* 47: 235–48.

Binford, Michael W., Mark Brenner, and Barbara W. Leyden. 1996. "Paleoecology and Tiwanaku Agroecosystems." In *Tiwanaku and Its Hinterland, Archaeology, and Paleoecology of an Andean Civilization*, vol. 1, *Agroecology*, edited by Alan L. Kolata, 89–108. Washington, DC: Smithsonian Institution Press.

Biwer, Matthew E., Willy Yépez Álvarez, Stefanie L. Bautista, and Justin Jennings. 2022. "Hallucinogens, Alcohol, and Shifting Leadership Strategies in the Ancient Peruvian Andes." *Antiquity* 96 (385): 142–58. https://doi.org/10.15184/aqy.2021.177.

Bonavia, Duccio. 2008. *The South American Camelids.* Monograph 64. Los Angeles: Cotsen Institute of Archaeology, University of California, Los Angeles.

Boserup, Esther. 1965. *The Conditions of Agricultural Growth: The Economics of Agrarian Change under Population Pressure.* New York: Aldine Publishing.

Boulange, Bruno, and Jaen E. Aquize. 1981. "La Sédimentation Actuelle dans le Lac Titicaca et de Son Bassin Versant." *Rev. Hydrobiologic Tropical* 14 (4): 269–87.

Bourdieu, Pierre. 1977. *Outline of a Theory of Practice.* Cambridge: Cambridge University Press.

Bouysse-Cassagne, Thérèse. 1992. "Past and Present Aymara Populations." In *Lake Titicaca: A Synthesis of Limnological Knowledge*, edited by Claude Dejoux and André Iltis, 488–94. Dordrecht, the Netherlands: Kluwer Academic.

Boyd, Robert, and Peter J. Richerson. 1988. *Culture and the Evolutionary Process.* Chicago: University of Chicago Press.

Brack Egg, Antonio. 1999. *Diccionario Enciclopédico de Plantas Útiles del Perú.* Cusco: Centro de Estudios Regionales Andinos Bartolomé de la Casas.

Braudel, Fernand. 2023. *The Mediterranean and the Mediterranean World in the Age of Philip II.* Berkeley: University of California Press.

Brightman, Marc, and Jerome Lewis. 2017. *The Anthropology of Sustainability: Beyond Development and Progress.* New York: Palgrave Macmillan. http://ebookcentral.proquest.com/lib/dickinson/detail.action?docID=4939332.

Broughton, Jack M., and James F. O'Connell. 1999. "On Evolutionary Ecology, Selectionist Archaeology, and Behavioral Archaeology." *American Antiquity* 64 (1): 153–65. https://doi.org/10.2307/2694351.

Browman, David L. 1978a. "The Temple of Chiripa (Lake Titicaca, Bolivia)." In *III Congresso Peruano "El Hombre y la Cultura Andina" Actas y Trabajos*, edited by Matos M. Ramiro, 2:807–13. Lima: Universidad Nacional Mayor de San Marcos.

Browman, David L. 1978b. "Toward the Development of the Tiahuanaco (Tiwanaku) State." In *Advances in Andean Archaeology*, 327–49. The Hague: Mouton.

Browman, David L. 1989. "Chenopod Cultivation, Lacustrine Resources, and Fuel Use at Chiripa, Bolivia." In *New World Paleoethnobotany: Collected Papers in Honor of Leonard W. Blake*, edited by Eric E. Voigt and Deborah M. Pearsall, 137–72. Missouri Archaeologist 47. Columbia: Missouri Archaeological Society.

Browman, David L. 1994. "Titicaca Basin Archaeolinguistics: Uru, Pukina and Aymara AD 750–1450." *World Archaeology* 26 (2): 235–51.

Browman, David L. 1998. "Lithic Provenience Analysis and Emerging Material Complexity at Formative Period Chiripa, Bolivia." *Andean Past* 5: 301–24.

Bruno, Maria C. 2006. "A Morphological Approach to Documenting the Domestication of *Chenopodium* in the Andes." In *Documenting Domestication: New Genetic and Archaeological Paradigms*, edited by Melinda Zeder, Daniel Bradley, Eve Emshwiller, and Bruce D. Smith, 32–45. Berkeley: University of California Press.

Bruno, Maria C. 2007. "Excavations in the AQ (Ayrampu Qontu) Sector." In *Kala Uyuni: An Early Political Center in the Southern Lake Titicaca Basin, 2003 Excavations of the Taraco Archaeological Project*, edited by Matthew S. Bandy and Christine A. Hastorf, 19–23. Contributions of the Archaeological Research Facility 64. Berkeley: University of California, Berkeley.

Bruno, Maria C. 2008. "Waranq Waranqa: Ethnobotanical Perspectives on Agricultural Intensification in the Lake Titicaca Basin (Taraco Peninsula, Bolivia)." PhD diss., Washington University, St. Louis.

Bruno, Maria C. 2009. "Practice and History in the Transition to Food Production." *Current Anthropology* 50 (5): 703–6.

Bruno, Maria C. 2011. "Farmers' Experience and Knowledge: Utilizing Soil Diversity to Overcome Rainfall Variability on the Taraco Peninsula, Bolivia." In *Sustainable Lifeways: Cultural Persistence in an Ever-Changing Environment*, edited by Naomi Miller, Katherine Moore, and Kathleen Ryan, 210–43. Philadelphia: University of Pennsylvania Press.

Bruno, Maria C. 2014a. "Beyond Raised Fields: Exploring Farming Practices and Processes of Agricultural Change in the Ancient Lake Titicaca Basin of the Andes." *American Anthropologist* 116 (1): 1–16.

Bruno, Maria C. 2014b. "Processes of Prehistoric Crop Diversification in the Lake Titicaca Basin of the South American Andes." In *Plants and People: Choices and*

Diversity through Time, edited by Alexandre Chevalier, Elena Marinova, and Leonor Peña-Chocarro, 86–91. Woodbridge, CT: Oxbow Press.

Bruno, Maria C. 2023. "Archaeobotanical Insights into Kañawa (*Chenopodium pallidicaule* Aellen) Domestication: A Rustic Seed Crop of the Andean Altiplano." *Agronomy* 13 (8): 2085. https://doi.org/10.3390/agronomy13082085.

Bruno, Maria C., José M. Capriles, Christine A. Hastorf, Sherilyn C. Fritz, D. Marie Weide, Alejandra I. Domic, and Paul A. Baker. 2021. "The Rise and Fall of Wiñaymarka: Rethinking Cultural and Environmental Interactions in the Southern Basin of Lake Titicaca." *Human Ecology* 49 (2): 131–45. https://doi.org/10.1007/s10745-021-00222-3.

Bruno, Maria C., and Christine A. Hastorf. 2016. "Gifts from the Camelids: Archaeobotanical Insights into Camelid Pastoralism through the Study of Dung." In *The Archaeology of Andean Pastoralism*, edited by José M. Capriles and Nicholas Tripcevich, 55–65. Albuquerque: University of New Mexico Press.

Bruno, Maria C., and Mary Leighton. 2007. "Additional Excavations in the KU Area—N894/E639." In *Kala Uyuni: An Early Political Center in the Southern Lake Titicaca Basin, 2003 Excavations of the Taraco Archaeological Project*, edited by Matthew S. Bandy and Christine A. Hastorf, 35–40. Contributions of the Archaeological Research Facility 64. Berkeley: University of California, Berkeley.

Bruno, Maria C., Eduardo Machicado Murillo, Vannesa Jiménez, José M. Capriles Flores, and Kathryn Killackey. 2006. "Excavaciones en Sonaji 2005. Proyecto Arqueológico Taraco: Informe de las Excavaciones de la Temporada Del 2005 en los Sitios de Sonaje y Kala Uyuni." Report submitted to the Unidad Nacional de Arqueología de Bolivia, La Paz.

Bruno, Maria C., Milton Pinto, and Wilfredo Rojas. 2018. "Identifying Domesticated and Wild Kañawa (*Chenopodium pallidicaule*) in the Archaeobotanical Record of the Lake Titicaca Basin of the Andes." *Economic Botany* 72 (2): 137–49. https://doi.org/10.1007/s12231-018-9416-4.

Bruno, Maria C., and Andrew P. Roddick. 2011. "Trinchera Este-Oeste de 8 × 2m (N893/E641)." In *Excavaciones en Kala Uyuni: Informe de la Temporada 2009 del Proyecto Arqueológico de Taraco*, 44–55. Report submitted to the Unidad Nacional de Arqueología de Bolivia, La Paz.

Bruno, Maria C., and William T. Whitehead. 2003. "*Chenopodium* Cultivation and Formative Period Agriculture at Chiripa, Bolivia." *Latin American Antiquity* 14 (3): 339–55.

Buechler, Hans C. 1969. "Land Tenure and Use." In *Land Reform and Social Revolution in Bolivia*, edited by Dwight B. Heath and Charles J. Erasmus, 176–99. New York: Praeger.

Buechler, Hans C., and Judith-Maria Buechler. 1971. *The Bolivian Aymara*. New York: Holt, Rinehart and Winston.

Burke, Melvin. 1971. "Land Reform in the Lake Titicaca Region." In *Beyond the Revolution: Bolivia since 1952*, 301–39. Pittsburgh, PA: University of Pittsburgh Press. https://digitalcommons.library.umaine.edu/eco_facpub/6.

Bush, Mark B. 2020. "New and Repeating Tipping Points: The Interplay of Fire, Climate Change, and Deforestation in Neotropical Ecosystems1." *Annals of the Missouri Botanical Garden* 105 (3): 393–404. https://doi.org/10.3417/2020565.

Cadena, Marisol de la. 2015. *Earth Beings: Ecologies of Practice across Andean Worlds*. Durham: Duke University Press.

Canessa, Andrew. 2012. *Intimate Indigeneities: Race, Sex, and History in the Small Spaces of Andean Life*. Durham: Duke University Press.

Capriles, José M. 2006. "A Zooarchaeological Analysis of Fish Remains from the Lake Titicaca Formative Period (ca. 1000 BC–AD 500) Site of Kala Uyuni, Bolivia." MA thesis, Washington University, St. Louis.

Capriles, José M. 2013. "State of the Fish: Changing Patterns in Fish Exploitation and Consumption during Tiwanaku (AD 500–1100) in Iwawi, Bolivia." In *Advances in Titicaca Basin Archaeology—2*, edited by Abigail Levine and Alexei Vranich, 105–16. Los Angeles: Cotsen Institute of Archaeology, University of California, Los Angeles.

Capriles, José M., and Christine A. Hastorf. Forthcoming. "Absolute Dating of Chiripa." In *Archaeology at Formative Chiripa 1998–2018: Production, Engagement, and Longevity; Excavations of the Taraco Archaeological Project at Chiripa, Bolivia*, edited by Christin A. Hastorf. Berkeley: Archaeological Research Facility, University of California, Berkley.

Capriles, José M., and Eduardo Machicado Murillo. 2011. "Kala Uyuni 2009, Sector Sur (N884/E664): ASD 7 y ASD 8." In *Excavaciones en Kala Uyuni: Informe de la Temporada 2009 del Proyecto Arqueológico de Taraco*, 56–75. Report submitted to the Unidad Nacional de Arqueología de Bolivia, La Paz.

Capriles, José M., Katherine M. Moore, Alejandra I. Domic, and Christine A. Hastorf. 2014. "Fishing and Environmental Change during the Emergence of Social Complexity in the Lake Titicaca Basin." *Journal of Anthropological Archaeology* 34: 66–77.

Cardenas, Martín. 1989. *Manual de Plantas Económicas de Bolivia*. La Paz: Editorial Los Amigos del Libro.

Carter, William, and Mauricio Mamani. 1982. *Irpa Chico: Individuo y Comunidad en la Cultura Aymara*. La Paz: Libreria Editorial Juventud.

Chávez, Sergio J. 1992. "The Conventionalized Rules in Pucara Pottery Technology and Iconography: Implications for Socio-Political Development in the Northern Lake Titicaca Basin." PhD diss., Michigan State University.

Chávez, Sergio J., and Karen L. Mohr-Chávez. 1975. "A Carved Stela from Taraco, Peru, Puno, Peru and the Definition of an Early Style of Stone Sculpture from the Altiplano of Peru and Bolivia." *Ñawpa Pacha* 13: 45–90.

Chew, Sing C. 2001. *World Ecological Degradation: Accumulation, Urbanization, and Deforestation 3000 BC–AD 2000*. Walnut Creek, CA: Altamira Press.

Chiou, Katherine L., Christine A. Hastorf, Víctor F. Vásquez, Teresa Rosales Tham, Duccio Bonavia, and Tom D. Dillehay. 2017. "Chile Pepper Distribution and Use." In *Where the Land Meets the Sea: Fourteen Millennia of Human History at Huaca Prieta, Peru*, edited by Tom D. Dillehay, 645–55. Austin: University of Texas Press.

Cipolla, Lisa M. 2005. "Preceramic Period Settlement Patterns in the Huancané-Putina River Valley, Northern Titicaca Basin, Peru." In *Advances in Titicaca Basin Archaeology—1*, edited by Charles Stanish, Amanda Cohen, and Mark S. Aldenderfer, 55–64. Los Angeles: Cotsen Institute of Archaeology, University of California, Los Angeles.

Clapperton, Chalmers M. 1993. *Quaternary Geology and Geomorphology of South America*. Amsterdam: Elsevier.

Cohen, Amanda B. 2010. "Ritual and Architecture in the Titicaca Basin: The Development of the Sunken Court Complex in the Formative Period." PhD diss., University of California, Los Angeles.

Cohen, Amanda B., and Andrew P. Roddick. 2007. "Excavations in the AC (Achachi Coa Kkollu) Sector." In *Kala Uyuni: An Early Political Center in the Southern Lake Titicaca Basin, 2003 Excavations of the Taraco Archaeological Project*, edited by Matthew S. Bandy and Christine A. Hastorf, 41–65. Contributions of the Archaeological Research Facility 64. Berkeley: University of California, Berkeley.

Cohen, Mark N. 1977. *The Food Crisis in Prehistory*. New Haven, CT: Yale University Press.

Cole, Jeffrey A. 1985. *The Potosí Mita, 1573–1700: Compulsory Indian Labor in the Andes*. Stanford, CA: Stanford University Press.

Conklin, William J. 2013. "The Cultural Implications of Tiwanaku and Huari Textiles." In *Visions of Tiwanaku*, edited by Alexei Vranich and Charles Stanish, 65–86. Monograph 78. Los Angeles: Cotsen Institute of Archaeology, University of California, Los Angeles.

Couture, Nicole C. 1993. "Excavations at Mollo Kontu, Tiwanaku." Master's thesis, University of Chicago.

Couture, Nicole C. 2002. "The Construction of Power: Monumental Space and Elite Residence at Tiwanaku, Bolivia." PhD diss., University of Chicago.

Couture, Nicole C. 2004. "Monumental Space, Courtly Style, and Elite Life at Tiwanaku." In *Tiwanaku: Ancestors of the Inca*, edited by Margaret Young-Sanchez, 126–49. Denver: Denver Art Museum.

Couture, Nicole C., and Kathryn Sampeck. 2003. "Putuni: A History of Palace Architecture at Tiwanaku." In *Tiwanaku and Its Hinterland: Archaeological and Paleoecological Investigations of an Andean Civilization*, vol. 2, *Urban and Rural Archaeology*, edited by Alan L. Kolata, 226–63. Washington, DC: Smithsonian Institution Press.

Craig, Nathan, Mark Aldenderfer, P. A. Baker, and Catherine Rigsby. 2010. "Terminal Archaic Settlement Pattern and Land Cover Change in the Rio Ilave, Southwestern Lake Titicaca Basin, Peru." In *The Archaeology of Anthropogenic Environments*, edited by Rebecca M. Dean, 35–53. Carbondale: Center for Archaeological Investigations, Southern Illinois University Carbondale.

Craig, Nathan, Mark S. Aldenderfer, Catherine A. Rigsby, Paul A. Baker, and Luis Flores Blanco. 2011. "Geologic Constraints on Rain-Fed Qocha Reservoir Agricultural Infrastructure, Northern Lake Titicaca Basin, Peru." *Journal of Archaeological Science* 38 (11): 2897–2907. https://doi.org/10.1016/j.jas.2011.05.005.

Crosby, Alfred W. 2003. *The Columbian Exchange: Biological and Cultural Consequences of 1492*. 30th anniversary ed. Westport, CT: Praeger.

Cross, Scott, Paul A. Baker, Geoffrey O. Seltzer, Sherilyn C. Fritz, and Robert B. Dunbar. 2000. "A New Estimate of the Holocene Lowstand Level of Lake Titicaca, Central Andes, and Implications for Tropical Paleohydrology." *The Holocene* 10 (1): 21–32.

Cross, Scott, Paul Baker, Geoffrey O. Seltzer, Sherilyn C. Fritz, and Robert B. Dunbar. 2001. "Late Quaternary Climate and Hydrology of Tropical South America Inferred from an Isotopic and Chemical Model of Lake Titicaca, Bolivia and Peru." *Quaternary Research* 56: 1–9.

Crumley, Carole L. 1994. "Historical Ecology: A Multidimensional Ecological Orientation." In *Historical Ecology: Cultural Knowledge and Changing Landscapes*, 1–16. Sante Fe, NM: School for American Research Press.

Cutler, Hugh C., and Martín Cárdenas. 1947. *Chicha: A Native South American Beer*. Botanical Museum Leaflets 13, no. 3. Cambridge, MA: Botanical Museum, Harvard University.

da Cunha, Manuela Carneiro. 2017. "Traditional People, Collectors of Diversity." In *The Anthropology of Sustainability: Beyond Development and Progress*, edited by Marc Brightman and Jerome Lewis, 257–72. Palgrave Studies in Anthropology of

Sustainability. New York: Palgrave Macmillan. https://doi.org/10.1057/978-1-137-56636-2_15.

Dean, Emily, and David Kojan. 2001. "Ceremonial Households and Domestic Temples: 'Fuzzy' Definitions in the Andean Formative." In *Past Ritual and the Everyday*, edited by Christine A. Hastorf, 109–35. Krober Anthropological Society Papers, no. 85. Berkeley: University of California, Berkeley.

de Certeau, Michel. 1984. *The Practice of Everyday Life*. Translated by Steven Rendall. Berkeley: University of California Press.

Denevan, William M. 1995. "Prehistoric Agricultural Methods as Models for Sustainability." *Advanced Plant Pathology* 11: 21–43.

Denevan, William M. 2001. *Cultivated Landscapes of Native Amazonia and the Andes*. Oxford: Oxford University Press.

Dennell, R. W. 1976. "The Economic Importance of Plant Resources Represented on Archaeological Sites." *Journal of Archaeological Science* 3 (3): 229–47. https://doi.org/10.1016/0305-4403(76)90057-1.

Descola, Philippe. 1994. *In the Society of Nature: A Native Ecology in Amazonia*. Cambridge: Cambridge University Press.

de Wet, J. M. J., and Jack R. Harlan. 1975. "Weeds and Domesticates: Evolution in the Man-Made Habitat." *Economic Botany* 29: 99–107.

Dincauze, Dena F. 2000. *Environmental Archaeology: Principles and Practice*. Cambridge: Cambridge University Press.

Douglas, Mary. 2018. "Deciphering a Meal." In *Food and Culture: A Reader*, 4th ed., edited by Carole Counihan, Penny Van Esterik, and Alice Julier, 29–47. New York: Routledge.

Emshwiller, Eve. 2006. "Origins of Polyploid Crops: The Example of the Octoploid Tuber Crop *Oxalis tuberosa*." In *Documenting Domestication: New Genetic and Archaeological Paradigms*, edited by Melinda A. Zeder, Daniel G. Bradley, and Bruce D. Smith, 153–68. Berkeley: University of California Press.

Erickson, Clark L. 1976. "Chiripa Ethnobotanical Report: Flotation Recovered Archaeological Remains from an Early Settled Village on the Altiplano of Bolivia." Honors thesis, Washington University, St. Louis.

Erickson, Clark L. 1988a. "An Archaeological Investigation of Raised Field Agriculture in the Lake Titicaca Basin of Peru." PhD diss., University of Illinois, Urbana-Champaign.

Erickson, Clark L. 1988b. "Raised Field Agriculture in the Lake Titicaca Basin." *Expedition* 30 (3): 8–16.

Erickson, Clark L. 1996. *Investigación Arqueológica del Sistema Agrícola de los Camellones en la Cuenca del Lago Titicaca del Perú*. La Paz: PIWA and El Centro de Información para el Desarrollo.

Erickson, Clark L. 1999. "Neo-Environmental Determinism and Agrarian 'Collapse' in Andean Prehistory." *Antiquity* 73 (281): 634–42.

Erickson, Clark L. 2000. "The Lake Titicaca Basin: A Precolumbian Built Landscape." In *Imperfect Balance: Landscape Transformations in the Precolumbian Americas*, edited by D. Lentz, 311–56. New York: Columbia University Press.

Erickson, Clark L. 2006. "The Domesticated Landscapes of the Bolivian Amazon." In *Time and Complexity in Historical Ecology: Studies in Neotropical Lowlands*, edited by William Balée and Clark Erickson, 235–78. New York: Columbia University Press.

Escalante Moscoso, Javier F. 1997. *Arquitectura Prehispánica en los Andes Bolivianos*. La Paz: CIMA.

Fabricant, Nicole. 2010. "Between the Romance of Collectivism and the Reality of Individualism: Ayllu Rhetoric in Bolivia's Landless Peasant Movement." *Latin American Perspectives* 37 (4): 88–107. https://doi.org/10.1177/0094582X10373352.

Falconer, Steven E., and Charles L. Redman. 2009. "The Archaeology of Early States and Their Landscapes." In *Polities and Power: Archaeological Perspectives on the Landscapes of Early States*, 1–10. Tucson: University of Arizona Press.

FAO (Food and Agriculture Organization of the United Nations). 2011. "Andean Agriculture | Globally Important Agricultural Heritage Systems (GIAHS) | Food and Agriculture Organization of the United Nations | GIAHS | Food and Agriculture Organization of the United Nations." 2011. https://www.fao.org/giahs/giahsaroundtheworld/designated-sites/latin-america-and-the-caribbean/andean-agriculture/en/.

Fisher, Chelsea. 2020. "Archaeology for Sustainable Agriculture." *Journal of Archaeological Research* 28 (3): 393–441. https://doi.org/10.1007/s10814-019-09138-5.

Flannery, Kent V. 1969. "Origins and Ecological Effects of Early Agriculture." In *The Domestication and Exploitation of Plants and Animals*, edited by P. J. Ucko and G. W. Dimbley, 73–100. London: Duckworth.

Flores, Edmundo. 1955. "Taraco: Monografía de un Latifundio del Altiplano Boliviano." *El Trimestre Económico* 22 (86 [2]): 209–29.

Flores Ochoa, Jorge A. 1987. "Cultivation in the Qocha of the South Andean Puna." In *Arid Land Use Strategies and Risk Management in the Andes: A Regional Anthropological Perspective*, edited by David L. Browman, 271–96. Boulder: Westview Press.

Fontenla Alvarez, Ruth, Hannah Sistrunk, and Maria C. Bruno. 2011. "Sector Norte de la Gran Trinchera Norte-Sur (N902/E650)." In *Excavaciones en Kala Uyuni: Informe de la Temporada 2009 del Proyecto Arqueológico de Taraco*, 18–33. Report submitted to the Unidad Nacional de Arqueología de Bolivia, La Paz.

Ford, Richard I. 1994. "Ethnobotany." In *The Nature and Status of Ethnobotany*, 2nd ed., viii–xxxii. Ann Arbor: Museum of Anthropology, University of Michigan.

Fowler, Catherine S. 1996. "Historical Perspectives on Timbisha Shoshone Land Management Practices, Death Valley, California." In *Case Studies in Environmental Archaeology*, edited by Elizabeth J. Reitz, Lee A. Newsom, and Sylvia J. Scudder, 87–101. New York: Plenum Press.

Franco Inojoso, José María. 1940. "Informe sobre los Restos Arqueológicos de la Misión Kidder en Pukara, Puno (Enero a Julio de 1939)." *Revista del Museo Nacional* 9 (2): 255–77.

Franquemont, Christine, Timothy Plowman, Edward Franquemont, Steven R. King, Christine Niezgoda, Wade Davis, and Calvin R. Sperling. 1990. *The Ethnobotany of Chinchero, an Andean Community in Southern Peru*. Botany New Series No. 24. Chicago: Field Museum of Natural History.

Franquemont, Edward. 1986. "The Ancient Pottery from Pucara, Peru." *Ñawpa Pacha* 24: 1–30.

Fritz, Gayle J., Maria C. Bruno, BrieAnna S. Langlie, Bruce D. Smith, and Logan Kistler. 2017. "Cultigen Chenopods in the Americas: A Hemispherical Perspective." In *Social Perspectives on Ancient Lives from Paleoethnobotanical Data*, edited by Matthew P. Sayre and Maria C. Bruno, 55–75. Cham, Switzerland: Springer.

Gade, Daniel W. 1970. "Ethnobotany of Cañihua (*Chenopodium pallidicaule*), Rustic Seed Crop of the Altiplano." *Economic Botany* 24: 55–61.

Gamble, Clive. 1999. *The Palaeolithic Societies of Europe*. Cambridge: Cambridge University Press.

Garreaud, René. 1999. "Multiscale Analysis of the Summertime Precipitation over the Central Andes." *Monthly Weather Review* 127: 901–21.

Gell, Alfred. 1992. *The Anthropology of Time: Cultural Constructions of Temporal Maps and Images*. Oxford: Berg.

Giddens, Anthony. 1979. *Central Problems in Social Theory: Action, Structure and Contradiction in Social Analysis*. Berkeley: University of California Press.

Gold, Mary V. 2007. "Sustainable Agriculture: Definitions and Terms | Alternative Farming Systems Information Center | NAL | USDA." 2007. https://www.nal.usda.gov/legacy/afsic/sustainable-agriculture-definitions-and-terms#toc2.

Goldstein, Paul S. 1993a. *House, Community, and the State in the Earliest Tiwanaku Colony: Domestic Patterns and State Integration at Omo M12, Moquegua*. Domestic

Architecture, Ethnicity, and Complementarity in the South-Central Andes. Iowa City: University of Iowa Press.

Goldstein, Paul S. 1993b. "Tiwanaku Temples and State Expansion: A Tiwanaku Sunken-Court Temple in Moquegua, Peru." *Latin American Antiquity* 4 (1): 22–47.

Goldstein, Paul S. 1998. "Moquegua y el Imperio Tiwanaku." In *Moquegua, los Primeros Doce Mil Años*, edited by Karen Wise, translated by Monika Barrionuevo, 45–48. Arequipa, Peru: Museo Contisuyo.

Goldstein, Paul S. 2003. "From Stew-Eaters to Maize-Drinkers: The Chicha Economy and the Tiwanaku Expansion." In *The Archaeology and Politics of Food and Feasting in Early States and Empires*, edited by Tamara L. Bray, 143–72. New York: Springer.

Goodman Elgar, Melissa. 2004. "Microstratigraphy and Soil Analysis." In *Taraco Archaeological Project: Report on 2003 Excavations at Kala Uyuni*, 86–94. Report submitted to the Unidad Nacional de Arqueología de Bolivia, La Paz.

Gosden, Chris, and Lesley Head. 1994. "Landscape—A Usefully Ambiguous Concept." *Archaeology in Oceania* 29 (3): 113–16.

Gose, Peter. 1994. *Deathly Waters and Hungry Mountains: Agrarian Rituals and Class Formation in an Andean Town*. Toronto: University of Toronto Press.

Gose, Peter. 2018. "Mountains and Pachakutis. Ontology, Politics, Temporality." In *Powerful Places in the Ancient Andes*, edited by Justin Jennings and Edward R. Swenson, 55–90. Albuquerque: University of New Mexico Press.

Graeber, David, and David Wengrow. 2021. *The Dawn of Everything: A New History of Humanity*. New York: Picador.

Graf, Kurt. 1981. "Palyonological Investigations of Two Post-Glacial Peat Bogs Near the Boundary of Peru and Bolivia." *Journal of Biogeography* 8: 353–68.

Graffam, Gray. 1990. "Raised Fields without Bureaucracy: An Archaeological Examination of Intensive Wetland Cultivation in the Pampa Koani Zone, Lake Titicaca, Bolivia." PhD diss., University of Toronto.

Graffam, Gray. 1992. "Beyond State Collapse: Rural History, Raised Fields, and Pastoralism in the South Andes." *American Anthropologist* 94 (4): 882–904.

Grobman, Alexander, Duccio Bonavia, Tom D. Dillehay, Dolores R. Piperno, José Iriarte, and Irene Holst. 2012. "Preceramic Maize from Paredones and Huaca Prieta, Peru." *Proceedings of the National Academy of Sciences* 109 (5): 1755–59.

Grun, Paul. 1990. "The Evolution of Cultivated Potatoes." *Economic Botany* 44 (3 [Supplement]): 39–55.

Guaman Poma de Ayala, Felipe. 1615. "September, Cycle of Sowing Maize (1165–1166) [1166]: Guaman Poma, Nueva Corónica y Buen Gobierno (1615)." http://www5.kb.dk/permalink/2006/poma/1166/en/text?open=id2978806.

Guédron, Stéphane, Christophe Delaere, Sherilyn. C. Fritz, Julie Tolu, Pierre Sabatier, Anne-Lise Devel, Carlos Heredia, Claire Vérin, Eduardo Q. Alves, and Paul A. Baker. 2023. "Holocene Variations in Lake Titicaca Water Level and Their Implications for Sociopolitical Developments in the Central Andes." *Proceedings of the National Academy of Sciences* 120 (2): e2215882120. https://doi.org/10.1073/pnas.2215882120.

Guillet, David. 1987. "Terracing and Irrigation in the Peruvian Highlands." *Current Anthropology* 28 (4): 409–30.

Guttman-Bond, Erika. 2010. "Sustainability out of the Past: How Archaeology Can Save the Planet." *World Archaeology* 42 (3): 355–66.

Haas, W. Randall, and Carlos Viviano Llave. 2015. "Hunter-Gatherers on the Eve of Agriculture: Investigations at Soro Mik'aya Patjxa, Lake Titicaca Basin, Peru, 8000–6700 BP." *Antiquity* 89 (348): 1297–1312.

Haas, W. Randall, Ioana C. Stefanescu, Alexander Garcia-Putnam, Mark S. Aldenderfer, Mark T. Clementz, Melissa S. Murphy, Carlos Viviano Llave, and James T. Watson. 2017. "Humans Permanently Occupied the Andean Highlands by at Least 7 Ka." *Royal Society Open Science* 4 (6): 170331. https://doi.org/10.1098/rsos.170331.

Hallam, Elizabeth, and Tim Ingold. 2016. *Making and Growing: Anthropological Studies of Organisms and Artefacts*. New York: Routledge.

Hand, Carol. 2016. *Sustainable Agriculture*. Cutting-Edge Science + Technology. Minneapolis, MN: Essential Library.

Hanselman, Jennifer A., William D. Gosling, Gina M. Paduano, and Mark B. Bush. 2005. "Contrasting Pollen Histories of MIS 5e and the Holocene from Lake Titicaca (Bolivia/Peru)." *Journal of Quaternary Science* 20 (7–8): 663–70. https://doi.org/10.1002/jqs.979.

Harkey, Anna, and Lee Steadman. 2011. "Cerámica de la Temporada 2009 en Kala Uyuni." In *Excavaciones en Kala Uyuni: Informe de la Temporada 2009 del Proyecto Arqueológico de Taraco*, 76–85. Report submitted to the Unidad Nacional de Arqueología de Bolivia, La Paz.

Harlan, Jack R., and J. M. J. de Wet. 1965. "Some Thoughts on Weeds." *Economic Botany* 19: 16–24.

Hastorf, Christine A. 1999. *Early Settlement at Chiripa, Bolivia: Research of the Taraco Archaeological Project*. Contributions of the University of California Archaeological Research Facility 57. Berkeley: Archaeological Research Facility, University of California, Berkeley.

Hastorf, Christine A. 2003. "Community with the Ancestors: Ceremonies and Social Memory in the Middle Formative at Chiripa, Bolivia." *Journal of Anthropological Archaeology* 22: 305–32.

Hastorf, Christine A. 2005. "The Upper (Middle and Late) Formative in the Titicaca Region." In *Advances in Titicaca Basin Archaeology—1*, edited by Charles Stanish, Amanda B. Cohen, and Mark S. Aldenderfer, 65–94. Los Angeles: Cotsen Institute of Archaeology, University of California, Los Angeles.

Hastorf, Christine A. 2009. "Agriculture as Metaphor of the Andean State." In *Polities and Power: Archaeological Perspectives on the Landscapes of Early States*, edited by Steven E. Falconer and Charles L. Redman, 52–72. Tucson: University of Arizona Press.

Hastorf, Christine A. 2012. "Steamed or Boiled: Identity and Value in Food Preparation." *Journal for Ancient Studies* 2 (Special Volume): 213–42.

Hastorf, Christine A. 2016. *The Social Archaeology of Food: Thinking about Eating from Prehistory to the Present*. Cambridge: Cambridge University Press.

Hastorf, Christine A. 2017. "The Actions and Meanings of Visible and Hidden Spaces at Formative Chiripa." *Ñawpa Pacha* 37 (2): 133–54. https://doi.org/10.1080/00776297.2017.1390925.

Hastorf, Christine A., and Maria C. Bruno. 2020. "The Flavors Archaeobotany Forgot." *Journal of Anthropological Archaeology* 59 (September): 101189. https://doi.org/10.1016/j.jaa.2020.101189.

Hastorf, Christine A., Matthew Bandy, William Whitehead, Lee Steadman, Katherine Moore, Jose Luis Paz Soria, Andrew Roddick, et al. 2005. "Proyecto Arqueológico Taraco Informe de las Excavaciones de la Temporada del 2004 en los Sitios de Kumi Kipa, Sonaji y Chiripa." Report presented to the Unidad Nacional de Arqueología de Bolivia, La Paz.

Hastorf, Christine A., Katherine M. Moore, Irene E. Smail, Rachael Penfil, Patrick Ryan Williams, Danielle J. Riebe, and Kelly J. Knudson. 2022. "Formative Exchange in the Andean Titicaca Basin: Isotopic Camelid Data and Lithic Sourcing: Evidence from the Taraco Peninsula, Bolivia." *Ñawpa Pacha* 43 (1): 27–53. https://doi.org/10.1080/00776297.2022.2066300.

Hastorf, Christine A., William T. Whitehead, and Sissel Johannessen. 2005. "Late Prehistoric Wood Use in an Andean Intermontane Valley." *Economic Botany* 59 (4): 337–55.

Hastorf, Christine A., and Melanie F. Wright. 1998. "Interpreting Wild Seeds from Archaeological Sites: A Dung Charring Experiment from the Andes." *Journal of Ethnobiology* 18 (2): 211–27.

Hawkes, J. G. 1990. *The Potato: Evolution, Biodiversity, and Genetic Resources.* London: Belhaven Press.

Hayden, Brian. 1990. "Nimrods, Piscators, Pluckers, and Planters: The Emergence of Food Production." *Journal of Anthropological Archaeology* 9: 31–69.

Heckler, Serena. 2009. "Introduction." In *Landscape, Process, and Power: Re-evaluating Traditional Environmental Knowledge*, 1–18. New York: Berghahn Books.

Heiddeger, Martin. 1971. *Poetry, Language, Thought.* Translated by Alfred Hofstader. New York: Harper & Row.

Heiser, Charles B. 1979. "Origins of Some Cultivated New World Plants." *Annual Review of Ecology and Systematics* 10: 309–26.

Higueras-Hare, Alvaro. 1996. "Prehispanic Settlement and Land Use in Cochabamba, Bolivia." PhD. diss., University of Pittsburgh.

Hildebrand, Elisabeth A. 2003. "Motives and Opportunities for Domestication: An Ethnoarchaeological Study in Southwest Ethiopia." *Journal of Anthropological Archaeology* 22 (4): 358–75.

Hirsch, Eric. 1995. "Landscape: Between Place and Space." In *The Anthropology of Landscape: Perspectives on Place and Space*, edited by Eric Hirsch and Michael O'Hanlon, 1–30. Oxford: Clarendon Press.

Hodder, Ian, and Scott Hutson. 2003. *Reading the Past: Current Approaches to Interpretation in Archaeology.* Cambridge: Cambridge University Press.

Hu, Di. 2022. *The Fabric of Resistance: Textile Workshops and the Rise of Rebellious Landscapes in Colonial Peru.* Tuscaloosa: University of Alabama Press.

Hughes, J. Donald. 2011. "Ancient Deforestation Revisited." *Journal of the History of Biology* 44 (1): 43–57. https://doi.org/10.1007/s10739-010-9247-3.

IGM (Instituto Geográfico Militar). 1991. "Taraco." Series H731, Sheet 5844 IV. La Paz: Instituto Geográfico Militar.

IGM (Instituto Geográfico Militar). 1994. "Carta Geologíca de Bolivia, Hoja Tiahuanacu." La Paz: Instituto Geografíco Militar.

Iltis, André, and Philippe Mourguiart. 1992. "Higher Plants: Distribution and Biomass." In *Lake Titicaca: A Synthesis of Limnological Knowledge*, edited by Claude Dejoux, 241–51. Dordrecht: Kluwer Academic Publishers.

INE. 2012. "Ine-Bolivia: Redatam (CEPAL)—Diseminación de Información Estadística." Resultados Censo de Población y Vivienda 2012. http://datos.ine.gob.bo/binbol/RpWebEngine.exe/Portal?BASE=CPV2012COM&lang=esp.

Ingold, Tim. 2011. *The Perception of the Environment: Essays on Livelihood, Dwelling and Skill.* New York: Routledge.

IPGRI, PROINPA, and IFAD. 2005. *Descriptores para Cañahua (*Chenopodium pallidicaule *Aellen).* La Paz: Fundación PROINPA.

Isbell, William. 1997. *Mummies and Mortuary Monuments: A Postprocessual Prehistory of Central Andean Social Organization.* Austin: University of Texas Press.

Isbell, William H., and Patricia J. Knobloch. 2006. "Missing Links, Imaginary Links: Staff God Imagery in the South Andean Past." In *Andean Archaeology III: North and South*, edited by William H. Isbell and Helaine Silverman, 307–51. New York: Springer. https://doi.org/10.1007/0-387-28940-2_14.

Isbell, William H., and Gordon McEwan. 1991. "A History of Huari Studies and Introduction to Current Interpretations." In *Huari Administration Structures*, 1–9. Washington, DC: Dumbarton Oaks.

Jackson, John Brinckerhoff. 1984. *Discovering the Vernacular Landscape.* New Haven, CT: Yale University Press.

Janusek, John Wayne. 1994. "State and Local Power in a Prehispanic Polity: Changing Patterns of Urban Residence in Tiwanaku and Lukurmata, Bolivia." PhD diss., University of Chicago.

Janusek, John Wayne. 2002. "Out of Many, One: Style and Social Boundaries in Tiwanaku." *Latin American Antiquity* 13 (35–61).

Janusek, John Wayne. 2003a. "The Changing Face of Tiwanaku Residential Life: State and Local Identity in an Andean City." In *Tiwanaku and Its Hinterland: Archaeological and Paleoecological Investigations of an Andean Civilization*, vol. 2, *Urban and Rural Archaeology*, edited by Alan L. Kolata, 264–96. Washington, DC: Smithsonian Institution Press.

Janusek, John Wayne. 2003b. "Vessels, Time, and Society: Toward a Ceramic Chronology in the Tiwanaku Heartland." In *Tiwanaku and Its Hinterland: Archaeological and Paleoecological Investigations of an Andean Civilization*, vol. 2, *Urban and Rural Archaeology*, edited by Alan L. Kolata, 30–89. Washington, DC: Smithsonian Institution Press.

Janusek, John Wayne. 2004a. "Household and City in Tiwanaku." In *Andean Archaeology*, edited by Helaine Silverman, 183–208. Oxford: Blackwell.

Janusek, John Wayne. 2004b. *Identity and Power in the Ancient Andes.* London: Routledge.

Janusek, John Wayne. 2004c. "Tiwanaku and Its Precursors: Recent Research and Emerging Perspectives." *Journal of Archaeological Research* 12 (2): 121–83.

Janusek, John Wayne. 2005. "Residential Diversity and the Rise of Complexity in Tiwanaku." In *Advances in Titicaca Basin Archaeology—1*, edited by Charles Stanish, Amanda B. Cohen, and Mark S. Aldenderfer, 143–71. Los Angeles: Cotsen Institute of Archaeology, University of California, Los Angeles.

Janusek, John Wayne. 2008. *Ancient Tiwanaku.* Cambridge: Cambridge University Press.

Janusek, John Wayne. 2013. "Social Diversity, Ritual Encounter, and the Contingent Production of Tiwanaku." In *Visions of Tiwanaku*, edited by Alexei Vranich and Charles Stanish, 197–209. Los Angeles: Cotsen Institute of Archaeology, University of California, Los Angeles.

Janusek, John Wayne. 2018. *Khonkho Wankane: Archaeological Investigations in Jesus de Machaca, Bolivia*. Contributions of the Archaeological Research Facility 68. Berkeley: Archaeological Research Facility, University of California, Berkeley.

Janusek, John Wayne. 2020. "Cosmopolitical Bodies: Living Monoliths, Vital Tectonics, and the Production of Tiwanaku." In *Sacred Matter: Animacy and Authority in the Americas*, 233–66. Washington, DC: Dumbarton Oaks.

Janusek, John Wayne, and Alan L. Kolata. 2004. "Top-Down or Bottom-Up: Rural Settlement and Raised Field Agriculture in the Lake Titicaca Basin, Bolivia." *Journal of Anthropological Archaeology* 23: 404–30.

Janusek, John Wayne, Patrick Ryan Williams, Mark Golitko, and Carlos Lémuz Aguirre. 2013. "Building Taypikala: Telluric Transformations in the Lithic Production of Tiwanaku." In *Mining and Quarrying in the Ancient Andes: Sociopolitical, Economic, and Symbolic Dimensions*, edited by Nicholas Tripcevich and Kevin J. Vaughn, 65–97. Interdisciplinary Contributions to Archaeology. New York: Springer. https://doi.org/10.1007/978-1-4614-5200-3_4.

Jarvis, David E., Yung Shwen Ho, Damien J. Lightfoot, Sandra M. Schmöckel, Bo Li, Theo J. A. Borm, Hajime Ohyanagi, Katsuhiko Mineta, Craig T. Michell, and Noha Saber. 2017. "The Genome of *Chenopodium quinoa*." *Nature* 542 (7641): 307.

Jennings, Justin. 2010. *Beyond Wari Walls: Regional Perspectives on Middle Horizon Peru*. Albuquerque: University of New Mexico Press. https://muse.jhu.edu/book/1574.

Jennings, Justin, and Edward R. Swenson, eds. 2018. *Powerful Places in the Ancient Andes*. Archaeologies of Landscape in the Americas. Albuquerque: University of New Mexico Press; School for Advanced Research Press. https://search.ebscohost.com/login.aspx?direct=true&db=e000xna&AN=1874596&site=ehost-live&scope=site.

Johannessen, Sissel, and Christine A. Hastorf. 1990. "A History of Fuel Management (AD 500 to the Present) in the Mantaro Valley, Peru." *Journal of Ethnobiology* 10 (1): 61–90.

Johns, Timothy. 1989. "A Chemical-Ecological Model of Root and Tuber Domestication in the Andes." In *Foraging and Farming: The Evolution of Plant Exploitation*, edited by David R. Harris and Gordon C. Hillman, 504–19. London: Unwin Hyman.

Johnson, Alan, and Timothy Earle. 2000. *The Evolution of Human Societies*. 2nd ed. Stanford, CA: Stanford University Press.

Kerssen, Tanya M. 2015. "Food Sovereignty and the Quinoa Boom: Challenges to Sustainable Re-Peasantisation in the Southern Altiplano of Bolivia." *Third World Quarterly* 36 (3): 489–507. https://doi.org/10.1080/01436597.2015.1002992.

Kessler, Michael, and Peter Driesch. 1993. "Causas e Historia de la Destrucción de Bosques Altoandinos en Bolivia." *Ecología en Bolivia* 21: 1–18.

Kidder, Alfred. 1943. *Some Early Sites in the Northern Lake Titicaca Basin*. Cambridge, MA: Peabody Museum.

Kidder, Alfred. 1956. "Digging in the Titicaca Basin." *University of Pennsylvania Museum Bulletin* 20 (3): 16–29.

Kimmerer, Robin. 2013. *Braiding Sweetgrass: Indigenous Wisdom, Scientific Knowledge and the Teachings of Plants*. Minneapolis: Milkweed Editions.

Kistler, Logan, S. Yoshi Maezumi, Jonas Gregorio de Souza, Natalia A. S. Przelomska, Flaviane Malaquias Costa, Oliver Smith, Hope Loiselle, et al. 2018. "Multiproxy Evidence Highlights a Complex Evolutionary Legacy of Maize in South America." *Science* 362 (December): 1309–13.

Klarich, Elizabeth A., and Nancy Román Bustinza. 2012. "Scale and Diversity at Late Formative Period Pukara." In *Advances in Titicaca Basin Archaeology—3*, edited by Alexei Vranich, Elizabeth A. Klarich, and Charles Stanish, 105–20. Ann Arbor: Museum of Anthropology, University of Michigan. http://www.jstor.org.dickinson.idm.oclc.org/stable/10.3998/mpub.11395967.11.

Klein, Herbert S. 1993. *Haciendas and Ayllus: Rural Society in the Bolivian Andes in the Eighteenth and Nineteenth Centuries*. Stanford, CA: Stanford University Press.

Klein, Herbert S. 2003. *A Concise History of Bolivia*. Cambridge: Cambridge University Press.

Knapp, A. Bernard, and Wendy Ashmore. 1999. "Archaeological Landscapes: Constructed, Conceptualized, Ideational." In *Archaeologies of Landscape: Contemporary Perspectives*, edited by Wendy Ashmore and A. Bernard Knapp, 1–32. Malden, MA: Blackwell.

Kolata, Alan L. 1986. "The Agricultural Foundations of the Tiwanaku State: A View from the Heartland." *American Antiquity* 51 (4): 748–62.

Kolata, Alan L. 1989. *Arqueología de Lukurmata*. La Paz: Los Amigos del Libro.

Kolata, Alan L. 1991. "The Technology and Organization of Agricultural Production in the Tiwanaku State." *Latin American Antiquity* 2 (2): 99–125.

Kolata, Alan L. 1993. *The Tiwanaku: Portrait of an Andean Civilization*. Oxford: Blackwell.

Kolata, Alan L. 2003a. "The Social Production of Tiwanaku: Political Economy and Authority in a Native Andean State." In *Tiwanaku and Its Hinterland: Archaeological and Paleoecological Investigations of an Andean Civilization*, vol. 2, *Urban and*

Rural Archaeology, edited by Alan L. Kolata, 449–72. Washington, DC: Smithsonian Institution Press.

Kolata, Alan L. 2003b. "Tiwanaku Ceremonial Architecture and Urban Organization." In *Tiwanaku and Its Hinterland: Archaeological and Paleoecological Investigations of an Andean Civilization*, vol. 2, *Urban and Rural Archaeology*, edited by Alan L. Kolata, 175–201. Washington, DC: Smithsonian Institution Press.

Kolata, Alan L., Michael W. Binford, Mark Brenner, John W. Janusek, and Charles Ortloff. 2000. "Environmental Thresholds and the Empirical Reality of State Collapse: A Response to Erickson (1999)." *Antiquity* 74 (284): 424–26.

Kolata, Alan L., and Charles Ortloff. 1996. "Tiwanaku Raised-Field Agriculture in the Lake Titicaca Basin of Bolivia." In *Tiwanaku and Its Hinterland, Archaeology, and Paleoecology of an Andean Civilization*, vol. 1, *Agroecology*, edited by Alan Kolata, 109–52. Washington, DC: Smithsonian Institution Press.

Kolbert, Elizabeth. 2014. *The Sixth Extinction: An Unnatural History*. New York: A&C Black.

Kosiba, Steve. 2018. "Cultivating Empire." In *The Oxford Handbook of the Incas*, edited by Sonia Alconini and R. Alan Covey, 227–46. Oxford: Oxford University Press.

Kosiba, Steve. 2020. "The Nature of the World, the Stuff of Politics: Exploring Animacy and Authority in the Indigenous Americas." In *Sacred Matter: Animacy and Authority in the Americas*, edited by Steve Kosiba, John W. Janusek, and Thomas B. F. Cummins, 1–35. Washington, DC: Dumbarton Oaks.

Krebs, Charles J. 1989. *Ecological Methodology*. New York: Harper & Row.

La Barre, Weston. 1938. "Native American Beers." *American Anthropologist* 40 (2): 224–34.

La Barre, Weston. 1948. "The Aymara Indians of the Lake Titicaca Plateau, Bolivia." In *Memoirs*, 50: 250, plates. Menasha, WI: American Anthropological Association.

Laguna, Pablo. 2011. "Mallas y Flujos: Acción Colectiva, Cambio Social, Quinua y Desarrollo Regional Indígena en los Andes Bolivianos." PhD diss., Wageningen University.

Laland, Kevin N., and Michael J. O'Brien. 2010. "Niche Construction Theory and Archaeology." *Journal of Archaeological Method and Theory* 17 (4): 303–22. https://doi.org/10.1007/s10816-010-9096-6.

Langlie, BrieAnna. 2008. "Paleoethnobotanical Analysis of Formative Chiripa, Bolivia." Honors thesis, University of California, Berkeley.

Langlie, Brieanna Sylvia. 2016. "Farming through the Auca Runa: Agricultural Strategies and Terraces during the Late Intermediate Period, Altiplano, Peru." PhD diss., Washington University in St. Louis.

Lee, Midori. 1997. "Paleoethnobotanical Report of Five Yaya-Mama Sites from the Lake Titicaca Basin." Master's Thesis, University of Missouri.

Lémuz-Aguirre, Carlos. 2001. "Patrones de Asentamiento Arqueológico en la Peninsula de Santiago de Huatta, Bolivia." Licenciatura Thesis, Universidad Mayor de San Andres.

Lenters, John D., and Kerry H. Cook. 1997. "On the Origin of the Bolivia High and Related Circulation Features of the South America Climate." *Journal of the Atmospheric Sciences* 54: 656–77.

Leon, Jorge. 1964. *Plantas Alimenticias Andinas*. Boletín Técnico, no. 6. Lima: Instituto Interamericano de Ciencias Agrícolas Zona Andina.

Lepofsky, Dana, and Ken Lertzman. 2005. "More on Sampling for Richness and Diversity in Archaeobiological Assemblages." *Journal of Ethnobiology* 25 (2): 175–88.

Levieil, Dominique, and Benjamin Orlove. 1992. "The Socio-Economic Importance of Macrophytes." In *Lake Titicaca: A Synthesis of Limnological Knowledge*, edited by Claude Dejoux and André Iltis, 505–10. Dordrecht, the Netherlands: Kluwer Academic.

Levine, Abigail. 2012. "Competition, Cooperation, and the Emergence of Regional Centers in the Northern Lake Titicaca Basin, Peru." PhD diss., University of California, Los Angeles.

Levine, Abigail. 2020. "The Sunken Court Tradition in the South Central Andes." In *Archaeological Interpretations: Symbolic Meaning within Andes Prehistory*, edited by Peter Eeckhout, 19–40. Gainesville: University Press of Florida. https://doi.org/10.5744/florida/9780813066448.003.0002.

Levine, Abigail, Charles Stanish, P. Ryan Williams, Cecilia Chávez, and Mark Golitko. 2013. "Trade and Early State Formation in the Northern Titicaca Basin, Peru." *Latin American Antiquity* 24 (3): 289–308. https://doi.org/10.7183/1045-6635.24.3.289.

Logan, Amanda L. 2006. "The Application of Phytolith and Starch Grain Analysis to Understanding Formative Period Subsistence, Ritual, and Trade on the Taraco Peninsula, Highland Bolivia." MA thesis, University of Missouri.

Logan, Amanda L. 2020. *The Scarcity Slot: Excavating Histories of Food Security in Ghana*. Oakland: University of California Press. https://doi.org/10.1525/luminos.98.

Logan, Amanda L., Christine A. Hastorf, and Deborah M. Pearsall. 2012. "'Let's Drink Together': Early Ceremonial Use of Maize in the Titicaca Basin." *Latin American Antiquity* 23 (3): 235–58.

López, María Laura, María C. Bruno, and María Teresa Planella. 2015. "El Género Chenopodium: Metodología Aplicada a la Identificación Taxonómica en Ejemplares Arqueológicos. Presentación de Casos de Estudio de la Región Sur-Andina."

In *Avances y Desafíos Metodológicos en Arqueobotánica: Miradas Consensuadas y Diálogos Compartidos desde Sudamérica*, edited by Carolina Belmar and Verónica Lema, 89–121. Santiago: Universidad SEK.

López, María Laura, Aylen Capparelli, and Axel Emil Nielsen. 2011. "Traditional Post-Harvest Processing to Make Quinoa Grains (*Chenopodium quinoa* var. *quinoa*) Apt for Consumption in Northern Lípez (Potosí, Bolivia): Ethnoarchaeological and Archaeobotanical Analyses." *Archaeological and Anthropological Sciences* 3 (1): 49–70.

Loza de la Cruz, Freddy Lucio. 1998. "Flora y Vegetación Arvense en Dos Comunidades Campesinas del Altiplano Norte (Prov. Omasuyos, La Paz)." Licenciatura Thesis, Universidad Mayor de San Andrés.

Lucas, Gavin. 2005. *The Archaeology of Time*. Themes in Archaeology. London: Routledge. https://doi.org/10.4324/9780203004920.

Machicado Murillo, Eduardo. 2008. "Las Tumbas de la Península de Taraco, Bolivia." Licenciatura thesis, Universidad Mayor de San Andrés.

Manzanilla, Linda, and E. K. Woodward. 1990. "Restos Humanos Asociados a la Pirámide de Akapana (Tiwanaku, Bolivia)." *Gaceta Arqueológica Andina* 20: 83–107.

Marsh, Erik J. 2012a. "A Bayesian Re-assessment of the Earliest Radiocarbon Dates from Tiwanaku, Bolivia." *Radiocarbon* 54 (2): 203–18.

Marsh, Erik J. 2012b. "The Founding of Tiwanaku: Evidence from Kk'araña." *Ñawpa Pacha* 32 (2): 69–187.

Marsh, Erik J. 2015. "The Emergence of Agropastoralism: Accelerated Ecocultural Change on the Andean Altiplano, 3540–3120 Cal BP." *Environmental Archaeology* 20 (1): 13–29.

Marsh, Erik J., Daniel Contreras, Maria C. Bruno, Alexei Vranich, and Andrew P. Roddick. 2021. "Comment on Arnold et al. 'Drought and the Collapse of the Tiwanaku Civilization: New Evidence from Lake Orurillo, Peru' [*Quat. Sci. Rev.* 251 (2021): 106693]." *Quaternary Science Reviews* 269 (October): 107004. https://doi.org/10.1016/j.quascirev.2021.107004.

Marsh, Erik J., Andrew P. Roddick, Maria C. Bruno, Scott C. Smith, John W. Janusek, and Christine A. Hastorf. 2019. "Temporal Inflection Points in Decorated Pottery: A Bayesian Refinement of the Late Formative Chronology in the Southern Lake Titicaca Basin, Bolivia." *Latin American Antiquity* 30 (4): 798–817. https://doi.org/10.1017/laq.2019.73.

Martin, Gary J. 1995. *Ethnobotany: A Methods Manual*. London: Chapman & Hall.

Mason, John. 2003. *Sustainable Agriculture*. 2nd ed. Collingwood, Australia: Landlinks Press.

Matsuoka, Yoshihiro, Yves Vigouroux, Major M. Goodman, Jesus Sanchez G., Edward Buckler, and John Doebley. 2002. "A Single Domestication for Maize

Shown by Multilocus Microsatellite Genotyping." *Proceedings of the National Academy of Sciences* 99 (9): 6080–84.

Mayer, Enrique. 2002. *The Articulated Peasant: Household Economies in the Andes.* Boulder, CO: Westview Press.

McEwan, Cheryl. 2022. "Multispecies Storytelling in Botanical Worlds: The Creative Agencies of Plants in Contested Ecologies." *Environment and Planning E: Nature and Space* 6 (2): 1114–37. https://doi.org/10.1177/25148486221110755.

Melton, Mallory A., Matthew E. Biwer, and Rita Panjarjian. 2020. "Differentiating Chuño Blanco and Chuño Negro in Archaeological Samples Based on Starch Metrics and Morphological Attributes." *Journal of Archaeological Science: Reports* 34 (December): 102650. https://doi.org/10.1016/j.jasrep.2020.102650.

Mesa, José de, Teresa Gisbert, and Carlos D. Mesa Gisbert. 2003. *Historia de Bolivia.* La Paz: Editorial Gisbert y Cia.

Miller, Melanie J. 2005. "What's in That Pot? Using Stable Isotope Analysis to Understand Cuisines of the Taraco Peninsula, Bolivia, 1500 BC–AD 1000." Honors thesis, University of California, Berkeley.

Miller, Melanie J., Maria C. Bruno, José M. Capriles, Iain Kendall, Richard P. Evershed, and Christine A. Hastorf. 2022. "Eating from the Earth on the Shores of Lake Titicaca: A Multimethod Approach to Understanding the Diets of Taraco Peninsula Inhabitants." In *Transforming Foods in the Ancient Andes: Archaeological and Ethnohistorical Studies of Food, Diet, and Cuisine*, edited by Marta Alfonso-Durruty and Deborah E. Blom, 89–108. Tucson: University of Arizona Press.

Miller, Melanie J., José M. Capriles, and Christine A. Hastorf. 2010. "The Fish of Lake Titicaca: Implications for Archaeology and Changing Ecology through Stable Isotope Analysis." *Journal of Archaeological Science* 37 (2): 317–27. https://doi.org/10.1016/j.jas.2009.09.043.

Miller, Melanie J., Iain Kendall, José M. Capriles, Maria C. Bruno, Richard P. Evershed, and Christine A. Hastorf. 2021. "Quinoa, Potatoes, and Llamas Fueled Emergent Social Complexity in the Lake Titicaca Basin of the Andes." *Proceedings of the National Academy of Sciences* 118 (49): e2113395118. https://doi.org/10.1073/pnas.2113395118.

Miller, Naomi F. 1985. "Paleoethnobotanical Evidence for Deforestation in Ancient Iran: A Case Study of Urban Malyan." *Journal of Ethnobiology* 5 (1): 1–19.

Miller, Naomi F., and Tristine Lee Smart. 1984. "Intentional Burning of Dung as Fuel: A Mechanism for the Incorporation of Charred Seeds into the Archaeological Record." *Journal of Ethnobiology* 4 (1): 15–28.

Mitchell, Don. 1996. *The Lie of the Land: Migrant Workers and the California Landscape.* Minneapolis: University of Minnesota Press.

Mohr, Karen Lynne. 1966. "An Analysis of the Pottery of Chiripa, Bolivia: A Problem in Archaeological Classification and Inference." PhD Thesis, University of Pennsylvania.

Mohr-Chávez, Karen. 1988. "The Significance of Chiripa in Lake Titicaca Basin Developments." *Expedition* 30 (3): 17–26.

Montes de Oca, Ismael. 1995. "Geografía y Clima de Bolivia." *Bulletin de l'Institut Français d'Études Andines* 24 (3): 357–68.

Moore, Henrietta L. 2017. "What Can Sustainability Do for Anthropology?" In *The Anthropology of Sustainability: Beyond Development and Progress*, edited by Marc Brightman and Jerome Lewis, 67–80. Palgrave Studies in Anthropology of Sustainability. New York: Palgrave Macmillan. https://doi.org/10.1057/978-1-137-56636-2_4.

Moore, Katherine M. 1999. "Chiripa Worked Bone and Bone Tools." In *Early Settlement at Chiripa, Bolivia: Research of the Taraco Archaeological Project*, edited by Christine A. Hastorf, 73–93. Contributions of the University of California Archaeological Research Facility, no. 57. Berkeley: Archaeological Research Facility, University of California, Berkeley.

Moore, Katherine M. 2011a. "Grace under Pressure: Responses to Changing Environments by Herders and Fishers in the Formative Lake Titicaca Basin, Bolivia." In *Sustainable Lifeways: Cultural Persistence in an Ever-Changing Environment*, edited by Naomi F. Miller and Kathleen Ryan, 244–72. Philadelphia: University of Pennsylvania Museum of Archaeology and Anthropology.

Moore, Katherine M. 2011b. "Zooarqueología en Kala Uyuni: Proyecto Arqueológico Taraco Temporada 2009." In *Excavaciones en Kala Uyuni: Informe de la Temporada 2009 del Proyecto Arqueológico de Taraco*, 86–98. Report submitted to the Unidad Nacional de Arqueología de Bolivia, La Paz.

Moore, Katherine M., Maria C. Bruno, José M. Capriles, and Christine A. Hastorf. 2010. "Integrated Contextual Approaches to Understanding Past Activities Using Plant and Animal Remains from Kala Uyuni, Lake Titicaca, Bolivia." In *Integrating Zooarchaeology and Paleoethnobotany: A Consideration of Issues, Methods, and Cases*, edited by Amber M. VanDerwarker and Tanya M. Peres, 173–203. New York: Springer. https://doi.org/10.1007/978-1-4419-0935-0_8.

Moore, Katherine M., David Steadman, and Susan deFrance. 1999. "Herds, Fish, and Fowl in the Domestic and Ritual Economy of Formative Chiripa." In *Early Settlement at Chiripa, Bolivia: Research of the Taraco Archaeological Project*, edited by Christine A. Hastorf, 105–16. Contributions of the University of California Archaeological Research Facility 57. Berkeley: University of California.

Morlon, Pierre, Jean Bourliaud, Raymond Réau, and Dominique Hervé. 1996. "Una Herramienta, un Símbolo, un Debate: La Chaquitaclla y Supersisencia en la Agricultura Andina." In *Comprender la Agricultural Campesina en los Andes Centrales: Perú-Bolivia*, 38–83. Lima: Institut Français de'Études Andines-Centro Bartolomé de las Casas.

Morrison, Kathleen. 1995. *Fields of Victory: Vijayanagara and the Course of Intensification*. Contributions of the University of California Archaeological Research Facility 53. Berkeley: Archaeological Research Facility, University of California, Berkeley.

Mujica, Elias. 1988. "Peculiaridades del Proceso Histórico Temprano en la Cuenca del Norte del Titicaca: Una Propuesta Inicial." *Boletín del Laboratorio de Arqueología* 2: 75–124.

Murphy, Fiona, and Pierre McDonagh. 2016. *Envisioning Sustainabilities: Towards an Anthropology of Sustainability*. Newcastle-upon-Tyne: Cambridge Scholars Publishing. http://ebookcentral.proquest.com/lib/dickinson/detail.action?docID=4820044.

Murra, John V. 1984. "Andean Societies." *Annual Review of Anthropology* 13: 119–41.

MUSEF Editores. 2019. *Vistiendo Memorias: Miradas sobre la Indumentaria desde el MUSEF*. La Paz: Museo Nacional de Etnografía y Folklore-Fundación Cultural del Banco Central de Bolivia.

Nabhan, Gary P., Amadeo M. Rea, Karen L. Reichhardt, Eric Mellink, and Charles F. Hutchinson. 1982. "Papago Influences on Habitat and Biotic Diversity: Quitovac Oasis Ethnoecology." *Journal of Ethnobiology* 2 (2): 124–43.

Nair, Stella, and Jean-Pierre Protzen. 2013. *The Stones of Tiahuanaco: A Study of Architecture and Construction*. Los Angeles: Cotsen Institute of Archaeology, University of California, Los Angeles.

Nash, Donna J. 2019. "Craft Production as an Empowering Strategy in an Emerging Empire." *Journal of Anthropological Research* 75 (3): 328–60. https://doi.org/10.1086/704144.

National Research Council. 1989. *Lost Crops of the Incas: Little-Known Plants of the Andes with Promise for Worldwide Cultivation*. Washington, DC: National Academy Press.

Netting, Robert McC. 1993. *Smallholder, Householders: Farm Families and the Ecology of Intensive, Sustainable Agriculture*. Stanford, CA: Stanford University Press.

Nuñez, Lautero, and Tom Dillehay. 1979. *Movilidad Giratoria, Armonia Social y Desarollo en los Andes Meridionales: Patrones de Trafico e Interaccion Economica*. Antofogasta, Chile: Universidad del Norte.

Oakland, Amy. 1986. "Tiwanaku Textile Style from South Central Andes, Bolivia, and North Chile." PhD diss., University of Texas, Austin.

Ofstehage, Andrew. 2012. "The Construction of an Alternative Quinoa Economy: Balancing Solidarity, Household Needs, and Profit in San Agustín, Bolivia." *Agriculture and Human Values* 29 (4): 441–54. https://doi.org/10.1007/s10460-012-9371-0.

Onofre Mamani, Luperio. 1997. "Contemporary Aymara Agricultural Soil Categories." In *Archaeological Survey in the Juli-Desaguadero Region of Lake Titicaca Basin, Southern Peru*, edited by Charles Stanish, 125–27. Chicago: Field Museum of Natural History.

Orlove, Benjamin S., John C. H. Chiang, and Mark A. Cane. 2000. "Forecasting Andean Rainfall and Crop Yield from the Influence of El Niño on Pleiades Visibility." *Nature* 403: 68–71.

Orlove, Benjamin S., John C. H. Chiang, and Mark A. Cane. 2002. "Ethnoclimatology in the Andes." *American Scientist* 90: 428–35.

Orlove, Benjamin S., and Richard Godoy. 1986. "Sectoral Fallowing Systems in the Central Andes." *Journal of Ethnobiology* 6 (1): 169–204.

Ortloff, Charles R., and Alan L. Kolata. 1989. "Hydraulic Analysis of Tiwanaku Aqueduct Structures at Lukurmata and Pajchiri, Bolivia." *Journal of Archaeological Science* 16: 513–35.

Ortloff, Charles R., and Alan L. Kolata. 1993. "Climate and Collapse: Agro-Ecological Perspectives on the Decline of the Tiwanaku State." *Journal of Archaeological Science* 20 (2): 195–221.

Paduano, Gina M., Mark B. Bush, Paul A. Baker, Sherilyn C. Fritz, and Geoffrey O. Seltzer. 2003. "A Vegetation and Fire History of Lake Titicaca since the Last Glacial Maximum." *Palaeogeography, Palaeoclimatology, Palaeoecology* 194: 259–79.

Pauketat, Timothy R. 2001. "Practice and History in Archaeology: An Emerging Paradigm." *Anthropological Theory* 1 (1): 73–98.

Paz Soria, José Luis, and Maria Soledad Fernandez. 2007. "Excavations at the (KU) Kala Uyuni Sector." In *Kala Uyuni: An Early Political Center in the Southern Lake Titicaca Basin, 2003 Excavations of the Taraco Archaeological Project*, edited by Matthew S. Bandy and Christine A. Hastorf, 25–34. Berkeley: University of California, Berkeley.

Pearsall, Deborah M. 2015. *Paleoethnobotany: A Handbook of Procedures*. 3rd ed. Walnut Creek, CA: Left Coast Press.

Perry, Linda, Ruth Dickau, Sonia Zarrillo, Irene Holst, Deborah M. Pearsall, Dolores R. Piperno, Mary Jane Berman, et al. 2007. "Starch Fossils and the Domestication and Dispersal of Chili Peppers (*Capsicum* spp. L.) in the Americas." *Science* 315 (5814): 986–88. https://doi.org/10.1126/science.1136914.

Pestalozzi Schmid, Hans-Ulrich Anton, and Marco Antonio Torrez Nina. 1998. *Flora Ilustrada Altoandina: La Relación entre Hombre, Planta, y Medio Ambiente en el Ayllu Majasaya Mujlli*. Cochabamba: Herbario Nacional de Bolivia y Herbario Forestal Nacional "Martín Cárdenas."

Pikirayi, Innocent. 2019. "Sustainability and an Archaeology of the Future." *Antiquity* 93 (372): 1669–71. https://doi.org/10.15184/aqy.2019.182.

Plourde, Aimée Marcelle. 2006. "Prestige Goods and Their Role in the Evolution of Social Ranking: A Costly Signaling Model with Data from the Formative Period of the Northern Lake Titicaca Basin, Peru." PhD diss., University of California, Los Angeles.

Ponce Sangines, Carlos. 1981. *Tiwanaku: Espacio, Tiempo, y Cultura*. La Paz: Amigos del Libro.

Ponce Sangines, Carlos. 1993. "La Cerámica de la Época I (Aldeana) de Tiwanaku." *Pumapunku* 4: 48–89.

Popper, Virginia. 1988. "Selecting Quantitative Measurements in Paleoethnobotany." In *Current Paleoethnobotany: Analytical Methods and Cultural Interpretations of Archaeological Plant Remains*, edited by Christine A. Hastorf and Virginia Popper, 1–16. Chicago: University of Chicago Press.

Portugal Ortiz, Max. 1992. "Aspectos de la Cultura Chiripa: A la Memoria del Prof. Maks Portugal Zamora." *Textos Antropológicos* 3: 9–26.

Portugal Ortiz, Max. 1998. *Escultura Prehispánica Boliviana*. La Paz: Carrera de Arqueología y Antropología, Universidad Mayor de San Andrés.

Posnansky, Arthur. 1945. *Tihuanaco: The Cradle of American Man*. 2 vols. Translated by James F. Shearer. New York: J. J. Augustin.

Pulgar Vidal, Javier. 1972. *Ocho Regiones Naturales del Perú*. Lima: Editorial Universo.

Quirós, Carlos F., and R. Aliaga Cárdenas. 1997. "Maca. *Lepidium meyenii* Walp." In *Andean Roots and Tubers: Ahipa, Arracacha, Maca, and Yacon*, edited by Michael Hermann and Joachim Heller, 173–98. Rome: International Plant Genetic Resources Institute (IPGRI).

Rajala, Ulla, and Phil Mills. 2017. *Forms of Dwelling: 20 Years of Taskscapes in Archaeology*. Oxford: Oxbow Books.

Ramírez, Ricardo, David H. Timothy, Efraín Díaz B, and U. J. Grant. 1960. *Races of Maize in Bolivia*. Washington, DC: National Academy of Sciences; National Research Council.

Reilly, Sophie E. 2017. "Meals in Motion: Ceramic and Botanical Investigations of Foodways in the Late Formative and Tiwanaku IV/V, Lake Titicaca Basin, Bolivia." MA thesis, McMaster University. https://macsphere.mcmaster.ca/handle/11375/23108.

Rigsby, Catherine A., Paul A. Baker, and Mark S. Aldenderfer. 2003. "Fluvial History of the Rio Ilave Valley, Peru, and Its Relationship to Climate and Human History." *Palaeogeography, Palaeoclimatology, Palaeoecology* 194: 165–85.

Rindos, David. 1984. *The Origins of Agriculture: An Evolutionary Perspective*. Orlando, FL: Academic Press.

Rivera Casanovas, Claudia. 2003. "Ch'iji Jawira: A Case of Ceramic Specialization in the Tiwanaku Urban Periphery." In *Tiwanaku and Its Hinterland: Archaeological and Paleoecological Investigations of an Andean Civilization*, vol. 2, *Urban and Rural Archaeology*, edited by Alan L. Kolata, 296–326. Washington, DC: Smithsonian Institution Press.

Robb, John. 2007. *The Early Mediterranean Village: Agency, Material Culture, and Social Change in Neolithic Italy*. Cambridge: Cambridge University Press.

Roche, Michel, Jacques Bourges, José Cortes, and Roger Mattos. 1992. "Climatology and Hydrology of the Lake Titicaca Basin." In *Lake Titicaca: A Synthesis of Limnological Knowledge*, edited by Claude Dejoux and André Iltis, 63–83. Dordrecht, the Netherlands: Kluwer Academic.

Roddick, Andrew P. 2000. "Archaeological Approaches to Ritual in the Andes: A Ceramic Analysis of Ceremonial Space at the Formative Period Site of Chiripa, Bolivia." Master's Thesis, University of British Columbia.

Roddick, Andrew P. 2009. "Communities of Pottery Production and Consumption on the Taraco Peninsula, Bolivia, 200 BC–AD 300." PhD diss., University of California, Berkeley. https://www.proquest.com/openview/334982a5133fc588a0283c25186da8fe/1?pq-origsite=gscholar&cbl=18750.

Roddick, Andrew P. 2011. "El Muro Oeste de ASD2 y Superficies de Uso Externas." In *Excavaciones en Kala Uyuni: Informe de la Temporada 2009 del Proyecto Arqueológico de Taraco*, 34–43. Report submitted to the Unidad Nacional de Arqueología de Bolivia, La Paz.

Roddick, Andrew P. 2013. "Temporalities of the Formative Period Taraco Peninsula, Bolivia." *Journal of Social Archaeology* 13 (3): 287–309. https://doi.org/10.1177/1469605313485396.

Roddick, Andrew P., Maria C. Bruno, and Christine A. Hastorf. 2014. "Political Centers in Context: Depositional Histories at Formative Period Kala Uyuni, Bolivia." *Journal of Anthropological Archaeology* 36: 140–57.

Roddick, Andrew P., Ruth Fontenla Alvarez, and Sophie E. Reilly. 2017. "Análisis de Cerámica." In *Informe de Investigación: Proyecto Arqueología del Paisaje y Comunidades de Producción en la Península de Taraco, Bolivia, 2016*, 14–33. Report submitted to the Unidad Nacional de Arqueología de Bolivia, La Paz.

Roddick, Andrew P., and Christine A. Hastorf. 2010. "Tradition Brought to the Surface: Continuity, Innovation, and Change in the Late Formative Period, Taraco Peninsula, Bolivia." *Cambridge Archaeological Journal* 20 (2): 157–78.

Roddick, Andrew P., and John W. Janusek. 2018. "Moving between Homes: Landscape, Mobility, and Political Action in the Titicaca Basin." In *Powerful Places in the Ancient Andes*, edited by Justin Jenning and Edward R. Swenson, 287–322. Albuquerque: University of New Mexico Press.

Rodriguez, Juan Pablo, Sven-Erik Jacobsen, Christian Andreasen, and Marten Sørensen. 2020. "Cañahua (*Chenopodium pallidicaule*): A Promising New Crop for Arid Areas." In *Emerging Research in Alternative Crops*, edited by Abdelaziz Hirich, Redouane Choukr-Allah, and Ragab Ragab, 221–43. Environment & Policy 58. Cham, Switzerland: Springer. https://doi.org/10.1007/978-3-319-90472-6_9.

Rojas, W., J. L. Soto, M. Pinto, M. Jäger, and S. Padulosi. 2010. *Granos Andinos: Avances, Logros y Experiencias Desarrolladas en Quinua, Cañahua y Amaranto en Bolivia*. Rome: Biodiversity International. https://cgspace.cgiar.org/handle/10568/104701.

Rosen, Arlene Miller. 2007. *Civilizing Climate: Social Responses to Climate Change in the Ancient Near East*. Lanham, MD: AltaMira Press.

Rowe, John H. 1963. "Inca Culture at the Time of the Spanish Conquest." In *Handbook of South American Indians*, vol. 2, *Andean Civilizations*, edited by Julian H. Steward, 183–330. New York: Cooper Square Publishers.

Rowe, John H., and C. Brandel. 1969. "Pucara Pottery Designs." *Ñawpa Pacha* 7: 1–16.

Sammells, Clare A. 2010. "Ode to a Chuño: Learning to Love Freeze-Dried Potatoes in Highland Bolivia." In *Adventures in Eating: Anthropological Experiences in Dining from around the World*, edited by Helen R. Haines and Clare A. Sammells, 101–25. Boulder: University Press of Colorado.

Sammells, Clare A. 2012. "The City of the Present in the City of the Past: Solstice Celebrations at Tiwanaku, Bolivia." In *On Location: Heritage Cities and Sites*, edited by D. Fairchild Ruggles, 115–30. New York: Springer. https://doi.org/10.1007/978-1-4614-1108-6_6.

Santana-Sagredo, Francisca, Rick J. Schulting, Pablo Méndez-Quiros, Ale Vidal-Elgueta, Mauricio Uribe, Rodrigo Loyola, Anahí Maturana-Fernández, et al. 2021. "'White Gold' Guano Fertilizer Drove Agricultural Intensification in the Atacama Desert from AD 1000." *Nature Plants* 7 (2): 152–58. https://doi.org/10.1038/s41477-020-00835-4.

Sauer, Carl O. 1925. "The Morphology of Landscape." *University of California Publications in Geography* 2 (2): 19–54.

Schaedel, Richard P. 1952. "An Analysis of Central Andean Stone Sculpture." PhD diss., Yale University.

Seddon, Matthew T. 1994a. "Excavations in the Raised Fields of the Rio Catari Sub-Basin, Bolivia." Master's Thesis, University of Chicago.

Seddon, Matthew T. 1994b. "Lithic Artifacts." In *Archaeological Research at Tumatumani, Juli, Peru*, edited by Charles Stanish and Lee Steadman, 65–77. Anthropology New Series, no. 23. Chicago: Field Museum of Natural History.

Seddon, Matthew T. 1998. "Ritual, Power, and the Development of a Complex Society: The Island of the Sun and the Tiwanaku State." PhD diss., University of Chicago.

Seligmann, Linda J. 2023. *Quinoa: Food Politics and Agrarian Life in the Andean Highlands*. Champaign: University of Illinois Press.

Seltzer, Geoffrey O., Paul A. Baker, Scott L. Cross, Robert B. Dunbar, and Sherilyn C. Fritz. 1998. "High-Resolution Seismic Reflection Profiles from Lake Titicaca, Peru-Bolivia; Evidence for Holocene Aridity in the Tropical Andes." *Geology* 26 (2): 167–70.

Serrano Quezada, Rosmery. 2012. "Distribución de la Diversidad Genética y Etnobotánica de Cañahua (*Chenopodium pallidicaule* Aellen) en las Comunidades del Altiplano Norte." Licenciatura thesis, Universidad Mayor de San Andres, Carrera de Agronomía. http://repositorio.umsa.bo/xmlui/handle/123456789/8002.

Smith, Adam T. 2003. *The Political Landscape: Constellations of Authority in Early Complex Polities*. Berkeley: University of California Press.

Smith, Bruce D., John M. Marston, Jade d'Alpoim Guedes, and Christina Warinner. 2015. "Documenting Human Niche Construction in the Archaeological Record." In *Method and Theory in Paleoethnobotany*, edited by John M. Marston, Jade d'Alpoim Guedes, and Christina Warinner, 355–70. Boulder: University Press of Colorado.

Smith, Clifford T., William M. Denevan, and Patrick Hamilton. 1968. "Ancient Ridged Fields in the Region of Lake Titicaca." *Geographical Journal* 134 (3): 353–67.

Smith, Scott C. 2016. *Landscape and Politics in the Ancient Andes Biographies of Place at Khonkho Wankane*. Archaeologies of Landscape in the Americas Series. Albuquerque: University of New Mexico Press.

Smith, Scott C., and Maribel Pérez Arias. 2015. "From Bodies to Bones: Death and Mobility in the Lake Titicaca Basin, Bolivia." *Antiquity* 89 (343): 106–21. https://doi.org/10.15184/aqy.2014.32.

Soriano, Jewell. 2017. "Hacienda de Chiripa: The Rise of Haciendas and Development of a Community on the Taraco Peninsula." BA thesis, University of California, Berkeley.

Spooner, David M. 2005. "A Single Domestication for Potato Based on Multilocus Amplified Fragment Length Polymorphism Genotyping." *Proceedings of the National Academy of Sciences* 102: 14694–99.

Stahl, Ann Brower. 1993. "Concepts of Time and Approaches to Analogical Reasoning in Historical Perspective." *American Antiquity* 58 (2): 235–60. https://doi.org/10.2307/281967.

Stanish, Charles. 1994. "The Hydraulic Hypothesis Revisited: Lake Titicaca Basin Raised Fields in Theoretical Perspective." *Latin American Antiquity* 5 (4): 312–32.

Stanish, Charles. 2003. *Ancient Titicaca: The Evolution of Complex Society in Southern Peru and Northern Bolivia*. Berkeley: University of California Press.

Stanish, Charles. 2006. "Prehispanic Agricultural Strategies of Intensification in the Titicaca Basin of Peru and Bolivia." In *Agricultural Strategies*, edited by Joyce Marcus and Charles Stanish, 364–97. Cotsen Advanced Seminar Series, no. 2. Los Angeles: Cotsen Institute of Archaeology, University of California, Los Angeles.

Stanish, Charles. 2012. "Prehispanic Carved Stones in the Northern Titicaca Basin." In *Advances in Titicaca Basin Archaeology—3*, edited by Charles Stanish, Alexei Vranich, and Elizabeth A. Klarich, 121–40. Ann Arbor: University of Michigan Press. http://www.jstor.org.dickinson.idm.oclc.org/stable/10.3998/mpub.11395967.12.

Stanish, Charles, and Brian Bauer. 2004. *Archaeological Research on the Islands of the Sun and Moon, Lake Titicaca, Bolivia: Final Results from the Proyecto Tiksi Kjarka*. Monograph 52. Los Angeles: Cotsen Institute of Archaeology, University of California, Los Angeles.

Stanish, Charles, and Abigail Levine. 2011. "War and Early State Formation in the Northern Titicaca Basin, Peru." *Proceedings of the National Academy of Sciences* 108 (34): 13901–6. https://doi.org/10.1073/pnas.1110176108.

Stanish, Charles, and Lee Steadman. 1994. "Background to the Tumatumani Investigations." In *Archaeological Research at Tumatumani, Juli, Peru*, edited by Charles Stanish and Lee Steadman, 1–18. Anthropology New Series, no. 23. Chicago: Field Museum of Natural History.

Stanish, Charles, Edmundo de la Vega, Lee Steadman, Cecilia Chávez J., Kirk L. Frye, Luperio Onofre M., Matthew Seddon, and Percy Calisaya. 1997. *Archaeological Survey in the Juli-Desaguadero Region of Lake Titicaca Basin, Southern Peru*. Anthropology New Series, no. 29. Chicago: Field Museum of Natural History Press.

Steadman, David. 1996. "Animal Bone." In *Taraco Archaeological Project: 1996 Excavations at Chiripa, Bolivia*, edited by Christine A. Hastorf, 47–48. Berkeley: University of California, Berkeley.

Steadman, Lee. 1999. "The Ceramics." In *Early Settlement at Chiripa, Bolivia: Research of the Taraco Archaeological Project*, edited by Christine A. Hastorf, 61–72. Contributions of the University of California Archaeological Research Facility 57. Berkeley: University of California, Berkeley.

Steadman, Lee. 2007. "Ceramic Analysis." In *Kala Uyuni: An Early Political Center in the Southern Lake Titicaca Basin: 2003 Excavations of the Taraco Archaeological Project*, edited by Matthew S. Bandy and Christine A. Hastorf, 67–112. Contributions of the University of California Archaeological Research Facility 64. Berkeley: University of California, Berkeley.

Sukhotu, Thitaporn, and Kazuyoshi Hosaka. 2006. "Origin and Evolution of Andigena Potatoes Revealed by Chloroplast and Nuclear DNA Markers." *Genome* 49: 636–47.

Swartely, Lynn. 2002. *Inventing Indigenous Knowledge: Archaeology, Rural Development, and the Raised Field Rehabilitation Project in Bolivia*. New York: Routledge.

Swenson, Edward R., and Andrew P. Roddick. 2018. "Introduction: Rethinking Temporality and Historicity from the Perspective of Andean Archaeology." In *Constructions of Time and History in the Pre-Columbian Andes*, edited by Edward R. Swenson and Andrew P. Roddick, 11–34. Boulder: University Press of Colorado.

Szpak, Paul, and Katherine L. Chiou. 2020. "A Comparison of Nitrogen Isotope Compositions of Charred and Desiccated Botanical Remains from Northern Peru." *Vegetation History and Archaeobotany* 29 (5): 527–38. https://doi.org/10.1007/s00334-019-00761-2.

Tapia Vargas, Gualberto. 1994. *La Agricultura en Bolivia: Quimera del Desarrollo*. La Paz: Editorial Los Amigos del Libros.

Tilley, Christopher Y. 1994. *A Phenomenology of Landscape: Places, Paths, and Monuments*. Oxford: Berg.

Torero, Alfredo. 1987. "Lenguas y Pueblos Altiplánicos en Torno al Siglo XVI." *Revista Andina*, no. 10: 329–405.

Torres, Constantino Manuel. 1995. "Archaeological Evidence for the Antiquity of Psychoactive Plant Use in the Central Andes." *Annali dei Musei Civici-Rovereto* 11: 291–326.

Torres, Constantino Manuel. 2001. "Shamanic Inebriants in South American Archaeology: Recent Investigations." *Eleusis* 5: 3–12.

Torres, Constantino Manuel, and William J. Conklin. 1995. "Exploring the San Pedro de Atacama/Tiwanaku Relationship." In *Andean Art: Visual Expression and Its Relation to Andean Beliefs and Values*, edited by Penelope Dransart, 78–108. Aldershot, UK: Avebury.

Towle, Margaret A. 1961. *The Ethnobotany of Pre-Columbian Peru*. Chicago: Aldine.

Troll, Carl. 1968. "The Cordilleras of the Tropical Americas: Aspects of Climate, Phytogeographical and Agrarian Ecology." In *Geo-Ecology of the Mountainous Regions of the Tropical Americas*, 15–56. Bonn: Ferd. Dümmlers Verlag.

Tschopik, Harry. 1963. "The Aymara." In *Handbook of South American Indians*, vol. 2, *The Andean Civilizations*, edited by Julian H. Steward, 501–73. New York: Cooper Square Publishers.

Tsing, Anna Lowenhaupt. 2015. *The Mushroom at the End of the World: On the Possibility of Life in Capitalist Ruins*. Princeton, NJ: Princeton University Press. https://doi.org/10.1515/9781400873548.

Tsing, Anna Lowenhaupt. 2017. "A Threat to Holocene Resurgence Is a Threat to Livability." In *The Anthropology of Sustainability: Beyond Development and Progress*, edited by Marc Brightman and Jerome Lewis, 51–65. Palgrave Studies in Anthropology of Sustainability. New York: Palgrave Macmillan. https://doi.org/10.1057/978-1-137-56636-2_3.

Turner, Sam, Tim Kinnaird, Elif Koparal, Stelios Lekakis, and Christopher Sevara. 2020. "Landscape Archaeology, Sustainability and the Necessity of Change." *World Archaeology* 52 (4): 589–606. https://doi.org/10.1080/00438243.2021.1932565.

Ugent, Donald. 1970. "The Potato." *Science* 170 (3963): 1161–66.

UN Secretary-General and WCED (World Commission on Environment and Development). 1987. *Report of the World Commission on Environment and Development: Our Common Future*. New York: United Nations. https://digitallibrary.un.org/record/139811.

USDA, NRCS (Natural Resources Conservation Service). 2007. "The PLANTS Database." https://plants.usda.gov/home.

Vacher, Jean, Emmanuel Brasier de Thuy, and Maximo Liberman. 1992. "Influence of the Lake on Littoral Agriculture." In *Lake Titicaca: A Synthesis of Limnological Knowledge*, edited by Claude Dejoux and Andrés Iltis, 511–22. Dordrecht, the Netherlands: Kluwer Academic.

Valcárcel, Luis Eduardo. 1935. "Litoesculturas y Cerámica de Pukara." *Revista Del Museo Nacional* 4: 25–28.

Valencia, Bryan G., Mark B. Bush, Angela L. Coe, Elizabeth Orren, and William D. Gosling. 2018. "Polylepis Woodland Dynamics during the Last 20,000 Years." *Journal of Biogeography* 45 (5): 1019–30. https://doi.org/10.1111/jbi.13209.

Vavilov, Nikolai I., and Doris Löve. 1992. *Origin and Geography of Cultivated Plants*. New York: Cambridge University Press.

Vicente-Serrano, S. M., O. Chura, J. I. López-Moreno, C. Azorin-Molina, A. Sanchez-Lorenzo, E. Aguilar, E. Moran-Tejeda, F. Trujillo, R. Martínez, and J. J. Nieto. 2015. "Spatio-Temporal Variability of Droughts in Bolivia, 1955–2012."

International Journal of Climatology 35 (10): 3024–40. https://doi.org/10.1002/joc.4190.

Vranich, Alexei. 1999. "Interpreting the Meaning of Ritual Spaces: The Temple Complex at Puma Punku, Tiwanaku, Bolivia." PhD diss., University of Pennsylvania.

Vranich, Alexei. 2009. "The Development of the Ritual Core of Tiwanaku." In *Tiwanaku: Papers from the 2005 Mayer Center Symposium at the Denver Art Museum*, 11–34. Denver, CO: Denver Art Museum.

Vranich, Alexei, and Charles Stanish, eds. 2013. *Visions of Tiwanaku*. Monograph 78. Los Angeles: Cotsen Institute of Archaeology, University of California, Los Angeles.

Vuille, Mathias. 1999. "Atmospheric Circulation over the Bolivian Altiplano during Dry and Wet Periods and Extreme Phases of the Southern Oscillation." *International Journal of Climatology* 19: 1579–1600.

Walker, John H. 2011. "Social Implications from Agricultural Taskscapes in the Southwestern Amazon." *Latin American Antiquity* 22 (3): 275–95.

Walker, John H. 2012. "Recent Landscape Archaeology in South America." *Journal of Archaeological Research* 20 (4): 309–55. https://doi.org/10.1007/s10814-012-9057-6.

Wallace, Dwight. 1950. "The Tiahuanaco Styles in the Peruvian and Bolivia Highlands." PhD diss., University of California, Berkeley.

Wallert, Arie, and Ran Boytner. 1996. "Dyes from the Tumilaca and Chiribaya Cultures, South Coast of Peru." *Journal of Archaeological Science* 23: 853–61.

Weberbauer, August. 1945. *El Mundo Vegetal de los Andes Peruanos*. Lima: Estación Experimental Agrícola de la Molina.

Weide, D. Marie, Sherilyn C. Fritz, Christine A. Hastorf, Maria C. Bruno, Paul A. Baker, Stéphane Guédron, and Wout Salenbien. 2017. "A ~6000 Yr Diatom Record of Mid- to Late Holocene Fluctuations in the Level of Lago Wiñaymarca, Lake Titicaca (Peru/Bolivia)." *Quaternary Research* 88 (2): 179–92.

Weismantel, Mary J. 1998. *Food, Gender, and Poverty in the Ecuadorian Andes*. Prospect Heights, IL: Waveland Press.

Whitehead, William T. 2006. "Redefining Plant Use at the Formative Site of Chiripa in the Southern Titicaca Basin." In *Andean Archaeology III: North and South*, edited by William H. Isbell and Helaine Silverman, 258–78. New York: Springer.

Whitehead, William T. 2007. "Exploring the Wild and Domestic: Paleoethnobotany at Chiripa, a Formative Site in Bolivia." PhD diss., Berkeley: University of California, Berkeley.

Whitehead, William T., and Kirk Frye. 2003. "Mapping, Photography, Database." In *Taraco Archaeological Project: Report on 2003 Excavations at Kala Uyuni*, edited by Matthew Bandy and Christine A. Hastorf, 14–17. University of California, Berkeley.

Williams, Patrick Ryan. 2013. "Tiwanaku: A Cult of the Masses." In *Visions of Tiwanaku*, edited by Alexei Vranich and Charles Stanish, 27–40. Los Angeles: Cotsen Institute of Archaeology, University of California.

Wilson, Hugh D. 1990. "Quinua and Relatives (*Chenopodium* sect. *Chenopodium* subsect. Cellulata)." *Economic Botany* 44 (Supplement): 92–110.

Winterhalder, Bruce, Robert Larsen, and R. Brooke Thomas. 1974. "Dung as an Essential Resource in a Highland Peruvian Community." *Human Ecology* 2 (2): 89–104.

Wirrmann, Denis. 1992. "Morphology and Bathymetry." In *Lake Titicaca: A Synthesis of Limnological Knowledge*, edited by Claude Dejoux and André Iltis, 16–22. Dordrecht, the Netherlands: Kluwer Academic.

Wirrmann, Denis, Philippe Mourguiart, and Luis Fernando Oliveira de Almeida. 1990. "Holocene Sedimentology and Ostracod Distribution in Lake Titicaca—Paleohydrological Interpretations." In *Quaternary of South America and Antarctic Peninsula* 6: 80–129. Rotterdam: A. A. Balkema.

Wirrmann, Denis, Jean-Pierre Ybert, and Philippe Mourguiart. 1992. "A 20,000 Year Paleohydrological Record from Lake Titicaca." In *Lake Titicaca: A Synthesis of Limnological Knowledge*, edited by Claude Dejoux and André Iltis, 40–48. Dordrecht, the Netherlands: Kluwer Academic Publishers.

Wittfogel, Karl. 1956. "The Hydraulic Civilizations." In *Man's Role in Changing the Face of the Earth*, edited by Thomas William, 152–64. Chicago: University of Chicago Press.

Wittfogel, Karl. 1957. *Oriental Despotism*. New Haven, CT: Yale University Press.

Wright, Melanie F., Christine A. Hastorf, and Heidi A. Lennstrom. 2003. "Pre-Hispanic Agriculture and Plant Use at Tiwanaku: Social and Political Implications." In *Tiwanaku and Its Hinterland: Archaeological and Paleoecological Investigations of an Andean Civilization*, vol. 2, *Urban and Rural Archaeology*, edited by Alan L. Kolata, 384–403. Washington, DC: Smithsonian Institution Press.

Wylie, Allison. 2002. "The Reaction against Analogy." In *Thinking from Things: Essays in the Philosophy of Archaeology*, 136–53. Berkeley: University of California Press.

Zubieta, Ricardo, Jorge Molina-Carpio, Wilber Laqui, Juan Sulca, and Mercy Ilbay. 2021. "Comparative Analysis of Climate Change Impacts on Meteorological, Hydrological, and Agricultural Droughts in the Lake Titicaca Basin." *Water* 13 (2): 175. https://doi.org/10.3390/w13020175.

Zuloaga, Fernando O., and Osvaldo Morrone. 1999. *Catálogo de las Plantas Vasculares del República Argentina*. 2 vols. Monographs in Systematic Botany 74. St. Louis: Missouri Botanical Garden Press.

Index

Achachi Coa Collu (KUAC), 61, 114, 170; architecture, 33, 35, 36, 169; excavations at, 116–18; Middle Formative, 38, 145–50; plant remains at, 144–50; pottery remains at, 145–46; as ritual center, 152, 168; sunken courts at, 40, 171; winter solstice celebration, 131–33
Adesmia spinosissima, 97
Agrarian Reform (1953), 20, 27, 52, 74
agricultural cycle, 17, 21–22; and rainfall, 58–59, 64
agricultural landscape, 5–6, 13, 166. *See also* landscape(s)
agriculture, 5–6, 10, 17, 23, 50, 173; dryland, 70; early, 167–168; intensive/intensification, 22, 42, 62, 106, 170, 173, 175–76; sustainable, 12, 163, 178, 180. *See also* farming; taskscapes
Akapana platform mound, 43
Alnus sp., 96
alpaca (*Lama pacos*), 134
altiplano, 3, 4f, 15, 24; climate, 64–66, maize variety, 85, 86f; vegetation, 94–96. *See also* plant communities
Alto Pukara, 36, 38
amaranths (Amaranthaceae), 95, 100, 137
amkaraya (*Urocarpidium sheparadae*), 99
animal food, 74; aquatic plants as, 95, 103–4; domesticated plants, 110, 113, 124; weeds as, 5, 91–92, 106
animals, 13, 15, 41, 135–36; and agro-biodiversity, 91–92; cooking techniques and, 139–40. *See also* birds; camelids; fish
anthropomorphs, 41, 44
antler tools, 63
apus, 60
aquatic plants, 91, 95, 103–4, 137. *See also* Cyperaceae; *totora* reeds
archaeobotanical record, 13–14, 75–78, 106–7, 169–70; chenopods in, 80–82; maize in, 85–87; noncrop plants, 93–94; tubers in, 84–85
archaeology, 6, 12, 30; of inhabitation, 17, 166; of landscape, 13–15, 19, 20; of plants, 75–76. *See also* Chiripa; Kala Uyuni
Archaic period, 31–32, 184*n*4
architecture, 35; public, 32–33, 36, 37, 40, 42, 47, 146, 169, 170, 177
ash, and coca chewing, 113, 124
assistance, help (*yanapataña*), 165
Asteraceae, asterids (Sunflower family), 94, 95, 102, 136–37, 172
Ayaviri, 50
aykayka (*Sisrynchium chilense*), 101
ayllu, 165–66
Aymara speakers, 7–9

Page numbers followed by *f* indicate a figure; page numbers followed by *n* indicate an endnote.

Ayrampu Qontu (KUAQ), 38, 114, 115, 116f, 169, 171; in Middle Formative period, 145–50

Baccharis sp., 97
barley, 51, 74, 75, 91, 109; threshing, 112–13
barrios, Tiwanaku, 44–45
bedstraw (Rubiaceae), 101
birds, in archaeological record, 135, 151, 156, 159, 162
boiling, 140
Bolivian High, 64
Bolivian Revolution (1952), 20, 52
bone tools, 63
Brassicaceae, 51, 94, 101–2, 172, 179
Brassica rapa, 5, 14
Bruntland Commission, 12
Buddleja sp., 96
burials, 148; Middle Formative, 36, 37, 117, 148; plant remains in, 122; Late Formative, 120, 152; Tiwanaku period, 47–48, 121, 144, 159, 177, 178

cacti (Cactaceae), 102–3, 137, 138, 139, 144, 160, 170; in archaeobotanical record, 144–145, 147–149, 151, 155–158, 160
camelids, 13, 77, 41, 102, 134, 168, 173–74, 178; and cactus fruit, 102–3; dung, 73–74, 97–98, 101; Early Formative, 145; Late Formative, 151, 155, 159; Middle Formative, 149; Tiwanaku, 46, 48, 162, 163. *See also* grazing; herding.
canals, and raised fields, 68f
Capsicum spp., 137
catfish, 128
cattle, 5, 51
Cavia sp., 135
celebrations, ceremonies, 169; food in, 149–50, 156–57; winter solstice, 131–33
ceramics. *See* pottery
ceremonial/ritual architecture, 32–33; Tiwanaku, 43–44. *See also* sunken courts
chaff, as animal feed, 124
ch'alla, 62
chaquitaclla, chakitaclla, 56f, 62, 63
charcoal, 96, 97
charqui, 142–43
ch'ata, 61
chenopods (*Chenopodium*), 22, 78, 79, 87, 106, 137, 162, 168; in archaeobotanical record, 80–82, 124. *See also illama; kañawa*; quinoa

chhijchhipa (*Tagetes multiflora*), 136
chicha, 142, 144, 153, 171, 175
chicha de quinua, 142
Ch'iji Jawira, 47
chili pepper (*Capsicum* spp.), 137
Chiripa, 17, 22, 32, 38, 51, 66, 67, 68f, 131, 165, 166, 169, 171; archaeology, 30–31; crop storage at, 124, 170; description of current community, 25–28; economy and subsistence, 27–28; Middle Formative, 35, 146; Montículo, 30–31; plant remains, 75–76, 84, 86; raised fields, 50, 63, 177
Ch'isi, 84
Choquehuanca, 35
chronology, Lake Titicaca Basin, 28–30
chucaripupata, 38
chuchulla, 83, 112
Chuquito, Lago, 64–65, 66
Chunchukala, 43
chuño, 110, 112, 125, 129, 142, 169
chuño blanco, 112
chuntilla, 55, 89
chuqi, 83
clays, 62
climate change, 15, 16, 49, 60, 61, 65, 66
Clinopodium bolivianum, 127, 136
clothing, Aymara, 8
clover (*Trifolium amabile*), 100, 172
Coa Collu, 17, 28, 58; winter solstice celebration, 131–33
coca, 113, 120, 124
Cochabamba, and Tiwanaku, 46–47, 142
colonization, Spanish, 6, 50–51, 70, 179
community events, Chiripa, 27–28
community organization, 20, 23, 26–28, 165–66, 169, 175; Early Formative, 32–33; Late Formative, 42, 151; meals, 131, 133, 149; Middle Formative, 37; Tiwanaku, 47–49
comunidades indígenas, 51
cooking techniques, 139, 152, 160; boiling and roasting, 140–42; fermenting 142–42. *See also* food preparation
Choquepacha spring, 104
Coronopus didymus, 101, 102
crops, 5, 73t, 78, 87–88, 169; diversity of, 22, 74–75; losses of, 59–60; processing, 122–26, 174; rotation of, 79–80, 168, 176; storage of, 109–10
Cyperaceae, 95, 103–4, 137

deer, 135
demography, Colonial period, 51
Desaguadero River, 65
development, sustainable, 11–12
diatom studies, 66
digging tools, 55; archaeological evidence of, 62–63, 170. *See also* hoes, stone
disturbance, 16, 174; plants and, 93, 106, 172
diversity index, 105
droughts, 49, 59, 65, 66
dry season, 58, 169
dung: for fertilizer, 73–74, 92, 106, 173–74; as fuel, 77, 137–38; and herbaceous plants, 97–98, 101
dwell(ed)/dwelling, 16, 17, 166
dye plants, 101

Early Formative period, 21, 30t, 31–32, 62, 84, 86, 115, 117, 140; architecture, 32–33, 35; ceramics, 32; meals, 135, 136, 137, 139t, 144–45; plant remains, 76, 87, 88f, 96, 100, 104, 105, 125, 138
Earth, as animate, 60
Echinocactus, 148
El Alto, 10
elites, 44, 47
encomiendas, 51
ethnobotanical collection, wild/weedy plants, 90–91
Eucalyptus sp., 4, 96
Evolvulus sp., 95

Fabaceae, 75, 78–79, 94, 100. *See also by species*
farming, Indigenous farming systems, 9–10; development of, 6–7; early, 167–68; historic and modern, 179–80; intensification of, 175–77; sustainable, 91–92. *See also* agriculture
fava beans (*habas*), 5, 51, 74, 75, 79; harvest and storage, 109–10, 112
feasting, 18, 44, at Tiwanaku, 46–48
felines, 41
fermenting, 142–43
fertilizer, 73–74, 92, 106, 113, 173–74
field preparation, 59, 167, 172, 180; process of, 54–57
fields: fallow, 5, 170; maintenance of, 73–74; rotation of, 72, 74–75; and soil types, 57–58
field systems, 63; dating, 69–70

fish, fisheries, 4, 162, 185n3; in archaeological record, 134–35, 149, 151, 155, 169, 174; isotopic signature, 135–36; in meals, 127–30
fish stew, 149; preparation of, 127–30
food, foodways, 19, 126–27, 131, 133–34; archaeological evidence of, 76–77; at Kala Uyuni, 114; Early Formative period, 144–45; Late Formative period, 150–59; Middle Formative period, 145–150; preparations, 138–143; serving, 143–44; Tiwanaku period, 159–163. *See also* meals
Food and Agricultural Organization, Globally Important Agricultural Heritage System, 9
food preparation, 80; boiling and roasting, 140–42; ceremonial, 157–59; fermenting, 142–43. *See also* cooking techniques
foot plow (*chaquitaclla*), 56f, 62, 63
Formative Period, 6, 21, 22, 29–30, 69, 184n7
freeze-drying 125, 174; fermentation and, 142–43; tubers, 110–12, 168
fuel: in archaeological record, 152, 158, 160; dung, 46, 77; wood, 96–97

Galium sp., 101
garbage pits, at Tiwanaku, 45, 48–49
gender, 19; in agricultural work, 54, 72–73, 108–10, 113, 164, 167, 174, 176, 180; in fishing, 169; in meal preparation, 127, 131, 132
gene flow, 15, 16
geology, 15, 60–62
glaciers, 60
Globally Important Agricultural Heritage System (GIAHS), 9
goats, 51
goods: Inca tribute, 50; nonlocal, 42, 46
grasses (Poaceae), 94, 95, 98–99, 105, 145, 168, 179
grazing, 26, 67, 95, 96, 98, 101, 104, 168, 174
Green Revolution, 12
grinding stones, 62
guanaco (*Lama guanicoe*), 134
guinea pig (*Cavia* sp.), 135

habas, 74. *See also* fava beans
haciendas, 26, 51, 52, 58, 70, 180, 184–184n
hallucinogens, 120; San Pedro cactus (*Trichocereus pachanol*), 102, 148; in Tiwanaku, 44, 46, 47
hamlets, 32, 33

harvest/harvesting, 17–18, 55, 108–9, 174; crop production, 74–75, 83, 126, 165, 169, crop storage, 109–10; tubers, 63, 106, 109, 168, 174; seed plants, 112–13; totora, 91
hearths, cooking techniques, 36, 139
herbaceous plants: in camelid dung, 97–98; diversity of, 104–6; terrestrial, 98–102
herbs, 91, 126–37
herds, herding, 5, 22, 168–70, 173, 175; and aquatic plants, 103–4
hilltops, 61
hoes, stone, 62, 172
households, 19, 27–28, 45
Huancané, 38
Huanoquite (Peru), 80
Huari, 47
Huatta (Peru), 65, 69
human motifs, 41, 44
human remains: isotopic signatures, 155, 175; maize with, 148, 161

iconography: Late Formative, 40–41; Middle Formative, 35–36, 37; Wari and Tiwanaku, 44, 47
identity: Aymara, 8; Tiwanaku, 45
illama, *illamancus* (*Chenopodium pallidicaule* var. *pampalasta*), 100, 137–38, 168, 170, 174, 179; in archaeobotanical record, 80–81, 137–39, 144–45. *See also kañawa*
imilla, 83
Inca Empire, 50, 70
incense burners, 34, 162
Indigenous communities, 6, 10, 23; land repatriation, 27, 52; sovereignty, 180–81
ingredients, 23, 126, 127, 133–38
intensification, 22, 42, 62, 106, 170, 173, 175–76. *See also* agricultural: intensive/intensification
Intertropical Convection Zone (ITCZ), 64
iris family (Iridaceae), 101
irrigation systems, 58, 67
isañu, 74, 83, 109, 167, 179
isotopic signatures, 135–36, 155; maize in, 85, 175, 177
Iturralde family, 52, 183–84*n*3
Iwawi, 162

Janko Kala, 38
Juli-Pomata region, 69

k'ala laq'a, 57–58, 61
Kalasasaya platform, 43
Kalasasaya red-rimmed vessels, 39, 120, 184*n*5
Kala Uyuni (KUKU), 32, 33, 38, 45, 52, 62, 66, 136, 169, 171, 175; archaeobotany, 106–7; archaeology of, 114–21; crop processing and storage at, 122–26, 170; Late Formative, 39, 40, 42, 150–59; Middle Formative, 35, 145–50; plant remains from, 22–23, 75–76, 86, 121–22, 142; Tiwanaku period, 48, 49, 159–63, 177
kalla, 112, 125
kañawa; cañihua (*Chenopodium pallidicaule*), 22, 75, 79, 80, 87, 100, 176, 178; in archaeobotanical record, 81–82, 134, 137–38. *See also illama*
karachi (*Orestias* spp.), 128
KARATE, 90
Katari Basin, 177
kayña (*Tetraglochin cristatum*), 97, 106, 174
keñua (*Polylepis* sp.), 96–97, 104
Kerikala, 43
kerus, 45, 142, 144, 159*f*, 161, 162–63, 177
khoa (*Clinopodium bolivianum*), 127, 136
Khonkho Wankané, 38, 40, 41, 48, 120
k'ink'u, 62, 170
Kollu Kollu Formation, 61, 67
KUAC. *See* Achachi Coa Collu
KUAQ. *See* Ayrampu Qontu
KUKU. *See* Kala Uyuni
Kumi Kipa, 22, 38–39, 42, 48, 52; plant remains from, 76, 86; pottery, 39, 40
k'uphaña, 54–55

labor, 18: shared help (*yanapataña*) 18, 74, 165, 185*n*1; hacienda, 52, 180; intensification, 173, 175; raised fields, 70; tribute, 50–51. *See also* gender
laderas, 57, 170
lake levels, 22, 59; changes in, 61, 62, 64–67, 173
lakebed/lakeshore: fields (*milli*), 57, 65, 173; plant communities, 94–95
Lama sp., 6, 134. *See also* camelids
Lamiaceae, 127, 136
land, land use, 6, 27, 33, 58, 67, 74, 165–66, 169–70, 172–73, 175, 177, 181; agricultural, 67, 170; political composition, 19–20, 26, 52, 74; Spanish colonialization, 6, 51. *See also* lake levels

landscape(s): agricultural, 5–6, 10, 21, 23, 163, 167, 178–80; crops/cropscapes in, 87–88; defining, 12–13; historical, 14–16; lived and grown, 16–18; material, 13–14; meaningful, 20–21; social and political, 18–20; wild and weedy plants/plantscapes, 77, 90–91, 93, 95, 104–6, 168, 172
laq'a, 62
Late Formative period, 21, 30*t*, 38, 43, 84, 118, 120, 144, 167, 171–72, 175, 178; architecture, 40, ceramics, 39, 144, 160; Kala Uyuni, 151-53, 157; iconography, 40–41; Late Formative II, 48; meals, 134–36, 139*t*, 154–57, 162; plant remains, 76, 81–82, 84, 86–87, 88*f*, 96–97, 99–101, 106, 125, 134, 138, 154–58; political centers, 42; raised fields, 69, 173
Late Horizon, 49–50
Late Intermediate period, 49–50
layu-layu (Trifolium sp.), 100, 172
legumes (Fabaceae), 75, 94; in archaeological record, 78–79, 100. *See also by species*
lejia, 113
Lepichinia meyenii, 136
Lepidium sp., 101–2
Lightning Stones, 35, 116
lima, 5
livestock, 5; and aquatic plants, 103–4
llajwa, 130, 136
llama (*Llama glama*), 6, 134
Llusco, 35
Lukurmata, 3, 38, 40, 47–48, 104, 144, 177
Lupinus mutabilis, 75, 90; in archaeological record, 78–79

maca (*Lepidium meyenii*), 101
Maihueniopsis cf. *boliviana*, 102, 148, 151, 160
maize (*Zea mays*), 22, 46, 75, 78, 80, 140, 142, 148, 155, 160–63, 171, 176, 179; in archaeological record, 73, 83, 85–87, 88*f*, 134, 155, 158, 161; development of, 15–16; harvest and storage, 109, 110, 112; isotopic signature, 135, 136, 177; planting, 72, 74
mallkus, 27–28, 132
mallow family (Malvaceae), 95, 98, 168
material culture, 8; archaeology, 28–29
meals, 133–134; animal ingredients, 135–36; archaeological evidence of, 133–34; daily, 126–27, 130, 169, 171, 173–74, 176; plant ingredients, 134; special occasion, 131–33, 169–70, 171, 175, 177; spices/relish, 136–38. *See also* food, foodways
meat, freeze-dried, 142–43, 185*n4*
medicines, wild plants as, 91, 101, 102
middens, 33, 44, 45, 114, 143–44, 171, 175; archaeobotanical contexts, 122–24; at Kala Uyuni, 114–15; 118, 120, 146, 148, 152, 155, 160
Middle Formative period, 21, 30*t*, 62, 86, 99, 169, 170–71, 178; ceramics, 34, 146–47, 148–49; architecture, 35–36, 145–46; iconography (Yayamama-Pa-ajanu style), 35–37; Kala Uyuni, 114–118, 125; meals, 135, 139*t*; 145–150; plant remains, 76, 82*t*, 84, 86–87, 88*f*, 96–97, 99–100, 104–106, 125, 136, 138, 146–48, 149, 174; raised fields, 69–70, 173; villages, 33, 37
migrations, Tiwanaku, 44–45, 46–47
milli, 57, 65, 72, 109
mint family (Lamiaceae), 127, 136
m'ita, Inca Empire, 50
Mollo Kontu (Tiwanaku), 82
monoliths, stone, 35*f*, 60, 116
Montes, Ismael, 52, 58
Montículo (Chiripa), 25, 26*f*, 28, 146, 170, 183–84*n3*; archaeology, 30–31; architecture at, 36, 177
Moquegua Valley, 46, 142
Morales, Evo, 10
mounding, 58, 89. *See also th'aruña*
mound sites, and raised fields, 70
mountain peaks, as animate, 60
mustard family (Brassicaceae), 5, 14, 51, 94, 101–2, 172, 179

Nasca periods, 97
natural selection, 15, 16
nonhuman entities, 11, 13
ñustasa (*Brassica rapa* L.), 5, 14, 172

oats, 74, 75, 109
oca (*Oxalis* sp.), 5, 22, 74, 78, 83, 87, 109, 112, 167–68, 174, 179, 174, 179; in archaeobotanical record, 83*t*, 84, 85, 125; in meals 130, 132; tending, 89–90
Ocorani, 27, 166, 183–84*n3*
Odontesthes bonariensis, 128
offerings, 164, 169
ollas, 140
Omo, 46
Opuntia sp., 148; *soehrensii*, 102

Orestias sp., 128
Our Common Future (Bruntland report), 11
ovens, earth, 140–41f, 153
Oxalis sp. *See oca*

Pachamama, 60, 164
paleoclimate, 15, 61
Pampa Koani, raised fields at, 69–70, 176
papa lisa, 167, 179
parenchyma, 84, 144, 157, 160, 174
pastoralism, 5, 173
pejerry (*Odontesthes bonariensis*), 128
Pennisetum clandestinum, 94
pesticides, 90
phytoliths, 76, 77, 85, 155
pick (*chuntilla*), 55
pigs, 5, 51, 110
Piñami, 46
pine trees, 96
pits, 91, 160, 171; food materials in, 144–45; Late Formative, 152–53; and meal preparation, 138, 141–42; Tiwanaku, 45, 48–49, 121
Plantago sp., 95
plant communities, 94–95
planting, 55f, 56f, 58, 71–73, 167, 170, 172, 176, 180; field rotation, 74–75; help in, 164–65; timing of, 59, 67
plants, 13, 15; archaeological evidence of, 22–23, 75–77; diversity of wild/weedy, 92–93; Early Formative, 144–45; historical changes in, 15–16; at Kala Uyuni, 121–22; Late Formative, 151; Middle Formative, 146–50; noncrop, 93–94; Tiwanaku period, 159–63. *See also* crops; weeds; *various plants by type*
platforms, earthen, 40, 42, 43, 47
Pleiades, 59
plows, plowing, 52, 54, 55f, 72, 89
Podocarpus sp., 96
political centers, Late Formative, 38, 40
politics/political, 28; Early Formative, 33; of food, 23, 133; of food at Kala Uyuni, 148–49, 152, 155–56, 158–59; landscape, 18–20, 166, 172, 177–78; Late Formative, 39, 41–42, 121; Middle Formative, 37–38; Tiwanaku, 43–44
polities, multi-community, 38–43
pollen analysis, 95, 96
Polylepis sp., 96–97, 104
population growth, 33, 39, 44, 87, 172

Porophyllum ruderale, 130, 136
Potamogeton sp., 95, 103
potatoes (*Solanum* sp.), 5, 14, 22, 58, 78, 82, 87, 130, 140, 167–68, 174, 179; in archaeobotanical record, 83–85, 134, 136; freeze-drying, 110–12; harvesting, 108–9; in meals, 128–29, 130; planting, 72–73, 74; tending, 17–18, 89–90
pottery, pottery production, 17, 45, 86, 115, 120, 140, 142, 145, 160; Early Formative, 33; Late Formative, 39–40, 41, 42, 69, 151, 152, 156–57; Middle Formative, 33–34, 146–48; serving, 143–44, 174; Tiwanaku, 45
power imagery, 41
precious stones, 46
Pukara, 40, 41
pukaras, 50
Pukina speakers, 7, 8
Puma Punku platform, 43
puna, 94, 95, 98
Putuni, 45

q'ala, 170
Qalasasaya. *See* Kalasasaya
Qaluyu style pottery, 146
q'ellu apilla, 83
Qeya-style wares, 39, 42, 69, 120
qheni apilli, 83
qhulltayxasina, 56–57, 58
q'ochas, (sunken gardens), 63
Quechua speakers, 8
quicklime, 120
quill-quiña (*Porophyllum ruderale*), 130, 136
quinoa (*Chenopodium quinoa* L.), 5, 6, 22, 74, 75, 78, 79–80, 95, 142, 167–70, 174, 176–79; in archaeobotanical record, 81, 114, 134, 136, 144, 147, 148, 151, 152, 154, 157, 158, 160, 162, 163, 170; harvest and storage, 109–10; in meals, 134, 137, 139; preparation of, 139, 140, 142; processing and storage, 123–25; threshing, 112–13
quinoa negra, 81, 82, 168, 170; in archaeobotanical record, 82, 114, 124, 125, 138, 145, 152, 157; in meals, 139t
quishwara (*Buddleja* sp.), 96
Quispe, 17; meals, 126–30; resource use, 3–5
Quitobaquito, 93
Quitovac, 93
q'ullu, 57, 58

radiocarbon dates, of raised fields, 69–70
rainfall, 21, 180; and agricultural cycle, 57, 58–59; and lake level changes, 64–67
rainy season, 22, 58, 64, 169
raised fields, 20, 22, 46–49, 50, 63–64, 67, 68f, 69–70, 175–78; dating of, 69–70
Rebutia sp., 102, 148
Relbunium sp., 101, 184n1
reducciones, 51
religion, Tiwanaku, 43–44
resurgent communities, 6, 10, 23, 180
risk, 75, 109
rituals/ceremonies, 20, 175; agricultural, 59, 169, 175, 177–78; at Kala Uyuni, 116–17, 120–21, meals, 133, 146, 149, 152, 155–57; Early Formative, 32–33; Late Formative, 41–42, Middle Formative, 36–37, 117, Tiwanaku 43–44, 47, 49. *See also* ceremonial/ritual architecture
roasting, 142, 154; earth ovens, 140–41
rodents, in archaeological record, 135
rotation: crop, 79–80, 176; field, 72, 74–75
Rubiaceae, 101
Ruppia sp., 95, 103

salt trade, 46
salvia (*Lepichinia meyenii*), 136
San José, 17, 28, 58
San Pedro cactus (*Trichocereus pachanol*), 102, 148
San Pedro de Atacama, 47
Santa Rosa, 17, 28, 58, 131
Santiago de Huatta, 38
saponins, in quinoa, 139
scarcity, 82, 125, 178
Schoenoplectus californicus, 5, 91, 95, 103, 137, 169
sculpture, Middle Formative, 35–36
sedges, 95, 168, 169
seeds, processing, 112–13
selection, human, 15–16
señoríos, 49–50
serving, 145; communal, 148–49, 156; pottery, 143–44, 174
shamans, 59
sheep, 5, 51, 91; dung, 73–74
shrubs, 96–97
Sisrynchium sp. (Iridaceae), 101
Siwinka Qontu (SQ), 114, 118
snuff tablets, at Tiwanaku, 47

social-political complexity, and food production, 18–19
soils, 20, 60, 106, 168, 172, 174, 180; and field locations, 57–58; management of, 176–77; manipulation of, 62–63; phytoliths and starch grains in, 86, 155; types of, 21, 61–62
Solanum sp. *See* potatoes; tubers
Sonaji, 22, 38, 42, 48, 52, 62; plant remains from, 75–76, 83–84, 125; pottery, 39, 40
sovereignty, Indigenous, 180–81
Spanish conquest, 50; land and agriculture, 51–52
spices, 127, 136–37
springs, 67, 68f
SQ. *See* Siwinka Qontu
Staff God, Tiwanaku, 44
starch grains, 76, 77, 85, 125, 155, 161
stelae, stone sculpture, 171–78; Late Formative, 40–41; Middle Formative, 35–36; Tiwanaku, 43–44
stone tools, 170, 172
storage, crop, 59, 76, 109–10, 124–25, 170
suchi (*Trichomycterus rivulatus*), 128
suni, 94
sunken courts, 40, 43, 47, 169, 170, 171; Early Formative, 32–33; Middle Formative, 35–38, 146, 149. *See also* Achachi Coa Collu
sustainability, 5, 6, 20–21, 180–81; defining, 11–12

Tagetes multiflora, 136
TAP. *See* Taraco Archaeological Project
Taraco (municipality), 28, 51
Taraco, Peru (site), 36, 38, 40, 81
Taraco Archaeological Project (TAP), 6, 21
Taraco Formation, 61, 62, 67
Taraco Peninsula, 3; description of, 24–25
Taraco Peninsula Polity, 39, 42, 151–52
Tarasa tenella, 99
tarwi (*Lupinus mutabilis*), 75, 90; archaeological evidence for, 78–79
tasks, 3–5, 54, 126, 137, agricultural, 17–20, 27, 166, 167, 178
taskscapes, 17, 172, 176, 179, 180; agricultural, 23, 163, 164, 166, 176, 178
taxation, Colonial period, 51
temperatures, seasonal cycles of, 64
tempo(s), 15, 53, 60, 178
teosinte (*Zea mays* ssp. *parviglumis*), 85
terraces, terracing, 63, 70

Tetraglochin cristatum, 97, 106, 174
textiles, 45, 184n7; as eating surfaces, 143, 156, 174–75
th'aruña, 58, 89–90f, 91
threshing, 112–13
Tiquina, Strait of, 64–65, 66
Titicaca, Lake, 24; resources from, 3–4, 5, 169
Titicaca Basin, Lake, chronology of, 28–30
Tiwanaku, 14, 81, 82, 131, 142, 160; as ceremonial center, 43–44; influence of, 46–48, 176–78; Late Formative period, 38, 40; migrations to, 44–45, 46–47; residential sectors/barrios, 44–45
Tiwanaku period, 6, 21, 29–30, 48–49, 96, 121, 142, 144, 167, 173, 175–77; architecture, 43–44; ceramics, 45, 144; iconography, 44; Kala Uyuni, 118–119, 121; meals, 138, 142, 159, 161–163; plant remains, 76, 81–82, 84–85, 87, 88f, 97, 99, 103, 106, 138, 159–63; raised fields, 45, 69–70
Tiwanaku state, 8, 66, 70, 172, 175–76
Toledo, Francisco de, Viceroy, 51
tombs. *See* burials
topography, 21
totora reeds (*Schoenoplectus californicus*), 5, 91, 95, 103, 137, 169
tourism, winter solstice ceremony, 131–32
tractors, 55, 184n
trade, 37, 175; Late Formative, 42; maize, 85, 87; Tiwanaku, 46, 47; wood, 96, 104
traditional ecological knowledge, 9
trees, 96–97, 104
tribute, Inca Empire, 50
Trichocereus pachanol, 102, 148
Trichomycterus rivulatus, 128
Trifolium sp., 160; *amabile* (clover; *layu-layu*), 100, 172
tubers, 22, 72, 75, 78, 87, 167–69, 178; in archaeobotanical record, 83–85, 134, 137, 144, 147, 148, 151, 154, 158, 160, 162, 163; freeze-drying, 110–12; intensification of, 174–75; in meals, 126, 132, 134; as staple, 82–83. *See also by type*
Tumantumani, 38
tunta, 110, 112, 125, 142, 174

ullucu, 83, 84
United Nations, 11
Urocarpidium sp., 99
Uru speakers, 7, 8

Verbena sp. (Verbenaceae), 100–101, 172
vicuña (*Vicugna vicugna*), 134
vilca, 120
villages: Late Formative, 38–39; Middle Formative period, 33–38; Tiwanaku 43

waki, 165
wallaque, 149; preparation of, 127–30
Wari state, 47
waste disposal, Kala Uyuni, 122–23, 124. *See also* middens
w'atia, 140–41f, 153
weather, 59, 64, 91
weeds, weeding, 6, 22, 82, 89, 93–94, 174; as animal feed, 5, 91–92; in landscape, 14, 104–6
wheat, 51, 74, 75; threshing, 112–13
Wila Jawira project, 69–70
Wila Jawira River, 104
wild plants, 92, 160, 174, 176; in fields, 90–91; and landscapes, 104–6
Wiñaymarka Basin, Lake, 3, 24; seasonal fluctuation of, 64–65, 66. *See also* lake levels
winnowing process, 123–24
winter solstice ceremony, 131–33
wood use, 96–97
work projects, community, 165–66, 169
World Commission on Environment and Development, 11

yanapataña, 165
yatiris, 59
Yayamama/Pa-ajanu style, 36, 37
yunta, 54, 55f, 72, 89

Zea mays, ssp. *parviglumis*, 85. *See also* maize
zooarchaeological record, 13, 134–35, 173–74